LIFE PASSAGES:
WRITING EXERCISES FOR SELF-EXPLORATION

LIFE PASSAGES:
WRITING EXERCISES FOR SELF-EXPLORATION

Dr. Allan G. Hunter

Kroshka Books
New York

Senior Editors: Susan Boriotti and Donna Dennis
Coordinating Editor: Tatiana Shohov
Office Manager: Annette Hellinger
Graphics: Wanda Serrano
Editorial Production: Jennifer Vogt, Matthew Kozlowski,
     Jonathan Rose and Maya Columbus
Circulation: Ave Maria Gonzalez, Vera Popovich, Luis Aviles, Raymond Davis,
     Melissa Diaz, Vladimir Klestov and Jeannie Pappas
Marketing: Cathy DeGregory

Library of Congress Cataloging-in-Publication Data

Hunter, Allan G.
    Life Passages: Writing Exercises for Self-Exploration / by Allan G. Hunter
  p.cm.
Includes index.
ISBN 1-56072-787-X.
    1. Self-perception—Problems, exercises, etc. 2. Diaries—Authorship. I. Title.

BF697.5.S43 H86 2000
158.1—dc21

                                         00-025988

Copyright © 2002 by Allan Hunter
     Kroshka Books, a division of
     Nova Science Publishers, Inc.
     400 Oser Ave, Suite 1600
     Hauppauge, New York 11788-3619
     Tele. 631-231-7269   Fax 631-231-8175
     e-mail: Novascience@earthlink.net
     Web Site: http://www.novapublishers.com

Printed in the United States of America

In our daily lives problems are bound to arise. The biggest problems in our lives are the ones we inevitably have to face, like old age, illness, and death. Trying to avoid our problems or simply not thinking about them may provide temporary relief, but I think there is a better approach. If you directly confront your suffering, you will be in a better position to appreciate the depth and nature of the problem.

The Dalai Lama, *The Art of Happiness*

CONTENTS

ACKNOWLEDGEMENTS

I have endeavored throughout this book to acknowledge the sources from which ideas came. In order to keep the text clean and easy to read you will find that authors who are mentioned in these pages are also named in the index, so you can read more about them. I have found this less cumbersome than endnotes. If there are any omissions or errors the responsibility is mine.

In expressing my thanks for the many kindnesses I've received it's hard to know where to begin, so I'd like first of all to acknowledge the help and practical guidance of David and Rosie Whitley who have supported my efforts throughout. I owe thanks to Curry College, especially to the Faculty Welfare Committee and Dean David Fedo, without whose support and funding the manuscript might have remained as manuscript. At Curry College specific help was generously given by Dr. Ronald Warners (especially in the section concerning the Myers Briggs Type Inventory, and the chart on page 201) for which I can never be appreciative enough. I also want to thank Jane Adelizzi, Peter Hainer, Barbara Fournier, Joan Manchester, George Shamon, and Marguerite Wengler, each of whom helped and challenged me, each in different ways, and to all of whom I am very grateful.

To Frank and Nadya Columbus, I owe thanks for their very considerable encouragement.

The greatest debt, of course, is to my clients and my students at Curry College and at the Cambridge Center for Adult Education. They have been the willing and enthusiastic participants in these exercises, and some of their responses appear in these pages. I have protected their confidentiality, although I wish to say that helpful advice came from Sue Delaney, Marlena Erdos, Chris Foster, John Hearne, Melissa Katz, Mary Agnes Mullowney, and Jane Rudd. Useful feedback and material help also came in great measure from Beth Greely, Sam Savage, Jean Fain, and Dr. Janis Wagner. The staff at the Cambridge Center for Adult Education also have my enduring thanks. Without the help of Director James Smith, Program Directors Rebecca King and Paula Ogier I would not have been able to develop my initial ideas further. Pamela Post-Ferrante inspired the exercises on pages 176 and 179, both of which have proven so useful. Special thanks go to Lee Varon whose kindness helped to bring this book to being.

For inspiration, ideas, and the poem that appears on page 28, I am deeply indebted to Patty Nasca; John Hearne contributed the poem on page 19 as well as his good-humored insights; and Mercedes Munson graciously allowed me to reproduce her poems on page 19, and pages 86-87.

A special thanks goes to Mrs. Arline Ripley Greenleaf, who has been far more help than her modest nature would ever allow her to admit, and to whom my gratitude is immense.

Last, but most important, is the continuing debt I have to Cathy Bennett, and to Anna and Nick Portnoy. Without them none of this would have been written.

Chapter One

ABOUT THIS BOOK

Every life passage we go through shapes us, each one differently, each one forever. Often we tend to think there are only a few of these - childhood, adolescence, middle years, old age. In this book you'll find that there are many more, and I'd contend that it is only by understanding them that we can come to know fully who we are. Sometimes, though, it feels as if we're so busy living we just don't have the chance to put our lives in any sort of perspective.

This book can give you that chance, and supply that perspective.

For if we don't know where we've been and what we've been doing, how can we expect to learn from our experiences? And if we don't know where we are now, then how can we open up the future for ourselves?

In these pages you will find the tools you need to come to a deeper understanding of yourself, so you can claim your selfhood and live your life more fully. You'll learn that you can do much of this work yourself, and that you don't have to rely on the specialists for meaningful self-exploration to occur.

For ours is an age dominated by experts, and sometimes the reverence we have for them leaves us unsure about how to begin the work of unraveling the mystery of ourselves.

It wasn't always like this.

I'll explain by telling you a story. In the sixties, when I was a boy, every weekend I would watch the parents in our neighborhood go through a familiar series of rituals. The men would tinker with their cars - check the oil, adjust things, and the women would do household improvements, or sew, or they'd can and preserve foods. Today I'd venture that except in rural areas, these tasks are extinct. Modern cars don't lend themselves to the tinkering my father's generation thought of as normal. Computerized circuits and microchips are specialized service items. Even changing the oil, once a rite of adolescent car ownership, is now unpopular. So we go to the service station instead. Similarly, very few women preserve foods anymore. Who has the time? And as for as sewing one's own clothes....

We've stopped doing things for ourselves, and we've started paying other people to do them for us.

I do not wish to belittle the benefits of our age: far from it. All I wish to point out is that we routinely hire experts to do what we need. The trouble is that we have also given over a portion of our self-hood to the so-called experts. Anxious parents buy and read books on childcare, and then agonize over whether or not they are doing the right thing for their children. The newspapers tell us that inner cities are a mess and that social services, relief agencies, and social workers are there to ease the problem. Every day children are removed from their parents and handed over to state care facilities, and often for very good reasons. Yet behind this lies another message, one that is not so benign. Through it all comes the sense that we are perhaps not expert enough; we, the ordinary citizens, need the experts to tell us how to run our lives. I'm sure there are some benefits. But on the whole this 'expert culture' this 'consultant ethos' has had the effect of leaving us feeling de-skilled. And so that is the way we tend to run our lives. We feel ill, we call a doctor, or a dietician, or a trainer. We feel sad; we call a therapist or a counselor. We agree to take medications, perhaps, and accept what the psychiatrist has to say, even though we may only just have met him or her. We have money problems; we call a financial advisor, a stockbroker, a debt-restructuring consultant. More experts. There's a growing tendency to hand our lives over to the experts.

The other side of the coin is that I notice with delight the number of home improvement and do-it-yourself places that have sprung up over the last ten years. For me, just walking through these places is empowering. I see tools, products, and inventions that let me know I can improve my home myself. I don't necessarily have to pay a contractor who may or may not appear on time and finish the task inside a year. I can do it myself, if I choose to.

This book is a version of that empowerment. In these pages you will find a series of writing exercises (and sometimes drawing exercises, too) all of which are designed to help you reflect on your life so that you can understand yourself better. The exercises will give you the tools of the trade, as it were, that can enable you to undertake the vital work of personal exploration yourself, rather than having to rely on the experts - the psychiatrists, the analysts, the therapists - in the way that many of us tend to do now.

Please don't think I'm trying to by-pass these people. As with my previous book, *The Sanity Manual: the Therapeutic Uses of Writing*, which also uses writing exercises, I do not pretend that any book can automatically provide all the answers. What you can discover from these pages can be enormously useful, life-enhancing, and vital, but ultimately it depends upon your efforts, not mine, and not upon anyone else's. And sometimes a qualified counselor can be enormously helpful in aiding you in the process.

What I'm suggesting is that we can help ourselves by maintaining a sense of mental awareness. Just as an athlete has to be fit and supple before she can expect a trainer to bring out the best in her, so it is with our mental health. You may choose to visit a therapist. I, personally, think it is a very useful component of self-exploration for most people. But your progress will be immeasurably enhanced if you appear, like the athlete, in a relatively 'trained' state, an aware state.

Or perhaps a different comparison may help - also a physical one. The overweight individual who discovers at age sixty five that he has all sorts of health problems connected with poor diet and lack of exercise - such a person certainly needs the advice of a doctor. But this individual is inevitably far less prepared than the person who has kept fit, eaten wisely, and taken care of his body. The task of regaining full health is likely to be much easier for the fit person - indeed, the fit person may never experience the illness at all. That's what this book is. Fitness exercises for the Spirit.

There are several ways to use this book. You can turn straight to the sections that are most important to you. If divorce is causing you distress, you can choose to turn directly to that section, or to whichever chapters seem to answer your needs. Under each chapter heading you will find exercises that can help you with specific issues. If you choose to work this way, I'd advise you to read the next sections, and specifically the one entitled 'Getting Started', before you begin. It may help you to start with some assessment of yourself before you move on to your individual concerns. In fact, I'd strongly advise working your way through the chapters as far as 'Schooldays' before you select specific themes to examine. The reason for this is that the more you know about yourself the better you'll be able to use the chapters on your specific issues. Discussions of birth, the family, and school will help you with this.

Another way you can use this book is by reading it straight through as a way of elucidating human nature in general, and yours in particular. That is why I've organized the chapters as a chronological sequence of emotional landmarks or mileposts that we can all expect to encounter. These are the Life Passages of the title. We will all experience each of these life passages in one form or another in our lives. We may face these passages ourselves, directly; or it may be indirectly as we see those close to us struggling to understand their lives in the light of illness or divorce, perhaps. One thing we can be sure of. Whether it's us or someone else, each life passage will change us.

As you go through the exercises I will be attempting to do several things. The first is to raise awareness about your own experiences, the events you will write about, and to encourage reflection on them. Often we don't make time to think about what things may mean. The significance and value of an event can easily be lost this way. Just as a photograph album can surprise us with a rush of memories - 'Yes, I really did this' - so we can reclaim our past experiences and gain from them only if we take the conscious effort to recall them.

The second thing this book sets out to do is to provide some sort of a context for the information and the emotions that will arise, so you can see them more clearly. After all, it's not much help if you access a poignant and beautiful memory and then are not sure what to do with the emotions that emerge. The paragraphs that follow each exercise are there to make suggestions to you, the reader, so that you can put these memories, or stories, into some sort of context that will enable you to see them in a clearer light. If you are working alone this will be an important way for you to put your responses into a new perspective. If you have arranged to work with a friend and compare results, or if you are working with a group or a class then you may find it helpful to note what the others' responses were. Often people who are quite dissimilar in all outward respects turn out to have faced similar difficulties, and can learn from each other as well as offer support. It is context that allows each of us to see that our concerns may well be important, that they are also concerns others have dealt with, and found solutions for. An unclimbed mountain peak has a forbidding quality to it. When we know that others have made it to the top before us the task can seem far less daunting, and we know we're not alone.

Behind all this lie two questions: why do negative feelings linger so long? And why is it that we remember anger and pain more than we recall peace and happiness? The challenge facing us is that if we don't come to terms with the negative emotions, they will inevitably weaken us, sap our energy, and undermine any sense of inner peace. The aim is to shed those items that weaken us. Think, for a moment, of a successful vacation you may have had. Remember how you came back feeling refreshed, thinking how much more fun life had been over the previous few days? Remember how you wanted to bring that frame of mind with you into the everyday world of work? Yet four days later I'll bet you were back in the grind and you couldn't believe how quickly all the good feelings had faded. See how quickly the negative feelings cut into the positive ones? We know what makes us happy, and we know what makes us unhappy. What we're less good at doing is seeing how we choose, so often, to accept things that are not in our best interests. In order to do this, in order perhaps to return to a job we dislike, we have to pretend that we don't know what we actually do know about happiness. In the spirit of 'compromise' or 'being sensible' we close our minds to our experiences. By writing about them we can see what is really going on, so we can reassess many aspects of our lives.

It's my aim for you to access the insight and wisdom each writing exercise can put you in touch with. In this way you can reclaim your life experiences, feel them, value those feelings, and then be able to move beyond them. You could say that retrieving these memories and thoughts is the reclaiming of knowledge, and that the understanding of them is the first step towards wisdom.

That is why I have found writing these exercises so successful in my work with clients over the past two decades. They are short - they may ask you to write a response to a question, for example - and each can completed in less than five minutes. No longer is needed than that. This may seem very sudden, but sometimes one's first response is the best, and I certainly wish you to value those initial reactions, and to trust them too. You'll also find that the exercises are cumulative - they lead on one to another, and each seeks to extend and deepen the understandings already uncovered.

Why do I insist on a writing exercise? Simply because at the end of each exercise you, the reader, will be able to see, clearly before you, an evolving record of your progress, in which that progress itself is visible and can be referred to again. This is important. I have come across frequent instances of clients who have gone to therapy, made a break-through and an hour later they have 'forgotten' almost all of it. Repression and denial have taken over, and they work more swiftly than we realize. I'm reminded of a client of mine who used to turn up to our sessions at one point in our work together and ask, "Now what was it we talked about last time? I felt so good when I left, but when I got home I couldn't remember a thing..." When I insisted that she take notes for herself during the sessions she was able to move ahead much more rapidly. All too often, in my experience, simply talking about issues is not enough - although it's often a very good start. We all spend so much of our time talking, and often a blur of spoken words can actually obscure what is important. A written exercise, on the other hand, is a physical record that cannot be so easily denied.

Writing can slow us down just enough so that we once again pay full attention to what we are feeling and expressing. This slowing down is often a Godsend for the more articulate and lively people I have worked with. In fact several of my clients have benefited greatly when I've given them Play-Doh or modeling clay during our sessions. As clients knead the clay they find it has the effect of slowing down the stream of words and focusing the mind on what they are saying, so they can hear themselves fully for the first time.

In all the exercises in these pages I want to emphasize the process rather than the end product. The things you will discover as you write are far more important than whether or not your prose rivals Tolstoy's. It's important to recall, though, that Tolstoy was only able to become the writer he was because he had spent a vast amount of time discovering, first and foremost, who he was. Once he knew that, his fiction flowed more rapidly than it could otherwise have done.

When we reclaim ourselves in this way we can begin to deal with some of the aspects of our lives that have caused us grief and before they can, in the future, cause further upset.

At intervals throughout the book you'll find sections that urge you to review your writing as a whole. It's a good idea to read those sections no matter which way you choose to use the book, since those pages will ask you to consider your writing not just from the point of view of what you said, but how you may be choosing to say it. Very often we can see habitual patterns emerging, and noticing them is a way of asking whether or not there may be another way to respond. It's as if we're all wearing spectacles - some are rose tinted, some are deep blue. It's only when we know we're wearing them that we can take them off and see things differently, perhaps challenging our preconceptions as we do so. Preconceptions are like noses: Everyone has one but we always look straight past our own. The reflective sections can help us with this.

At this point it's probably a good idea to move straight into an exercise, but before we do here is a word of caution: if you find during the course of doing these exercises that you are feeling frightened or deeply agitated I would advise you to get professional help. The purpose of these exercises is to uncover issues and emotions within you that may need attention. If some of them feel too big for you to deal with yourself then you may need the experts to help you. There's no point in delaying under those circumstances.

Chapter Two

GETTING STARTED: WHO ARE YOU?

Although I call all these activities writing exercises, writing may be accomplished in a number of ways, and does not always have to mean picking up a pen - at least not straight away. Some people use pens, or computers, or typewriters; some prefer to use a special notebook or a file. Whatever you use, make it comfortable, easy for yourself. One woman preferred to speak her responses into a tape recorder, and she would then play back her answers, ponder, and add more. Another woman used a video camera, trained on herself. Still other writers have added pictures to their writing responses, some have even chosen to dance their responses and video tape them. Whatever you do in reply to these questions - making a song, building a collage - is wonderful as long as you are able to review what you produce, so you can reassess it later. For many of us, writing is the best option, but I certainly don't want to exclude other possibilities.

EXERCISE 1:

❖ Write your name. What do you like about your name? What do you dislike? Write two or three responses if you can.
❖ If you could change your name, or if you became a media star, would you change your name? What would it be?
❖ Where did you get your name? How has it changed? What nicknames did you have at different times in your life? What did those names say about you?

If you prefer, you can respond to the following:

❖ Write the story of your name and provide a description of a moment that seems to sum up what you find endearing or comforting about your name, or any regrets you have about it.

Most people don't have much say in what names they receive, and sometimes people have very strong feelings about that. Johnny Cash's famous song 'A Boy Named Sue' gives a humorous insight into a man who tracks down his father in order to kill him, for naming him Sue. The last stanza of the song has the father explaining that he knew he wouldn't be around to raise his son, and that by giving him a girl's name he made sure his son would grow up tough, able to defend himself. Happy ending to song. Real life doesn't quite work like that. The Canadian researcher W.B. Darling kept his first two names as initials, for he knew he could never live down his parents' sentimental action that had written 'Welcome Baby Darling' in the name section of the Birth Certificate.

We can all think of other examples, I'm sure, both humorous and actual. What it all suggests, though, is that there's a sense of identity that exists independently of our given identity - which may in fact may be onerous to us. The young man with the aristocratic name dating from the arrival of the Mayflower, or the man with James Perkins IV as his given name, may feel oppressed by the weight of family pressures to conform, to succeed, or even to take over the family business. This may be either comforting in the sense of continuity it suggests, or it may be crushing. One young man discovered that his older brother had been named after his father's brother, who had died in World War Two, and that he himself had been named after his father's best friend who had died in an air crash. As a result of doing the exercise he was made aware of the fact that his father had, in a sense, wished to replace his dead friends with his sons, and that there was a sense of having to live up to an expectation that was never fully made clear. What were the expectations that came with your name?

When we come to the section about inventing a name, responses have often been wonderful fantasy fulfillments. A young man of German descent with a name that others found hard to pronounce invented a romantic Spanish-sounding name which he felt reflected a dashing, decisive figure - something he wasn't. A woman with an unusual Hungarian surname longed for what she called a 'waspy, easy-to-remember' name, and settled on Lightfoot. Since she was also athletic and a team coach, she felt this would be reassuringly close to who she really was and wanted to be.

You may notice that some parts of this question are designed to encourage fantasy responses, whereas others may appear more analytic. Fantasy should always be respected, since often, for some people, it is the more convenient, more vital way to proceed. We are not all analytic, certainly, and it would be counter-productive to force you, the reader, into a mode that may not agree with your preferred way of being.

This is why the next series of questions are more narrative inclined. 'Write the story...' This approach may well appeal more to those of you who have specific memories of events, or a strong overall impression of a certain time. In some ways this is the opposite of the analytic approach, since it is likely to give rise to memories of a particular event or mood. Writing down this story or event may well be a way of recapturing a whole series of insights that bear directly on one's family life and that cannot, yet, be broken into manageable chunks to be analyzed.

If you have chosen this approach, you may wish to return to your response and see what other stories grow out of this one. Remember, as you explore them, that they are our way of making sense of reality in a way that is synthetic rather than analytic; the story-teller feels the whole, intuitively, where the analyzer sees parts more easily. Neither way is better nor worse than the other, they're just different. Just similarly the fantasist or humorist who made up his or her own name may find it revealing. We laugh at good comedy because we recognize in it an accurate but exaggerated representation of our own lives.

Again, for those of us with the ability to use other intelligences, as defined by Howard Gardner, it may be easier to think of songs we associate with our names, or pictures, or even scents. One woman related hating Bob Dylan's song 'Sara' because one of her boyfriends always used to sing it to her, and she felt she wasn't at all like the woman of the song. Another woman had the misfortune to be given a name that was later used for a popular fragrance that she didn't care for. I say 'unfortunately' because at one point she found herself being given bottles of this perfume for birthdays and Christmas by those who thought they were being thoughtful and witty. Other women have reported being compared to females in literature and even to women in famous oil paintings because of their names. My childhood friends Elizabeth Taylor and Kate Moss were both very attractive, to be sure, but they never looked much like the film star or the model who made their names a daily burden to them, and one young woman named Virginia was sick, she declared, of being compared to Virginia Woolf just because they both wrote fiction.

The responses in this exercise, then, are intended to give you the chance to look at who you are independent of your name, family position, and the projections your friends may put on you. It is only by reflecting on who you are that you can become fully aware of how you function. In addition, once we can see ourselves as individuals in a context of others, we can see more clearly where we are.

Here is a follow-up exercise for you to do.

EXERCISE 2:

❖ Research your name. What does it mean? Look it up in a dictionary of names or an encyclopedia. Does the derivation match your image of yourself?
❖ What are the stories about famous people with the same name?
❖ Is your name biblical or historical?
❖ Were you named after someone in your family or a family friend? What are the stories told about that person?

A middle-aged woman reported that she had never liked her name, Ruth, very much until she began to research it in the Bible. She said she found the stories of Ruth to be both inspiring and strengthening, and she grew to love the name she had been given, finding more of herself in it than she had imagined. After that, whenever she felt herself under stress, she would recall her name and her strengths, and feel calmer and more capable.

Others have reported similar feelings of strength when they researched their surnames and were able to trace them back to their point of origin. In America, with its waves of Ellis Island immigration and the name changes that occurred there (intentional and accidental) this can be a particularly important task, since where we have come from can often shed light on how we came to be where we are now. Americans of African descent have long been sensitive to this. Malcolm X used the letter X as a way of highlighting that he refused to accept his 'slave name'. Other nationalities have similar tales to tell, from the Frenchmen named Etoile, who upon arrival changed his name to the anglicized Starr, to the Jewish people who alter their names for their colleagues at work - Devora becomes Debbie, Weneke becomes Wendy - to the waiters at my local Chinese restaurant who call themselves by the nearest anglicized equivalent of their names, and whom I greet as Christine, May, or David. While such alterations are convenient, they can also cause a loss of the sense of connection to a tradition. This exercise is designed to re-discover that tradition.

Here is another exercise that may work for those of you who prefer the story approach:

EXERCISE 3:

❖ Write a narrative story in which someone with your name does a series of actions you would not normally do.

This exercise can be as wild and fantastic as you wish. One rather timid young man wrote a narrative in which the main figure was a swash-buckling, romantic, devil-may-care kind of fellow, who always got away with everything he did. This was a fairly clear case of the fantasy being used to enjoy wishful thoughts, and he was able to identify his areas of timidity by this contrast. As a result he found it easier to acknowledge his shyness with women, his cautiousness, and his fear of authority. He enjoyed this exercise because it allowed him to disassociate from his name and his established personality. People, he realized, expected him to be timid, and he found it hard to break out of that expectation. This realization in turn allowed him to ask why he had permitted himself to remain so confined by what were essentially others' impressions of him, and what he might be able to do to reclaim his life.

Another example may help, here. A very shy man in his thirties was an accomplished student of Portuguese. Whenever he arrived in Portugal, his sister reported, he became a completely different person - outgoing, happy, friendly. It was only when he left his identity as an English speaker behind, and in fact left all the expectations of the social system he'd just come from, that this side of him could emerge. Interestingly, he would not allow his English name to be used when in Portugal. He was William for his friends at home and Guillermo in his other, happier, life. This man was living out a version of this exercise. It's an example I find particularly attractive because many people travelling in parts of the world that are foreign to them do find that they engage with a different self. Willie Rushton's comedy 'Shirley Valentine' is about exactly that as the heroine, a bored British woman, goes to Greece and discovers a whole new self.

We can also see, in this exercise, the things we absolutely would never do under any circumstances and may find horrifying. A woman wrote about a character who was violent and beat up others. After completing this exercise she was able to identify those things she felt most afraid of - in this case callous physical violence. Looking deeper she began to confront some serious issues about the violence in her family and the terror that had evoked. As she wrote about this she was able to see that, in a sense, she expected her relationships with men to have the capability of turning violent, even though that was the very last thing she wanted consciously. This expectation had placed her in a mindset of perpetual suppressed fear of men, even though on the surface she had 'good' relationships with men.

In each instance - and I could give many more - the exercise has allowed for a deeper knowledge of the self. That is what this book is about. I wish to empower you, the reader, by giving you a method for self-reflection so that you can better understand yourself. I'll give you the tools, and show you how to use them.

This leads in turn to a number of points for you to consider. The sorts of experiences, memories and stories that you will be able to reclaim as a result of doing these exercises are not to be trivialized. I ask you to honor what you find. At times the realizations you may reach will be liberating, and this is good. However, it has to be said that at other times, before the process is complete, the realizations may be uncomfortable, or embarrassing. If there is a sense of shock and discomfort you, the reader, should be aware that this means you are dealing with an important issue, one that deserves careful assessment. Just as in the gym the trainers used to mutter, 'no pain, no gain', so, with these writing exercises we can say that pain is a sure sign that you have identified the topic that needs more work.

It may be that you feel it easier to stop work when you reach this point of discomfort, but I would urge you to reconsider. Be good to yourself when this happens: that means you will need to be sensitive to yourself and your needs. If you're feeling fragile, don't try to tough things out. Accept that you are in an uncomfortable place and know that you will get through it soon. Treat it as if you had a cold - look after yourself so it doesn't turn into pneumonia. At the same time you may wish to keep an ongoing record of events, in diary form, just to keep all the thoughts in perspective. How does the world seem to you in the light of your new understandings? Writing about it can help.

In actual fact, writing about it will be essential, because the rest of the world may not be very sympathetic if you attempt to talk about your unhappiness or confusion. Many people are afraid of looking inside themselves, and they are afraid of those who choose to do so. Even loved ones and significant others may be less than supportive. In my experience women often suffer from this. One middle-aged woman began to encounter resistance from her husband, because he was afraid she'd change and 'not need him anymore'. He found her growing self-awareness threatening, and he was confused and frightened. The situation calmed down only after the woman and her husband agreed to do the exercises together. She continued to work analytically and questioningly. He found it easier to write narratives and fantasy pieces rather than anything more analytic, which he felt to be too direct and exposing. On occasions you, too, may find it easier to write about other people rather than yourself. It is always easier to see what others do than to turn the searchlight upon oneself. At the same time, starting with others is often a most valuable method of honing one's own skills until one can look directly inwards. In this way you can reclaim your wisdom - wisdom and insight you may not realize you had - and then mobilize them for yourself. And that is why I offer choice in each exercise.

Here's another exercise that leads off from this. It's based on one suggested by Joseph Campbell and Sam Kean, but I've adapted it over the years that I've used it.

EXERCISE 4:

❖ Empty your pockets, or pocketbook. What do the contents say about you? What do you think an archaeologist would say if he or she found these objects a thousand years from now?

❖ What are the myths or stories that you attach to these objects?

❖ Which are you favorite objects to touch? Why?

This is a chance to play detective, and the process can be a great deal of fun. If possible, have someone else with you for this, and that person can make suggestions about your items, and you about his or hers.

What can we expect to find? Some people like to carry keys, for example. Yet keys are bulky, cumbersome, and noisy. One might conclude that it's not easy to lug around all that weight. For some people, though, keys are consoling, and losing one's keys a matter of panic. Keys are symbols of power. They unlock things. The keys to the office, to the car, and so on, all of these are about power and control. One young woman always kept her keys chained to a small wallet containing her driver's license, credit cards, and library card. When it was pointed out to her that if she were ever to lose her keys the finder would have access to her house as well as her credit cards, she replied that she knew it seemed illogical to do things that way, but she found it essential to keep all her 'vital resources' (as she called them) together, or she'd lose them separately.

Many men seem to like bundles of keys with tags that have significance to them, or with bottle openers attached (for those who are beer drinkers and proud of it), or even small tools. Some men who have done his exercise have reported carrying a small pocket knife that they have become attached to over the years. The loss of such a knife is always seen as being intensely annoying, even depressing. This is part of the 'be prepared' mentality so many men have written about. The man who carried a Swiss Army knife just in case his old Ford had mechanical troubles still carried it years after he had graduated to a new Mercedes with an impeccable record of reliability. He didn't feel complete without the knife, and it was a powerful clue to his practical, thoughtful, personality.

On a different tack, one young man used to keep used theatre tickets and bus tickets from European vacations in his jacket pockets. Just like the ski-lift pass dangling from one's jacket months later, or the tee-shirt that says Zimbabwe or Harvard (although the owner may have been to neither place), these items are intended to signal that the possessor is a savvy world traveler, someone to be taken seriously. Similarly, many teenagers and adolescents carry items designed to make them seem tougher than they are. Army surplus clothing can signal, by association, that this is a person who has experienced some extreme situations. Logically, of course, it means nothing, but the myth of association says something more glamorous.

REFLECTION ON EXERCISE 4:

❖ What do you think your pockets' contents say about you? Do you carry more or less stuff than you absolutely need? How many of these objects could you do without? Which ones do you feel naked or lost without? Which ones would you take on vacation? What memories are attached to those objects? Write a narrative explaining those memories and their importance to you. Or if you prefer, write about a time you lost one of those objects, say your wallet or purse. Another possibility is to write about these objects being found by someone else and being used for purposes they were never intended for.

One man wrote about a lucky Roman coin he carried being sold so the finder could buy drugs. It was the exact opposite of the personal feeling he had for this ancient coin, the luck he felt it brought him, and the connection it gave him to a thousand years of history. Many of the spiritual values he held dearest were concentrated in this one coin. It reflected aspects of his identity he'd never realized before, and never fully acknowledged. The question could be phrased a different way, perhaps: what are the messages you send your self every day by the things you carry with you?

A woman in her late forties wrote with annoyance about how she felt compelled to carry around a large purse with things in it for every conceivable occasion. As she wrote and explored this she was able to link her over-equipped state to her fears about being without a place she could truly call a home. As a child she had never felt fully comfortable with her adoptive parents, and so she carried these items now as a way of feeling secure that she would not have to ask help from anyone. Further exploration led her to realize that her apartment (in which she did not feel 'at home') was crammed full of items she had accumulated in an effort to compensate for the loss of articles from her adoptive home that had been stolen after she had moved out. The message she sent to herself every time she picked up her bag was that it was dangerous not to be fully prepared, and that objects were a consolation that didn't fully make up for real, personal, losses. Eventually this exercise, and the literal weight of her bag - which had become so heavy that she had strained her shoulder and needed to visit a chiropractor - caused her to make conscious what she was 'saying' to herself in a non-verbal way, so that she could stop the behavior and reach some understanding.

Another example was the man who had kept a key ring with a heart decoration given to him by the woman for whom he had almost left his wife the previous year. After doing this exercise he realized that every time he took out his keys he was reminding himself of other doors he still fantasized about opening, even though he knew the relationship was over. The sexual symbolism of keys in locks was not lost on him. He threw out the keyring a few days later and felt it to be a relief, he said.

Every day the things we carry with us work as messages we send ourselves, messages that tell us what we ought to consider important, or what we once considered vital, but which may not be useful anymore. What messages are you sending yourself, every day? Tim O'Brien's famous essay about soldiers in Vietnam is entitled, simply, "The Things Carried". In it he describes the objects that men took into combat with them as good luck charms. Everything from prayer books to a girl-friend's stockings to a single playing card tucked inside a helmet strap makes an appearance as a totem object. Each object had a powerful story for the man who carried it. What are the stories you carry with you?

All of the preceding exercises have to do with the enquiry into who you are, and have to do with naming. They can also work as a way of thinking about others. Just as the cartoon character romantic carves his girlfriend's name into the bark of a tree, focusing on her name, so we can think of others in the same way by asking whether their names fit them. The frail individual christened Samson or Hercules (Hercule is a popular French name), may become more understandable, at least at first, if we think of the name he has to live with. And we should remember that names carry a huge weight of emotion behind them. If you want to get into real trouble, try telling someone she or he has a silly name! Even the person who dislikes his name intensely will not thank you for a comment like that.

Yet naming is exactly what we will be doing, in many different forms, in a good number of the exercises in this book. I'll be inviting you to write about aspects of yourself so that you can identify and name emotions you felt at the time, and the emotions you feel now, writing about it. You will, in fact, be naming the experience as a first step to understanding it more fully. So, for example, if we think of the man I mentioned earlier who discovered he was named after the deceased best friend of his father, we could say that he had identified and named an area of conflict. Clearly his father had hopes for him. The message seemed to be: 'I want my son to be just like...' This could be a loving hope or a tyrannical wish - or possibly both at the same time. With this realization the man began to sense another aspect, specifically the depth of his father's loss when the friend died, and the hope that he could be close to his son on an equal footing. The young man had at first been angry at the seeming impossibility of having to live up to the name of a person he'd never met. It wasn't until he reflected on the issue that he could see his father's love, caring, and loneliness, as well as his hopes. Throughout these exercises I'll be asking you to find the emotional core behind the event, and then to consider that core more fully. Just as we are more than our names, so these exercises are more than just one-emotion deals.

EXERCISE 5:

In this exercise I'd like you to complete the sentence: "I'm writing this because..." Now take what you wrote to complete the sentence, and use it as the start of the next sentence, adding 'because' and then completing that sentence. When you have done that, take the addition, and do the same again in a new sentence. Continue for as long as you can.

Here is an example of how this worked for a woman of thirty six:
I'm writing this because I want to look deeper inside myself.
I want to look deeper inside myself because I know there's more.
I know there's more in there because I often feel sad.
I often feel sad because I'm lonely.
I'm lonely because I'm afraid....

From the example I think it's fairly obvious how this exercise can work. "It's like peeling layers off the proverbial onion," as one woman wrote when she reflected on it. This simple sentence completion has the ability to allow us to ask those questions we may most want to shy away from, and yet it can give us the space to recognize that we may already have the answers, if we'd allow ourselves to see them, to know them. Each of you has come to this book determined to explore yourself, and learn more. Each of you is likely to be a little afraid of this task, and you'll tend to want to avoid it if you can. This is natural. The exercise puts the power firmly back in your hands and assures you that this task of discovery is yours, and that you can do it.

It's a technique that you can return to. It was suggested to me by a client who had used a version of it in her own writing, and I do not know who first discovered it. Over time I've found that it can be adapted to meet many circumstances. In journal work sometimes it can be very useful for writers to re-read their writing and then ask themselves why they're writing this. "I'm writing this because I want to try and get straight what happened when my father left," as one man wrote. Another put it differently: "I'm writing this to avoid having to write about..." On each occasion we can challenge ourselves to come clean, to name what's really going on, for that is sometimes the hardest thing to do.

Chapter Three

More Exercises for Getting Started

Here is another exercise that may prove helpful in reflecting on who you are. It was originally suggested to me by Pat Nasca and I've adapted it over the years to its present form.

EXERCISE 1:

Find a sheet of paper approximately 8 inches by 12 inches, larger if possible. You'll need a piece of paper that is dark brown - I usually use old grocery bags - some glue and some pencils. Green would be a good color to have.

Take the dark brown paper. For this exercise you are to tear the paper: no cutting allowed! Tearing the paper, I'd like you to create the shape of a tree, and glue it to the larger sheet of paper. When you've finished look at what you have created. Write a reaction to it.

Does it sound bizarre? Well, there's method to this. Tearing the paper relieves us from the usual dilemma of feeling that our tree will not be 'good enough'. After all, if we have to improvise, we can't be criticized for lacking finesse, can we? That is the message we send ourselves, and the unconscious and conscious defenses tend to relax, so we can play. In fact, this exercise can bring us back to the stage of unfettered creativity that we lost when we began to worry that the products we generated might not be acceptable. This takes us back to about the age of five or six, when we all felt able to draw, paint, create, and be effective. I say 'all', because that is generally true.

If you found you could not do this exercise it's a fair guess that your creative and playful side was inhibited some time before you reached school. That would tend to indicate a parental force that worked to discount those feelings. A woman, who described herself as the conformist of the family, knew she had given up this aspect of herself very early in her childhood in order to gain parental praise. In our subsequent work together we spent some time attempting to release her from this 'sensible' voice, as she called it, so that she could uncover her creativity. This was not a minor point. As it emerged over time, she felt, at age fifty-three, that she had failed to get her life started because she couldn't nurture or believe in her dreams. This showed itself in a hesitation - which had lasted thirty years - to buy an apartment. It just wasn't 'sensible' for a single woman to have her own place, she said. She was supposed to meet a man, marry, and move to his place. This had not happened, and she had remained stuck. After all, she'd always done as her parents had told her to, so why hadn't life happened as she'd been told it would? Her life, and her creativity, had remained on hold.

This is the first thing one can learn from this exercise. Ask yourself: how open are you to playing? Phrased another way, how strong is the Internal Critic that stops you doing what you'd like to do?

The trees that have emerged when clients have done this exercise have been many and varied. Look at yours. Did you give it branches? How many? What about leaves? And roots? I've seen trees that were spindly-looking things, the green pencil applied for the foliage, but no sense of branches. I've seen trees without leaves. A woman of forty in a poor marriage produced a tree whose roots were strong and extensive but the tree itself was without foliage. Instead it had a single drop of dew on a branch, which she compared to a tear. The sense that came through this picture was that she knew she had deep-rooted strengths, but that her best outward show, the leaves, were blasted by her husband's rages. As a diagram of herself and her life, it could hardly have been more accurate, or more poetically suggestive.

I give this example because we all have at least two sides to us - that which shows (the leaves), and that which we feel to be an inner strength (the branches, the roots). Do your branches support your leaves, as in a real tree? If not, this may indicate a sense that one's outward actions are not vitally linked to who one is. After all, we all know what a tree is - so we've no excuse for not being able to make cause and effect connections. How twisted were the branches and the roots? The tortured tree may reflect a suffering or even a melodramatic personality. Write some words of explanation beside your tree, thoughts you may have about what it shows. If you choose to decode it, it can be a useful diagram of the self, of where you are now.

Sometimes responses to this exercise have only surfaced much later, as people tend to see trees as powerful symbols of themselves, growing. One man of forty chose to quote from W.B.Yeats:

Though leaves are many, the root is one;
Through all the lying days of my youth
I swayed my leaves and flowers in the sun;
Now I may wither into the truth

He then added his own poem, which I quote:

Faltering in his career choices,
He is now open to see;
There are flowers in the picture,
Where once there was only seed.
Move Upward and Onward!

Now, life reveals there is
Always play time,
Just as fragrance will always recede.
Life, now, is known to be, the space between
The blossom and the seed.

John Hearne

In each case there is an identification of the self with the solid trunk of the tree, and a sense of the self growing and developing. In a very real way this exercise of constructing a tree can be seen as a self-portrait.

In a slightly different way a young woman writing about a tree chose to link the idea of roots to the centeredness and caring she saw in a friend, and distilled this into a poem.

Friendship
Like the roots grown from the tree of life
Stable and strong
Reaching deep into the majestic soil
Fanning her webbed tentacles
Absorbing the nutrients
To create not destroy
Life and love.

Mercedes Munson

I give these examples in detail because in response to this exercise many people have reported a renewed interest in creative activities. One woman immediately went out and bought several packets of crayons - which she then was very hesitant to use because she could hear her mother's voice saying: "What do you need them for?" When I ordered her, as 'homework', to do a drawing the imagined mother's voice was silenced, at least temporarily.

Since creativity can be so easily squelched - how many of us draw with pleasure now, compared to a first grade class where children can scarcely be restrained from drawing? - it's worth exploring further. In a sense each of the exercises in this book is like a 'reason,' or an excuse to examine things we'd have trouble approaching on our own. How many of us make time each day to find out what is going on in our deepest selves? Julia Cameron, in her book *The Artist's Way*, suggests that we all should write at least three pages every day no matter what. She calls them 'morning pages' because they help to set one up for the rest of the day. I personally think this is an excellent idea, and yet I recognize how hard it is to do this. Three pages seems like a lot. The blankness of the paper appalls us. Personally I hate blank paper. In order to write the first draft of this book I resorted to what usually works for me - I write by hand on the back of used computer print out paper. That way I can reassure myself that this is just a draft: it's not 'real' writing, and I can suspend my critical self for long enough to get the words down. But hand me a nice neat notebook and I'll freeze, at least initially. Ernest Hemingway had a similar problem, it is said. He used to make sure he finished each day's writing about half way down the page. That way, when he continued, he would be adding on rather than starting anew. A blank page held terrors for him.

I'm sure many of us can identify with that. A friend I know is a gifted public speaker, and he clutches his notes before each presentation. Yet the notes contain only the barest outline of what he has to say, and just above that is his meticulously worded opening. Once he has started he has no trouble. It's the start that is always so hard for him. He told me he used to start always with a quotation from some erudite source. That way he felt reassured; it wouldn't even be himself who started.

Whatever it takes to get us started, I'd suggest an exercise, any exercise, is a version of this, for without one nothing might happen at all.

Starting is always a difficult prospect. Joseph Conrad, the novelist, recorded in his memoirs how his editors, on seeing his first manuscript and agreeing to publish it, asked if he could produce another like it. Conrad was struck by this and recorded his reaction as follows: "Another I could do. Many others I was not sure of. But another…" He went on to produce a major novel or story collection on average every eighteen months, until he died thirty years later. He was a writer who constantly had trouble starting work, and who produced some of his finest writing when under pressure to meet periodicals' publishing deadlines. Creativity may not be a comfortable process, even for the truly gifted.

Eric Clapton, the world renowned guitarist, had a similar reluctance to start work, often dreaming up reasons not to come to the recording studio. Several times he even appeared with a note, written by Patty Boyd, his then girlfriend, excusing his absences - just like a naughty schoolchild, according to Glynn Johns, his producer at that time (WZRX, Clapton: Behind the Mask, 1996).

In my own work, coaching young writers or using writing as a therapeutic tool, I have found very often that the most encouraging and productive thing I can say to a client is, "That's an interesting comment. Can you tell me more about that?" Almost everyone can manage to write or say 'more', whereas asking someone to start again can stop the exploration dead in its tracks. If we are to reclaim our true creative selves, our true sense of our spirit, we may have to recognize that it will take some effort and even a few subterfuges. But it will be worth the trouble. So, as you look at what you have written, some of it may seem to be less than useful. Some of it may look promising: that's the part you might want to expand upon.

Building on the previous section I'd like you to try the following exercises as a way of reflecting more on who you are, and what that may mean for how you see the world.

EXERCISE 2:

Read the following poem.

The owl and the pussycat went to sea
In a beautiful pea-green boat
They took some honey and plenty of money
Wrapped up in a five pound note

They sailed away for a year and a day
To the land where the bong tree grows
And there in a wood
A piggy-wig stood
With a ring at the end of his nose.

Edward Lear's charming nonsense poem conjures up, for the most part, pleasing and slightly absurd images, as these two decidedly un-nautical creatures set out for far lands.

Imagine you are going on such a trip. What would you take? Who would you go with? What would you expect to find - hope to find - when you arrive? You can write a list, or a description, or draw a picture.

I've had many responses to this exercise. One woman, a gifted artist, spent several weeks perfecting her response - a series of pictures done in pastels, dramatizing the major events of the poem. Most striking was her initial picture in which two tiny creatures sat in a boat that was not pea-green, on surging and turquoise waves, underneath a vast blue-black sky. The feeling this picture conveyed was positively epic - suddenly the figures were not two rather silly animals but bold adventurers heading into an enormous, beautiful and wondrous future. In this woman's case the picture conveyed her sense of the wonder of future possibilities in her relationship, but to "explain" the picture in such naked terms would be to rob it of all its life. It was, above all, an optimistic picture.

Others have written lists of essential items to be taken along, and those lists have sometimes been extensive. Often the apprehension of the unknown, and the desire to be ready for anything, is expressed in the amassing of objects. How much did you choose to take with you? Were you optimistic, taking only things that would add enjoyment, or were you fearful, and intent on carrying extra lifejackets?

One man of twenty-two was quite clear that he'd need charts and 'a bilge pump' for when the boat sprang a leak. Other responses have included on the boat such figures as trained gourmet chefs, and the full crew of an oceanic liner. Since the type of boat in the poem is not specified (although Edward Lear's original sketches showed a rowing boat) some responses have assumed this to be a cruise ship heading for the Caribbean. For others this was a white-water rafting expedition, while one woman chose long barges such as one sees in Europe on canals. In each case the poem was hardly adhered to faithfully or even logically - white water rafting for a year and a day? Now that would be taxing.

The point of this exercise is to ask you to look ahead. How do you see your life ahead? Is it placid, rowing down a gentle river, or is it storm-tossed? And is that what you want? Many people enjoy storms. And who did you choose to take with you? Some people take siblings or parents in preference to spouses or significant others. What does your choice say about you? Some people choose to take those they've never met; film stars appear fairly often. I find for such people it is the fantasy that is clearly the most important aspect, and it's worth asking them to explore further what they may expect from someone they cannot know. The choice of a companion says a huge amount about what relationships are important to the individual, and what each person hopes for that relationship. Remember, cruises have always been romantic, and in these days of jet travel, one chooses to go on a boat because it is slow, relaxed and trouble-free. "I'd like to get you on a slow boat to China..." that much-broadcast song of early 1960s, was a love-song that spelled out how hard it was to get time alone with the person one might be attracted to.

There are other aspects of this exercise that may reward closer scrutiny, also. The size of the boat may indicate a desire for pleasure - the cruise liner, for example - while a smaller boat may hint at a valuing of emotional intimacy. In addition a sea voyage involves dealing with water, traditionally seen as moody, emotional, and challenging. Poseidon, the Greek god of the sea, and Neptune, his Roman counterpart, were both characterized as passionate, emotional and unstable, although very definitely male. If we add to this the fact that the sea moves to the tides, which are controlled by the moon - traditionally seen as a feminine force linked to the menstrual cycle - the watery element can be seen as symbolic of the female emotions also. Since the moon itself waxes and wanes, it is often connected to the idea of the ups and downs of the emotions. When looking at the way you respond to the sea, this exercise can give insight into how you feel about the emotional demands and expectations you see ahead. How comfortable are you with your emotions and the emotions of others?

Usually, when I give this exercise the responses describe events in broad daylight. Lear's poem actually mentions that the Owl sings to the Pussycat "to the sound of a small guitar" and looks up "at the moon above." This knowledge can lead people to provide a night scene. On the whole though, the night scenes I have come across have been very few in number, and those that I've encountered often have less to do with romance than with a sense that the individual has a dark night to pass through before reaching the sunlight again. If you produced a night scene, ask yourself if this is a representation of what you see ahead for yourself on your journey through emotionally demanding times.

Broadly speaking, fearful people tend to focus on the things they'll take with them. Optimists will tend to take less, or take items that have to do with physical comfort. Those who have strong family ties or relationships they wish to cultivate will concentrate on the duration of the journey and who they spend it with, rather than the destination. In this way the exercise can be seen as a metaphor for where you want your life to go, and under what circumstances, and what you expect your life to provide for you. If we expect life to be good to us, the chances are we won't settle for second best, and so the list of things, and the places you may discover on the journey, can indicate how you see yourself in relation to what the world will provide. One young man imagined having to subdue the hostile population of a small island, using his shotgun. His sense of violent struggle was entirely different from that of a woman of thirty-eight who had her five siblings on board the large cruise ship she was sailing in, and no destination was even being aimed for, let alone arrived at. The harmonious, pleasurable journey was everything, and arriving was purely coincidental.

The question this exercise asks us is to consider that, ultimately, we have to provide for ourselves on our journey through life. We have to make things happen. If we don't spell out to ourselves what we want and need, how can we hope to get it? If we don't see our fears and challenge them, how can we move beyond them? This whimsical exercise can help.

For younger people what's often most important is what they find at the end of the trip, "In the land where the bong tree grows." The ring in the pig's nose can be seen as a reward, or a trophy, earned at the end of the voyage. A man of twenty one saw himself arriving at the island only in his advanced years, and the ring was to be sent back to his relatives, after he was dead, to show what he had achieved. The ring in the original poem was used as a wedding ring for the Owl and Pussycat, as you may recall, and there have been any number of people who have written about taking a loved one on this trip and giving the ring to that person. In these instances the value of the ring is obvious. I would like to take it a little further, however. Just as one gives oneself in marriage, so we could see the ring as being a metaphor for one's relationship with oneself. Did you value the ring? Did you wear it, either on your hand, or as an earring, or even on a string around your neck? Did you hide it? It may be worth writing more about the story you produced in response to this poem.

In fact, if the ring can be seen as symbol of the achieved self it can work, as many symbols do, both ways. There are some people who will value the ring, wearing it around the neck for status. "I'd wear it to keep those pigs in order, let them know who's boss," wrote a man of twenty-three who had a history of struggling to gain respect. A young woman of twenty-four was equally sure she didn't need a ring at all, so confident was she of who she was. And so the symbol can work both ways. What's important here is how you felt about the ring. Another example may clarify this.

A woman who was a survivor of incest described how she would like to take her boyfriend on the trip to a desert island. When she had the ring she said she would stand with him on the edge of a large freshwater lagoon and throw the ring high in the air so it landed in the center of the water. This would be the sign of her connectedness to him. This wonderfully poetic statement links, I feel, the life-giving and refreshing aspects of the water (which, as I have suggested, has a great deal to do with the emotions) with a desire to throw off an old sexual attachment (symbolized by the ring) and have that experience washed clean so the new attachment can grow. It was fairly clearly a story of redemption and renewal.

And this leads me into a larger discussion, which I shall call 'the stories we tell ourselves'. The exercise we have been looking at is a very effective way of mirroring back to ourselves the unacknowledged 'stories' we may use to shape our past experiences, and which can, in turn, limit our future. If we see our lives as being spent on a leaky boat, lost in a watery waste, then we are telling ourselves 'the world is like this for me'. We can choose another version - we can choose anything we want to. We could select the luxury liner, heading towards a beautiful destination, if we wish. So why did you choose the boat you did? What we choose is worth looking at because it can reflect to us our ideas of 'luck'. "Just my luck!" a friend of mine used to say whenever anything went wrong. And when things went well he could be heard saying. "I don't believe it. Something's bound to go wrong soon..." I used to be amused by his pessimism until I realized that because he expected things to go badly, he looked only for events that would confirm his bleak outlook. As a result he was, literally, blinding himself to the good things that were around him. He just could not see them.

This is what I mean by 'the stories we tell ourselves'. There are many, from simple roles we find ourselves slipping into to the whole way we run our lives. A simple role may be something like this. I knew a man who pretended to be mechanically incompetent because he discovered that other men and women were only too anxious to come and help him out - and show off as they did so. The strategy worked, but at the expense of making the man believe he was less competent than he really was. This was an interesting example to me because that role is often played by women when they want men to do things for them. The manipulation of the gender stereotype is easily accomplished. The person sends out a signal that says 'please help poor little me', and those who wish to appear competent are happy to oblige. The trouble is that we may actually become the roles we adopt.

A more complex example of this sort of 'story' came to my attention some years ago when I was traveling in India. A young Indian man asked me why I was traveling and what job I had. I replied that I had given up my job as a teacher, sold everything and had set out traveling, and that I did not know what job awaited me in the future. He laughed, because, he explained, he couldn't believe anyone would do that. In his world, he said, no one would dare to leave a job, certainly not a teacher, unless there was another job waiting. His mindset, his 'story', was that one found a job and stayed in it. Mine was that I'd held one job and could track down another when the time came.

I give these examples because we all have these stories. If I had accepted the young Indian's story I would never have traveled as I did, and my life would have been the poorer for it. If he had accepted mine, he might well have risked poverty. Every story seems reasonable to the individual who owns it. There are, however, many culturally determined versions of these stories, which have become so pervasive as to be almost imperceptible to us. With this in mind let me outline a few. See if you recognize any of them. The chances are that you'll see aspects of several of these stories in your life.

1. The dangerous world.

Every night millions of Americans watch the news, or some 'real-life' police or rescue drama. The news is always bad news, of course, because disasters sell - and that's what the TV stations want so they can charge high prices for their advertising. We are, it would seem, in love with bad news. If we actually pay attention to this we'll see that we can fall into the trap of sending powerful negative messages to ourselves about how dreadful the world is. We may find ourselves not talking to strangers in public places for fear of being mugged or knifed. As we become more fearful we tend to notice more readily those things that confirm our view. Whether or not the world is as dangerous as we think it is, we find ourselves believing that it is.

Our sense of reality, then, is that the world is dangerous. And since we're too fearful to check our perceptions, we are unlikely to be able to emerge from our fear. Now, I'm not suggesting that the world is all sweetness and light. Surely it isn't. All I'm suggesting is that whenever we fear the worst in others we do not give them the chance to behave well. I realized long ago, when working with the emotionally disturbed, that if I acted as if I expected them to misbehave, they usually did. Yet when I gave them some responsibility and some respect, when I let them know that I expected them to be able to act appropriately, they almost always managed to. In the wider world, if we treat people with suspicion and fear we're unlikely to see the best of them.

This may sound trivial. You may think that I'm exaggerating. All I can say is that office managers everywhere are paying large amounts of company money to go to seminars that will tell them essentially the same thing - that respect breeds respect. If this works in a company, why not in the whole world? What sort of world do you want to live in?

2. Conspiracy Stories.

These spin off from the news. Everything (but everything these days) is far more sinister and devious than we ever imagined. We love this sort of thing. We must, because UFOs, cover-ups by the CIA, and FBI double-dealing are the regular fodder of publications like *The Enquirer, The Weekly World News* and so on, as well as of such seemingly respectable media as Discovery Channel TV, which has regular lengthy programs about UFOs and how the government is suppressing information. Note that those newspapers outsell many reliable newspapers, and that those TV shows, including programs like *The X-Files*, are extremely popular. What impact can this have on us? I've noticed that those who tend to gossip, who impute unpleasant motives to others, are often of the conspiracy school of thought. Talk to them and they'll tell you what's 'really going on' and very frequently it sounds as if there might be a conspiracy! That may be true or it may be a dangerous and limiting construct. Either way, ask yourself if you want to respond to the world in this way. Is this really what you want to think about every day, from the moment you wake up? There are, I'm sure, many conspiracies in the world. I, for one, do not recommend as a reaction to this that we all elect to live in fear.

The prevalence of conspiracy theories reveals two other deeply embedded beliefs that are often widely accepted without question. The first is that the world is filled with good guys and bad guys. Just as the early cowboy films insisted on the good guys wearing white hats and the bad guys wearing black hats (or being dressed as Indians, for example), so conspiracy theories tend to emphasize the us-and-them polarization. This sort of simplistic split is enacted over and over in Sylvester Stallone and Bruce Willis movies, in the Indiana Jones series, and even in Star Wars, as well as in sporting events where "the best team wins". This is rubbish of course. The 'best' team is the most successful one, and these days that is likely to mean the one with the most money to hire the biggest players and most skilled coaches. The team with the most money is much more likely to win, even when pitted against the team which is bonded together by mutual respect.

The second embedded story that comes out of this is that any conspiracy theory is merely a reversal of another familiar story. It's one which Starhawk points out in her book *Dreaming the Dark*. She calls it "The Great Man receives news and passes it on to the few." Conspiracies assume that there is a small body of people who know what's really going on, rather than what everyone thinks is going on. This is certainly echoed in most religious stories and even in their organizations. There have always been conclaves of the religious elite who decide what the masses should do. The Pope is allegedly infallible; the tablets of the laws were handed by God directly to Moses; Christ had his disciples and St. Paul set himself up as the person who decided how the church should be; the Ayatollahs in Iran declare what is holy, and so on. Yet each of these religions originally had a much greater openness than the times have more recently allowed. Christ originally preached directly to the crowds; there was no official view. Islam began as a religion that embraced others and was far more open to discussion and debate than seems to be the case today in many parts of the world. Judaism once reveled in the scholarly tradition of questioning the scriptures. Like the other religions it now seems to have its fair share of ultra-orthodox branches, all of which seem to be inflexible and ossified.

The danger point seems to be reached when any line of thinking is committed to paper - be it the Bible, the Torah, the Koran, the Communist Manifesto, or the complete Standard Edition of Freud. Freudians, Jungians, Adlerians and Kleinians fight just as bitterly as any religious faction that ever declared its independence, but they seem to shed less blood. A friend of mine informs me that even amid such organizations as the Macrobiotic Health Association there are purists who refuse to deviate from the 'official' line of Japanese macrobiotic dieting. However we look at it the imagery is clear. Some people 'know' and are 'experts' and the rest of us must listen. This is exactly the mindset I wish to challenge. We all lose a little of our self-motivation when we agree to put aside what we know and feel and let others tell us what we ought to know and should feel.

In daily life this may be something as ordinary as doing what we feel is expected of us by our neighbors. Or it may be that we accept without question something that a doctor prescribes for us, even though it seems to have strange side effects. Perhaps it takes the form of caving in to what the experts tell us about the way our child learns, and what he or she is capable of, when we know our child is able to do far more than they say. An example that springs to mind is of a woman of fifty who was told by doctor after doctor that there was no cure for her condition and that she would eventually have to have her bladder removed and wear an ostomy bag for the rest of her life, or live in pain. She refused to give in to medical orthodoxy and began exploring other non-traditional forms of medicine. After eighteen months of disappointments and frustrations she found the answers she needed. She is, at the time of writing, still not fully cured, but she is far better than she was, and she still has her bladder. It was through her journal working that she realized she did not have to accept the 'official' view of her condition.

This is not to say that there aren't many wonderful and knowledgeable people from whom we can learn a great deal. All I'm suggesting is that we should listen and be aware that our thoughts and feelings have value, too. This leads on to the next 'story', which is not really a story at all.

3. The language we use.

How do we explain things to ourselves? Too often we may phrase our thoughts in ways that are, whether or not we realize it, destructive. Whenever we find ourselves using words like 'should' and 'ought' and 'must' we are well advised to pay attention. For example, 'should' indicates that there is something that needs to be done that I haven't done. The fact that I haven't done it yet is blameworthy, and my feeling, which has caused the delay, is also blameworthy. So I punish myself twice over and I haven't done anything yet! Each time we use vocabulary like this we are in danger of tyrannizing ourselves into doing something, and reproaching ourselves at the same time. It's a double obligation. The antidote is to think in terms of 'I wish' and 'I want.' Look at the differences between these statements:

1. "I ought to go and get groceries…" (grumble mumble).
2. "I want to buy some groceries…" (I am in charge. I want food. I agree to take my responsibility even though I'm not mad about shopping).

Or an extreme example might be this:

3. "I have to go to that horrible supermarket and buy bags of groceries…"

Each is the same action. What varies in each case is the type of story we tell ourselves about what grocery shopping involves. If we set ourselves up for a negative experience that is exactly what we are most likely to achieve. The words we use can affect the way we feel about what we do.

Here's a brief exercise you can use for more understanding.

EXERCISE 3:

❖ Write a list of all the 'shoulds' you heard as a child, all the 'musts', all the 'oughts'. Write them in a column. Do about ten of these. More if you can.

❖ When you have your list write beside each one whether or not it sounds sensible today.

Some remembered 'shoulds' such as, "you should always leave the table feeling as if you could eat some more" may not seem very useful today. Other advice, like, "you should never borrow money from friends" may in fact be useful, depending on the friend. Mark the items that are still relevant to you today. Do about a dozen of these.

Did you find more items that were relevant than not? Did you identify any items you struggled against as a child that you might endorse now? Did you find some orders that you have rejected totally now that you are older?

One man confessed that at age forty-five he still refused to wear a seat belt in his car because he always recalled his parents telling him he should. An unfortunate side effect of this was that he never asked his ten year old child to buckle up, either. One might say that the on-going rebellion against his parents had outlived any symbolic usefulness it may once have had, and had now become potentially dangerous to a child who was not involved in the original struggles.

Another response, from a woman in her forties, was the following poem in which she discusses the strictness of her religious upbringing.

The Shoulds of Childhood

Creating saints
Out of sinners who no longer wear pigtails
But who still dream of forbidden caresses
In the middle of long afternoons.
The shoulds of voices
Once past, still present
Projecting
Future condemnations
Controlling every choice:
Deny all that you feel
Distrust all that is real
The reality above the need is the reality to be believed.
But who created me with desire?
Who planted this unquenchable fire within
Then gave me shoulds to fuel it even more?
Hell is within the should
                         Pat Nasca

The voice of 'should' and 'ought' has been identified variously by other writers as the voice of The Internal Critic, The Internal Parent, or the Superego, or any number of other names, including one I feel is particularly accurate, The Self-Hater. Think of that name. Think of what it conveys about what we do to ourselves. For I want to stress that this is something we do to ourselves, and therefore only we can release ourselves from it. We have heard the critical parental voice, and we've learned the lessons about what we're expected to do. The trouble is that we've learned them too well. Like soldiers who have been drilled never to do anything except on command, we have given away part of ourselves. We edit what we do before we do it.

The problem now becomes rather different. How can we turn The Self-Hater into The Self-Lover? But wait. Is that really the answer? If we do that aren't we just perpetuating the problem? The Self-Hater may be destructive at times, but The Self-Lover would seem to offer an easy path to complacency, self-indulgence, even narcissism, that ultimate form of self-absorption. I'd suggest an alternative possibility. The voice of self-hatred can almost always be traced to a critical parent figure who told us what he or she wanted us to do. This person, or persons, probably was only repeating the sort of coercion that he or she had to endure as a child. If we think back, though, it's not hard to imagine a scenario in which the adult tells the child what to do not out of a sense of tyranny, but out of a genuine sense of concern for the child and the family. "You have to wear a jacket and tie!" Those are words spoken by an adult who wants the family to be proper because he or she actually believes this will be a beneficial lesson, something that will help to form the child and make him more capable of success in the wider world. The action has somewhere buried in it genuine caring, just as when we give advice to a friend: "you should quit that job". There's should again.

If we can see the pin head of caring lost in the heap of chaff, we can see what to do with the voice of The Self-Hater. We cannot destroy it or silence it, and inverting it is no use. What we have to do is transform it. Appoint that 'should' voice as your official care-taker and permit it to speak only when the question is one of looking after yourself. Imagine the situation: I'm at a party and someone is encouraging me to drink, which I resist because I have to drive. My internal voice says, 'You shouldn't drink'. If I'm in rebellion against this parental voice I'll be tempted to disregard it entirely, and give in to the spirit of the party. Yet if I listen to this prompting as one that may be trying to protect me, I'll be far more likely to act wisely. That's what I mean by listening for the official care-taker.

Again, you may want to utilize 'I wish' or 'I'd like to' and 'I choose to' as often as you can. Instead of that voice hitting your inner ear as someone exerting power upon you as a helpless child, use it to elicit your own powers of taking care of yourself.

Should, as we have already seen, is a word that has a way of making us feel guilty about something. Another distinction that can be usefully made is that guilt and remorse are not the same thing. I'll take a moment, here, to deal with this because within this distinction lies another form of language that we may use to describe ourselves, and which is often hard to trace.

Guilt occurs when we feel we failed to be better than we were able to be. This is the most insidious of feelings because we can only do the best we can given who we are at the time, and guilt is the emotion that expects us to achieve more than we are able to. It's a little like criticizing a horse for not being a cow. And yet a version of this happens all the time. Parents often want their children to be something and that ambition may not have much to do with who each child actually is. So we internalize this over-hopeful expectation and it becomes a sense of guilt, a feeling that just because we are who we are we can never quite measure up. This manifests itself as a constant drain on our personal energy, a gloomy sense of being inadequate in the face of large demands, perhaps.

Another reaction might be for the child to try extra hard to come up to the expectations that the guilt has engendered. I will be the child my parent/teacher/grandparent wants! The danger here is that the individual will deny herself and her true nature in order to be sufficiently compliant and so win the affection and praise she craves. It's easy to see that someone who says yes to everyone receives, in the end, the respect of no one.

If we accept this definition of guilt we can see that it is, above all else, a static emotion. The person can never change and grow in a fundamentally life-giving way because he or she fears to antagonize others. Guilt keeps us stuck.

Remorse is quite different. Remorse comes from knowing we have hurt others, and from a desire to change that behavior. Remorse is the exact opposite of guilt because it always leads to change, if it is genuine. When we feel remorse we recognize we have done something amiss, something that we knew at the time we could have done better. In turn that gives us an awareness that we can approach those people who have been hurt and try to make amends. It may take some courage, but it allows us the chance to alter the relationship, to bring it back to a healthier state of mutual respect. This cannot happen with guilt. As Deborah Cowens writes:

> Guilt…tends to maintain its own patterns. This is the irony of guilt, because you would think that because it is so unpleasant, it would prevent us from repeating the same pattern, but it doesn't work that way. Guilt actually stops us from examining our pain. Guilt gives rise to a pain that is inarticulate, imprecise and opaque. Very often we're not sure why we feel guilty; all we know is that we do. But the underlying belief below the pain is that, somehow, we should have been a different person from the person we were. (p.152)

Perhaps an example might help. A relative described in detail how he had been loaned the family car when he was a teenager, and had been led to believe from his parents' attitude that he would, surely, do something wrong, something to hurt the car, just because he was the type of person he was. Even though he drove entirely without incident for several years he said that he never gave the car back without a sneaking feeling that he might have done it harm, just by using it. This was guilt in operation. It worked for the parents - the son was a careful driver because of it - but it left the son feeling tense, nervous, and unhappy. It stopped their relationship developing, because it implied that he was just not competent or grown up, yet.

When it was his turn to let his own teenager borrow the family car, he tried to be as calm as possible. Sure enough, the boy put a scrape on the passenger door in the first two weeks. The boy came to see his father, explained the damage, and between them they arranged to get it fixed. The son had to make the calls and deal with the garage, the father shared the cost. It seems that this was a good experience for both. When the son drives now he drives more safely. To put it in the father's words: "I used to drive carefully in fear, because I thought, this is my parents' car. My son drives our car safely out of a sense of responsibility, because he thinks of it as the car which we all have to take care to use wisely." The son is in this case not a junior partner being allowed to use what is not his. He's been welcomed as an equal and responsible person.

Guilt comes from outside, as in 'laying a guilt trip on someone', and it prevents change. Remorse leads to responsibility, and when people take responsibility they gain self-respect.

EXERCISE 4:

❖ Write down a list of things you have felt guilty about. Now, beside it, write a list of items you regretted but were able to come to terms with. Label the second list 'remorse'.

❖ Look at your list. Are there any items in the 'guilt' part that you could move into 'remorse,' if you were willing to deal with the people involved? Write about what that would take, if you were to do it.

Those who have done this exercise have reported that being able to redefine their feelings of guilt in this way, and examine the difference between guilt and remorse, can lead to a new awareness that can be truly liberating. "Once you stop apologizing for who you are life becomes far less exhausting!" wrote a man of thirty-six. Sometimes just being able to take a fresh look at a familiar problem can provide the necessary impetus to change. In general terms, one could say that this exercise gives us the opportunity to let go of certain fears and behaviors that are giving us pain. Naturally this is not always easy, because we've become accustomed to living that way, and we may even feel it to be morally wrong not to be in pain doubt. The choice is up to us.

There is an interesting side discussion to this topic, also. I've discovered over the years as I listen to clients that often all I have to do is be aware of repeated words or catch phrases, especially 'should', and I can begin to uncover some of the stories they tell themselves, some of the ways they shape their realities through the use of words.

There are, however, other stories that exist at a still more unconscious level, and I feel these are worth spelling out as well, since they are almost inseparable from ourselves. The first story is exactly that, the story of our lives, the sense of a beginning, a middle, and an end that shapes all our story telling. We shape experiences in this way in order to try and understand them, to make sense of them in the seamless forward rush of time. As such we have to break experience into more or less artificially selected chunks.

Perhaps this principle of shaping narrative was first formally articulated by Aristotle when he named the four elements of the drama. These are most easily explained as Situation, Complication, Climax and Catharsis. So, for example, Romeo's family is at war with Juliet's family (situation); Romeo and Juliet fall in love (first of a series of complications); they die for each other mistakenly (climax); and the ending is a sense of the evil of civil strife being purged, preparatory to a new beginning (catharsis). This is not a bad way of shaping a narrative, a play, or even a joke, but it is a shaping of reality that is being used for a specific purpose, usually to demonstrate a moral point, such as that civil war doesn't pay, in *Romeo and Juliet*. Our own life stories will fit no such easy pattern. Any Catharsis our deaths can provide will presumably not happen to us since the person who dies will rarely have the same sense of an ending that the survivors have. Most of us will die, I suspect, feeling that it's time to leave. Those who love us, who survive, may feel quite differently. If we have biographers it is eminently likely that their assessment of what our lives added up to, or 'meant' will be quite different from what we may feel as we expire. For example Ferdinand Marcos, the former dictator of the Philippines, was convinced that his nation would be convulsed by grief when he died. He was mistaken about that.

Another version of this type of story is to be seen in the name given to World War I, 'The Great War' as it is still called, and 'The War to End all Wars.' This was what the allies called it, but to Hitler it was a series of outrages to be redressed. The Second World War was immeasurable greater in scope and was referred to as 'The Big One' - with the implicit assumption that since that was the big one then there would be no chance of a larger one coming along. And yet - the Nazi and fascist elements of several countries have begun to rise again. Genocides from Cambodia to Bosnia have been based on the same sort of racial victimization as Hitler's holocaust. I could multiply the instances, but I think I've made the point. The stories that shape history only end because we choose to give them closure in our imaginations. Usually they are just the latest events in a series that will alter the meaning or value of the events that came before.

The celebrated Oxford historian Niall Ferguson has used this approach many times to question the accepted 'stories' of history, and in the process has asked provocative questions about how we shape reality by forcing it into a set pattern. He energetically opposes "any method that approaches history as a 'story' with a beginning, a middle, and an end - a fixed narrative that relegates contingency and alternative outcomes to the realm of science fiction and fantasy."

4. The American Dream.

A different story we tell ourselves is what I call 'The American Dream' or the 'If I Try I Will Succeed...' story. The American dream is a wonderful construct, and has certainly helped many people to feel empowered, and to make things happen in their lives. There is an unfortunate down-side however. If we all feel we have to be better, more successful, than our parents' generation then we put an enormous amount of pressure on ourselves. Those who are not so able or so adept as their parents may feel that they are failures, that they just didn't try hard enough. A woman in her forties put it like this: "There's my brother. He works hard, he tries hard, but he just doesn't make it. No one could try harder. And it makes him miserable." This man might not be a success, but he certainly isn't a failure, and I'm sure he doesn't deserve to feel miserable. And yet the missing factor in this equation can be something as intangible as luck. One may be a perfectly well-motivated person but one's luck may not be good, or one falls ill, or one has to choose whether to go on and be a success or care for those who need it.

The danger of success as a criterion of worthiness is that it presupposes that some people are more valuable than others just because they are successful, and thus they are more worthy of respect. In fact the world's most copious raw resource is people, and all countries waste cheap resources. Many of us may not have the chances others have, by accident of birth and circumstance. I'd suggest that the negative side of the American Dream is that there is a lessened possibility for Americans to feel they matter *unless* they can feel successful. It's a message that comes at us from our TV screens regularly, whether it be the Dow chemicals ad of the farmer proudly sending his daughter to agricultural college, or the Citibank voice-over that says "...because Americans want to succeed, not just survive." In many countries in the world survival sounds very attractive to most of the population; success is beyond their dreams. It makes us ask what success is, doesn't it? In America it is equated more often than not with wealth. Rarely is it coupled with the image of the working man doing his best, with dignity, and being aware of life's joys.

There is, in addition, another danger to this idea of hard-work-inevitably-breeds-success, and one that I often see in college-aged students. Many of them do work hard, do not succeed, and feel like failures. In the work that I've done with many of them, however, another element can emerge. This is that 'hard work', for some of them, means simply doing the same thing as always, but doing more of it. The difficulty here is that there's a difference between working hard and working well. In a world of bewilderingly rapid changes it is mental flexibility that is important. Grandfather may have made a fortune running a grocery store, but if a vast supermarket opens down the street, offering twenty-four hour service, hard work alone will not preserve the smaller store. One has to have a plan. Hard work, if truth is told, is never enough.

These are just some of the stories we may tell ourselves every day of our lives. Some of them will be reflected in your responses to the Owl and the Pussycat exercise. Others you may have found yourself becoming aware of in the sections that followed. Perhaps you want to take a moment, now, to write down your responses to these pages.

It's likely that there are many other stories that have not yet been detected, which we buy into regularly. Stories are our natural way of making sense of the world and of our experiences, but there's a price to be paid, as we've seen. In their purest form stories can stop us being fully present in the world. If we're constantly telling ourselves that we are going to be the great American success story we may indeed become rich and famous, but we may forget that the journey is as much a part of our lives as the destination. In the Owl and the Pussycat exercise, were you more concerned with the journey or with the destination?

When I worked with disturbed adolescents I noticed that some of them were so afraid of looking at themselves that they would create any drama at all to prevent them from having to confront their own fears of being empty. They claimed to be much happier when they were on the run, scrabbling to survive, than when they were well housed, fed, and able to think about why they did things. For several of them the story they seemed to need was what I called 'desperado'. Today we could see similar versions of this in many compulsive actions, from work addiction to promiscuity, to depression. It is, therefore, a good idea to ask ourselves regularly what stories we seem to be telling ourselves, and whether there might not be another story that would serve us better and help us to be present in the moment. Perhaps Joan Didion put it best in *The White Album* when she wrote: "We tell ourselves stories so that we can live."

Chapter Four

BIRTH AND THE FAMILY

Building on our experiences with naming, it's worth taking some time to consider one's family, and birth order in particular. I've adapted an exercise originally proposed by James Agati, and over the years in response to classroom needs it's become sufficiently different that I now consider it my own. In workshops I ask the participants to divide themselves up into groups - only children, first born, second born, third born (and later), and last born. If there is a gap of greater than four years between children I ask the later-born person to consider him or herself as being a first born. These people can float between the two groups and decide which one they belong to. I then ask each group to record all the messages they received as they grew up - the things they heard said to them by parents, and even the unspoken expectations they felt themselves to be under. Twins and adopted children are also asked to join the same categories, but to make their own lists if they feel their messages were different from those their group is recording. At the end of ten minutes or so I ask each group to read out these lists.

EXERCISE 1:

If you are working with others you may want to divide up, now, and produce your own lists. If you are working alone take a piece of paper and write down the words or phrases you remember your parents telling you. If you were the oldest child, perhaps they wanted you to look after your little brothers and sisters. Did they expect you to be responsible in that way? If you were not a first child you may have been compared to one of your siblings. 'Why can't you be more like so-and-so!' Were you ever told you were 'too little' to do certain things? These are the sorts of messages you may have received. Write them down.

When you have produced eight or more of these messages, review your list. What is the picture that you see emerging? Can you write about this?

What I find again and again is that the messages we recall have stayed with us, in one form or another, all our lives. These early imprintings have often not faded at all and have replicated themselves in all aspects of our being. Let's take a moment to see how this works.

When a first-child is born she enters a world that is usually parent-dominated. The child sees that the rules of living appear to be heavily in favor of these large, capable adults, and so she joins with that series of expectations. That way she is assured of love and acceptance. If the child is an only-child the bond is especially strong, and often the only child is treated by the adults as an equal participant in many of the family activities, in a way that is often less available for families with more than one child. Many only-children have reported their messages to be such things as, 'You can be anything you want to be. You can be better than us,' and 'Work hard at all you do'. These are wonderful positive messages, of course, but they also are tinged with a parental desire for the child to move rapidly into an adult world of achievement. In the adult world this child will have no trouble at all relating to employers and authority figures, and will have no compunction in challenging them since the child has always felt on an equal footing with the adults in her life. In contrast, the negative aspect can be that the only-child has become the focus of many frustrated parental hopes, and so she may be continually fearful of what the parents may think of her decisions.

Interestingly, only-children report higher levels of trust shared with their parents than any other group. This makes sense given the feelings of equality they are likely to encounter, and this factor never fails to astonish others who have a different birth order. "Total trust, one hundred percent. I tell them everything," said a first-born woman of twenty-two, and the woman beside her, a second-born aged twenty-four, simply said, "No way," and left it at that. This is a fairly typical reaction, in my experience.

The group of eldest children usually record messages that are substantially different from the second-borns, and that indicate they were expected to look after the others, be responsible, and take charge of the younger children. The down side is that they do not see themselves as being on the same footing with adults in the same way that the only-child very often is. As a result, such first-born children tend to find it easy to be administrators and make decisions. They're good at giving orders and don't expect any discussions, because their earliest experiences with siblings have been that they are right; they have been entrusted with authority, and the younger children haven't. This group may well turn out to be conformist in nature, often doing the right thing at the expense of their own desires or wishes. There may even be considerable resentment towards, and envy of, younger and seemingly less disciplined siblings.

Second-born children tend to feel overshadowed by the first-born, and their messages reflect this: 'Why can't you be more like...' and 'When you're his age you can too...' are typical. If the time gap between births is very close - a year or less - there is often fierce rivalry for attention. Second-born children tend to observe how the parents give praise, what the first-born does well, and then they try and develop their own abilities in a different direction. It can be too frustrating to compete with an older brother or sister who is, for example, very athletic, so the second-child may become bookish or develop a different sort of sporting interest. Second-born children tend, in this way, to find a niche for themselves, and will often feel like questioning the authority structure in the family, wondering out loud why it has to be his way, when the oldest child would not question, perhaps.

Bear in mind, here, that if there is a sufficiently long gap between children, and more than five years is a good rule of thumb, then it is quite possible that the second child will be treated in most respects the same way as the first child, since the two children are not in competition at all. Older sisters are frequently reported as being more like mothers to younger siblings in these cases, and the gap, if sufficiently large at any point, can turn that child into an 'honorary' oldest child, or even an only-child.

Another way in which the roles can be changed is if the oldest child rebels against parental authority by refusing that role of responsible conformity, in which case the second-born may well find that the parents expect him or her to fulfill that role by default. Sometimes this takes the form of the 'favorite' oldest child falling out of favor and being replaced by another child who now becomes the favorite - but the price is that the new favorite has to buy into the parents' rules. In this way, too, the second-born can achieve 'honorary' first born status, and may willingly acquiesce. It's always worth remembering that the first-born historically was the one to carry on the family traditions and inherit the bulk of the money. Even in families where there's no money there is often a strong sense of obligation to parental pressures to conform, and to be what they wish that child to be.

You may have noticed that in the preceding paragraph I used the word 'favorite'. This is very often a concern for second and later born children. They tend to wonder who is loved best by the parents, and where they may fit in. Eldest children rarely seem to report any doubts about this. Second-borns most often do, with only rare cases of it being a concern for later children.

Frank Sulloway, in his twenty years of research at Harvard, has shown through exhaustive statistical analysis that second-born children make up an overwhelming percentage of the world's revolutionaries, inventors, and political innovators, where first-borns tend to be leaders in a more conservative way. The second-born child learns early what it means to take on the existing power structure in order to try and get his or her own way, and will be well-practiced at questioning the established order.

Third-born and later children tend to be the great negotiators. They'll also be risk takers. After all, if the third-born sees the first-born riding a bike without training wheels for the first time, to parental approval, the third child is likely to think, 'Hey! I can do that! If I fail, then there's no disgrace because I'm so young; and if I succeed the pay-off is huge!' Armed with such thoughts, the child will be a risk taker, precocious, and also capable of tremendous achievements. This child, if he or she has younger siblings, will also be a negotiator - one who from infancy is seasoned at getting his or her own way, and playing people off against each other if that seems necessary. These children can become formidable politicians, and extraordinary manipulators. They learn early to read other people's characters and by adulthood they can often have a deep intuitive awareness of what others want but cannot say. They know how to deal with the elder siblings, so they go through life instinctively knowing how to manage their bosses. They can be gifted diplomats, or on the negative side, they can become dreadful gossips. Both aspects are ways of using information rather than strength or confrontation.

Third-borns and later children often report that they were clothed in hand-me-downs, and they may even be unsure about what actually belongs to them if the family is large.

The result in later life can be that these children are keen to have things that they know are theirs and may be meticulous about clothing and presentation. It can also work the other way, in that the child may come to believe that material objects are not going to be important or valued, and so this child can be careless with other people's possessions and even with things like business reports and accounting procedures.

The youngest child may well be an even better diplomat than the third child. Certainly the 'baby' is often the favorite of the parents and, like Jacob in the Bible, this favoritism can be the cause of sibling envy. The 'baby' can choose which role to take on - to be adult when that suits or to be helpless when that seems more convenient. The baby of the family can be very manipulative, very persistent, and inventive to a high degree. The same situation, however, can produce the individual who refuses to grow up or take responsibility, one who plays it helpless and gets others to do the real work.

This thumb-nail outline is not intended to be conclusive. For one thing, there are many more combinations available. What happens when single parents with children marry other single parents with children, for example? How does that alter the idea of birth order? And, in the end, all the examples discussed here depend upon the western model of a nuclear family. In India and Pakistan one frequently sees the extended family as a unit, with uncles, cousins, grandmothers and several sets of parents taking care of a large brood of children. Obviously such cases lead to a different sort of considerations. In the United States social workers have spent much effort in recent years attempting to define what a family might be, especially in poor and inner-city circumstances. The criteria vary, but they may include sharing accommodations, sharing meals and the sharing of child care, but not necessarily blood ties or overt financial links. If any of this is part of your background you may want to reflect on it in writing. What was different about your experience? One man responded by drawing up a communication chart for his family, in which he was able to trace just who was allowed to say what to whom, and who was allowed to question and challenge whom. What's important here is not that you should be squeezed into someone else's theory, but that you should be able to use this information for your own purposes.

As you read this, think of your family, think of your birth order. Do any of these categories seem to ring a bell for you? Agati claims that birth order is the single best predictor of adult character traits. Would you agree? If this seems too analytic, here is a narrative exercise for you.

EXERCISE 2:

❖ Imagine the widest impact your birth has had on your family, your community, your country, the world. Write about it.

You can answer this any way you wish. Some people choose fantasy, humor and exaggeration, imagining cheering crowds greeting the news. Laura Esquivel in *Like Water for Chocolate* describes Tita's birth in comic terms. Her mother was chopping onions in the kitchen and Tita began weeping in the womb. When she was born, she was already crying and the tears when they dried provided ten pounds of salt - which was later used for cooking. Just as this mythic exaggeration sets the tone for Tita's story in the novel, you can use this exercise to create a mythology of yourself. What was the maximum significance of your birth? Have fun.

This can lead us to another question.

EXERCISE 3:

❖ What are the stories told about your birth? What are the stories you have remembered about your birth?

One woman reported that her mother had said that at her birth she emerged smiling from the womb, and the doctors were all astonished. This story, which the mother swore was true, seemed to explain as well as describe the extraverting, ebullient adult she had become. Her story seemed apt and poetic, and served to remind her that, compared to most, she was upbeat, outgoing, and sociable. By contrast, a middle-aged man recalled his mother describing him as 'a big lump' of a baby, and how those three words had made him feel he was ungainly and a burden, loved but hardly the child his mother had wished for. In both cases this exercise gave these people small nuggets of information that they had accepted as somehow reflective of a deeper truth that lay beyond the story. Tita's birth, as related by Laura Esquivel, leads to sorrow and more tears, and the circumstances of birth would seem to play themselves out in life. What do you know about your birth? To what extent might the stories of your birth have shaped your expectations?

EXERCISE 4:

❖ Can you recall your baby names? What did your parents call you as a nickname?

Baby names can shape us much as anything. 'Little one' may seem neutral but what about 'Little Man' which I have often heard people say they were called? At one point that could be cute; at another, diminishing. The expectations in the word man may have extra weight, also. And what about names like 'Treasure' and 'Precious' and 'Jewel'? How do those feel beside 'Big Guy', 'Champ', and so on? What about less flattering names? Children often call each other cruel nicknames, and they stick: 'Stupid', 'Toad', 'Mouse', 'Rabbit', 'Dingo', 'Bunny'. All these may have positive or negative connections, and the connections change over time. How do you think people saw you then?

EXERCISE 5:

❖ Find a baby picture of yourself, at say one year old, or a picture at the age of four or less. What do you see? What do you remember? Now find a picture at age eight or so. Write about these.

It can be very enlightening to see ourselves in photographs. In baby pictures we may be surprised at how vulnerable we looked. At a year old we've already learned quite a bit about the world. You may want to do this exercise with a friend so you can compare pictures. One man didn't know what to say about his picture until he compared it with someone else's. 'I looked kind of bored and fed up', he said, 'whereas my friend's picture was of a lively, interested kid. I didn't realize how different things could be at that age.' What can you reconstruct from your pictures?

At age four most of us have not yet gone to regular schooling, so the photograph may reflect a relatively free and unsocialized child. Think your way into that child's world. What can you recall? What did you like to do?

By the age of eight we have come into contact with all sorts of things we like and all sorts of things we really don't like. We can no longer avoid eating our green beans or broccoli, we have to tidy our rooms, we have to behave. At age eight we can see a child coming to terms with the greater world, excited by it and still not allowed to do certain things. Look at your picture. What do you see?

This exercise can produce a flood of information. It's a good idea to return to it from time to time. Often it can be useful to pin these pictures up somewhere you can see them every day. Things will come to mind, in which case write them down. It's important to honor the memories, good and less good. One man recalled how rough the material of his short pants was, at the age of five, and how his mother sewed soft cotton onto the inner seams so it would not rub. Another man recalled how much he loved the rain hat he is shown wearing at a rakish angle. How much can you reconstruct?

EXERCISE 6:

❖ Think of your toys. Write a narrative of you and your favorite toy. Which toys have disappeared?

Toys are important to us. We lavish affection on our teddy bears and dolls. We built fantasy worlds around them, and we wept piteously when they were lost. These were objects of real significance to us at the time. Possibly they still are. Do you still preserve your toys? Every year college freshmen and freshwomen carry their teddies to their dorms. Many people collect toys, dolls, and antique playthings, often in an attempt to recreate a childhood delight that may not have been entirely fulfilled. It has long been held by psychiatrists that 'transitional objects' - usually cuddly toys or a special blanket - give substantial comfort to children. As they 'love' the toy it frees up the mother who might otherwise be the only source of comfort and affection, and this in turn allows the child to separate from her without being panicked. What was the comfort you derived from your toys?

EXERCISE 7:

❖ Describe a safe place.

All children need to feel safe. Toys, as in the preceding exercise, can help them feel safe. Sometimes real safety may not seem possible in very chaotic families. Yet, often a relative's arms may be sufficient. Even in the most loving families children like to have dens, or camps where they can be apart. Place a blanket over a table and watch as children aged about five head straight for this 'tent' or 'hut' and revel in its coziness. Tree houses, play houses, corners of the attic, all are popular. One man recalled squeezing himself down behind the couch, with his feet against the radiator, as a favorite safe place. Another man described having to run away from a raging and drunken father, and he'd hide in the wood shed until the crisis was over.

Your idea of a safe place may well find its expression today in your choice of home decoration, the amount of things you surround yourself with, and your choice of home. So called Pack-Rats, for instance, may have become that way because being surrounded by objects was more comfortable than facing the world without support. Writing about a safe place can help you confront what was not safe about your home life. It's far more effective than asking 'what was scary about your home?' That sort of question simply makes people clam up. What you perceived to be dangerous in your home life is what may tend to emerge, here, as you consider what places were safe for you. A safe place, in addition, can be the place in which you were able to use your imagination creatively without fear of adult (or sibling) interruption to deflate the game. It's always worth asking yourself what your imaginative world was like. Did you lose yourself in books? Did you have any special toys? Often people will say they had a favorite stack of comic books, or a favorite author, or a set of toy cars that only were played with alone in that safe place. A young man recalled that his 'best' toy soldiers would accompany him to the back of the closet, since he didn't trust that any of his friends could play with these toys and not lose various accessories. A young woman described how she set up an alternative bedroom in her closet. At night her mother would tuck her into her bed, turn off the light, and close the door. Then the girl would sneak into her alternative bed in the closet. She did this for two years before her mother found out. When they spoke about it, the girl revealed that she'd been terrified by a break-in at the house, and had developed this alternative, safe, strategy. What did you need to help you feel safe? What do you need now?

EXERCISE 8:

❖ Describe a comforting figure of your childhood.

Children need comforting figures - and they don't necessarily have to be parents or relatives. Strangely enough, they may not even be permanent figures. A friendly next-door neighbor, a person in the same building, a friend's mother, all can provide great comfort and love over a period of weeks or even years, and then be almost entirely forgotten. Who were the figures in your life? Where are they now? What did they provide that you did not feel able to receive at home? Sometimes the comforting figure is not human at all, but a pet, or even an imaginary friend. The richness of imagination that can create an imaginary playfellow or turn a dog into one's closest confidante is not something to be underestimated. It indicates the establishment of a private identity that is at least as vital as the public persona. When children don't get what they need, they manufacture it. Do you have any activities like that today? Hobbies, fantasy games, computer games - all are outlets of some need.

EXERCISE 9:

❖   What were your favorite clothes as a child?

If a safe place and a friendly neighbor can be important, clothes can have a similar significance. Clothes are comforting in the most basic way. A warm coat, a cozy sweater, the list is endless. They can also be fantasy fulfillments. The little boy who loved his cowboy suit so much he always wore it has now given place to the Batman suit or the Spiderman outfit, which in turn is displaced by the surfer T-shirt, the mountain-bike gear, the football shirt with the team logo. What were your favorite clothes? Did you, like one woman, recall a beautiful dress she wore to a relative's wedding? Or did you recall your first set of Levi's? Did you enjoy clothes (some people have described changing clothes four times a day as five year olds, just because they liked to do that) or did you prefer to wear something rugged that would get you through the day's games?

One man described, with dismay, how his mother always chose clothes for him that she thought looked nice, but she didn't ask his opinion. At age eleven he was simply given the clothes and told to wear them. His memory from that time was of being dressed in fashions he felt, rightly or wrongly, to be silly, and of never being warm enough. This exercise brought out feelings of rage and sadness for him. It might do the same for you, as you relive the experience. If so, explore those emotions. How do you feel about clothes, today?

EXERCISE 10:

❖   What did you collect as a child? What did you lose?

Often children collect odd things: bits of wire, corks, Star Wars toys, stones, marbles, stamps... Sometimes we treasure these items and keep collecting them. Just as often we lose the collections and don't realize until years later when we ask, 'Whatever happened to...?' Are there any things you regret losing?

One man related a fascinating tale of losing a teddy bear on a cross country trip. He was upset, but his mother imagined that he must be far more upset than in fact he was, and insisted that his father drive back one hundred miles to the last place the bear had been seen. The boy felt he'd better acquiesce even though he didn't care as much as his mother imagined he did, and when no bear was found, he accepted the mother's fantasy that a 'poor child' had found the bear and was now very happy. As he wrote about this, the man realized that even at that early age he had adopted the habit of second-guessing his mother and going along with her imagined ideas of who he was and what he needed. He found this realization to be disturbing, and he used it as a way of exploring his relationship with his mother in later years, also. On the other hand, one of the positive things that came out of this was his renewed sense of how his parents had valued him as a child who had feelings that were to be respected, even if, in this case, they erred on the indulgent side. As a vignette of how loving feelings became complicated in his childhood, one could hardly ask for a better example.

Other responses have been similarly revealing. A tale of having his favorite toy truck stolen from him by an older boy in the school yard was what one man wrote about, and another wrote about watching his father throw his toys away as he raged about how noisy and messy he was. In each case it allowed the individual to recall an occasion when the nature of the world seemed to change from kindly to hostile, and that things were never quite the same again.

This next exercise builds on the previous ones. It can be done in a few minutes, or can be spread out over a much longer span of time, as you wish.

EXERCISE 11:

❖ Draw a 'family tree' of your immediate family, rather than a detailed pedigree of an historical sort.

❖ Put those figures who were close to you and important, close to you in the chart. When you've finished the chart, you might want to underline the names of those who are important to you. You might want to write down what it is that makes them important. Are they powerful? Kind? Scary? Loving? Who did you leave out?

One man left his adopted younger sister out of his family's chart, because, as he said, "she didn't really become a part of us". This omission would prove to be well worth considering further. A woman left question marks next to her father's family because she'd never met them that she could recall. All she knew was that her father had had an argument with his family. Seeing that hole in the chart she realized her father must have made a deliberate decision to leave his family, and she was able to deduce that the split had something to do with her father's marriage to her mother. This set her thinking in an entirely new way about her parents' relationship.

You can add to this chart by placing non-blood relatives in the chart as 'honorary-family' - in a different color, if you wish. Often we find that non-family members are far more influential and important than true relations. An older gentleman recalled with mingled sadness and love how he had been 'adopted' by his best friend's father after his friend died. Even though his own father and mother were still alive, he felt far more affinity to this man, whom he called his Uncle. I mention this because it is not an unusual experience. At times it seems as if those who are not satisfied with their own families recreate the family they want when they venture out into the world. Whether it be the man who trusts his father-in-law because he can't get along with his own father, or the person who marries into the big, welcoming Italian family when he or she has few relatives left alive, there is always a tendency to make the family we need. Drawing this chart may help you to see if this was going on around you, or if you did something similar, yourself. A young woman of twenty-three, the only child of a single mother, found she was dissatisfied with the chart she had drawn until she reflected that she was about to move to her fiancé's family's house. "They're great," she said. "They're this big, welcoming family, and that's exactly what I want, because I never had that." Once she had made the connection she was able to rethink the whole exercise and come to some clarity about what she needed, and the life she wanted to have.

One young man found the idea of a chart to be too constricting, and he began to make a collage instead, with pictures of his family, or if these were not available, pictures of objects associated with them. By the time he had finished he had a huge poster-sized chart, full of colors and life (dull relatives were in black ink or black and white pictures) that expressed the way he felt about most of his family. For him the creative act of producing this collage was enormously helpful. He was able to depict what he could not easily describe in words, and he had found a creative outlet for his long-suppressed feelings about his family. Thus what had been at one point a topic too difficult and too depressing to talk about had become an invigorating experience, a reclaiming of his own particular gifts.

This can lead to another written exercise.

EXERCISE 12:

❖ Pick a moment when you felt furthest from your family, when you felt completely apart from them, and tell what happened.

Just like the old joke that teenagers all seem to tell, that they believe their family comes from another planet, or that they feel so alien themselves they believe they must have been adopted, this exercise seeks to identify those moments of bifurcation. It is at times like this - and they can be shocking to some - that we discover an identity apart from our families. It's at this point we begin to see that we have to live our lives without them. As we see how different we are from them we, effectively, face exile. The father who doesn't care for his son's politics and who yells at him for being 'communist' or 'republican' may seem simply to be part of a family squabble. But the first time it happens the child is likely to feel threatened at a profound level. How can he or she continue to live in the same house?

Building on this is another exercise.

EXERCISE 13:

❖ Imagine a dinner party and all your relatives are expected to attend. Whom would you place next to whom and why? You may even include deceased relatives, if you wish.

This is the stuff of either fantasy pleasure or crippling anxiety. Every Thanksgiving and Christmas substantial numbers of Americans become acutely anxious about whether or not their massed relatives are going to be civil to each other. Similarly, a large number of people really enjoy these festive days. In each case, though, they take care to try and keep those people who like each other in proximity. Whether it be the setting up of a children's table or remembering not to put Uncle Paul next to Uncle George because they always tell off-color jokes, certain arrangements need to be made. This imagined exercise can help us to see the tensions that may exist in the family. Like the chart, it may help us to see alliances, too. One man recorded that for long periods of his youth he thought his godfather was actually his brother's godfather, because they seemed to get on so much better with each other than he did. He defined their roles because he saw how they functioned, even though officially the role was different. This gave rise to a whole series of feelings of rivalry for his brother who always seemed to be everyone's favorite. A woman described a dinner in which she specified what everyone would eat, because her memory of Thanksgiving was of relatives who sometimes did not want to eat the dishes prepared by others, causing resentments and tensions. Since the young woman was herself a strict vegetarian, who would not eat anything connected with meat production, she had certainly some work to do on her own contribution to the tension!
A final exercise may help here.

EXERCISE 14:

❖ Write down all the home addresses you remember. Can you recall relatives' addresses? What about phone numbers? Have you ever revisited any of these places? Tell the story of such a visit. If you like, pick a place to revisit and imagine what it feels like to go back there. Describe what you see.

This is an exercise centered on memory, and all memory is selective. Most of us can remember our addresses from about the age of four, the age at which we are likely to have had that information drilled into us by our parents. One young woman wrote a response to this in which she recalled memorizing her address, repeating it over and over on the school bus, and being prepared for the teacher to ask her so she could get the gold star reward. But the teacher forgot to ask, so, timidly, she approached the teacher, made her request to be asked her address, and won the star. Twenty years later she recalled the event with a huge smile and a glow of pleasure. What she had reclaimed for herself was not just a nice memory, but a moment when she was making a successful transition to become a girl who knew her address, a successful and competent learner, and - this was important, too - a person who was not afraid to ask to have her knowledge recognized by others. It is, in fact, a hugely empowering memory. In recalling it the young woman reminded herself of her strengths.

The phone numbers we tend to recall may reflect our sense of whom we trusted. Typically, we recall the numbers of those we called 'if anything went wrong' or we remember a parent's number at work because we were expected to call that parent the moment we got home from school, to check in. Such numbers represent our safety-line to the rest of the world. It's worth exploring that information.

One woman wrote about how at age eight she would come home from school, call her mother at work to let her know she was home, then she'd take a carving knife from the kitchen draw. Armed, she'd curl up in the nook beside the fridge, not far from the phone, often with a book, to wait until her mother came home. She knew she'd never forget the phone number, nor would she ever forget the fear she had felt at being alone in the apartment. Eventually this memory led to a discussion of how she had been molested as a child. This allowed her to move on to other writing assignments in which she explored her fears at her own pace.

In the revisiting part of the exercise, people have given responses that are lyrical and often beautiful. Many have written about the way things seemed smaller and less impressive when revisited, and they often spend time considering the difference between childhood and adult perceptions. In imagined responses writers have a chance to be as specific as they wish - meeting old classmates engaged on a similar pilgrimage, for example, or seeing people now long dead, and being able to say things to them that never got said in reality. It can be an exercise that makes peace with the past.

A middle-aged man described driving to the site of his old school, with his foreign-born wife who had never seen the place. When he got there he saw, to his horror, that the whole building had been bulldozed a few weeks before. Rubble and an empty playing field were all that remained. By writing about it, he was able to acknowledge that he had wanted to show his wife something that would help explain who he was. The school's destruction made him realize that if she were ever to understand who he was, and how this school had shaped him, he'd have to do it in a more direct fashion. He'd hoped his wife would be able to feel intuitively far more than it was rational to expect anyone to be able to feel, and he began to rethink what he expected her to be able to deduce about him as a matter of course. Such a subtle discovery is, I think, one that could only benefit the relationship in the long term.

What does all this mean? The exercises have been encouraging you to reclaim memories or impressions by using a variety of methods. Often a memory will have, within it, a small item of information or an insight that you didn't realize was there, lurking behind the details. Sometimes a memory may be so powerful in itself that remembering it recalls all the emotions of that moment, also. When this happens you may find yourself feeling alone, unsupported, with these feelings welling up from the past. 'What do I do, now?' You may think. It's not my intention to bring you to a point of crisis and then walk away from you. What you may want to consider is that your strong feelings indicate a gold-mine of information you haven't yet used. You haven't made that gold your own yet.

A simple comparison may help. When a child burns his or her finger for the first time the cries of pain are deafening. When we reach adulthood we may burn our fingers, but we're unlikely to scream and carry on like a three year old, although we probably have a few choice phrases to resort to. The difference is that at age three we have probably never felt such pain before. We're shocked and to our minds, we're the only person in the world who has ever felt that way. That is our perception. As adults we know that we are not the only people to have ever felt that way, and in addition, we are quicker to learn. Oh yes, we may say, I had better make sure I don't do that again, and we get gloves or potholders, or whatever is needed. We have put the pain in context, and used this information, this learning, to move ahead.

That is how these chapters and this book can function. You will uncover the pain, the joys, as you write. The book can provide the contexts so that the pain is seen in perspective. The purpose of going back in time in these exercises is not to return to gloomy memories and wallow in them. Going back is only being used here in the service of going forward.

These are the first steps to beginning the process of understanding. Now it is up to you to reflect on your responses, to compare them to the examples in these pages, and to begin to put this information in context. You can then start to identify repeated ideas, patterns of thinking, concerns that seem to recur. This may take longer, but for now, you have done the most important thing, you have reclaimed neglected and repressed feelings.

As you look back at your childhood it may be worth bearing a few things in mind. Childhood is the time that shapes us most profoundly, since we are so unformed that we are almost entirely impressionable. The old saying attributed to the Jesuit order, 'give me a child before the age of seven, and I'll have him for life,' rings true. What it means is that a child before the age of seven can be shaped profoundly to accept religious or any other beliefs, and those beliefs are to all intents and purposes ineradicable. This is well-known to those engaged in political or religious indoctrination at all levels. Since those early years shape us so profoundly, if we are to understand ourselves we may need to review that time in detail, and even to compare our experiences with others. It's a task that takes time and care.

Another aspect that needs to be considered is that although childhood can be loving and wonderful - and often is - there is inevitably a down side. Children are less strong and less knowledgeable than adults, and adults are those who make the rules. It's unavoidable that many of our childhood experiences contain a measure of frustration. We hear the word 'no' a lot, often for reasons we don't understand. We may be criticized or victimized. 'It's not fair!' may be a phrase we recognize all too well. We want to fly planes, be doctors and have magic kingdoms, but we're only six and we're not even allowed to set our own bedtimes. Growing up is, necessarily, a time of conflict. If the memories you have written about seem to you to be very negative, bear this in mind: our pains are based on many things, some of which are inherent in living. Children feel profoundly, and with an abandon we can learn from. The three-year old watching wide-eyed as a clown performs, or who sees Mickey Mouse at Disneyworld and believes that this really is Mickey Mouse - that child can teach us a great deal about belief and joy.

The four year old who gives you a big sloppy kiss and says 'I love you' can also teach us a great deal about unconditional love. Just similarly, their sadness is deeper than we may easily be able to understand, at least at first.

For many people thinking about their own childhood does not resurface until they become parents themselves. Suddenly, all their memories begin to bubble up as they look at their own children. They may buy expensive model train sets that they themselves never had as children, and present them to their own offspring. This is a cliche, perhaps, but I've seen it first hand, the fathers playing with the replica Lionel train while the sons are in the next room with the video games. The kids are just being kids while the fathers are reliving their childhoods.

That is the positive image. If, however, we consider those who had substantially unhappy childhoods, a different picture may emerge. The man who was neglected and treated poorly as a child may well seek to replicate that situation when he is a father - and he may not be conscious of this. It's a truism that childhood abuse victims often go on to abuse other children, that battered children grow up to be batterers themselves. A less extreme but just as important consideration applies to all parents. These parents will tend to replicate aspects of their own childhood when they become parents - unless they can confront the past, make the negative aspects of it conscious, and endeavor to break any destructive patterns that were present. Sometimes we have to go back before we can go forward....

Men and women have frequently reported that, on becoming parents, they found themselves acting like their parents acted, even if they often did not like or approve of that style of child rearing. These ideas of 'right' and 'wrong' in child rearing are surprisingly heartfelt. I have come across instances of women who were best friends for twenty years, and who were then alienated as a result of seeing the way each chose to raise her children. Again, the gossips of any small town, or neighborhood, will be only too free with their descriptions about how so-and-so treats the children, or how someone else spoils the family. People who don't have an opinion on politics and who don't care about world issues become immovable when they discuss what should (there's that word 'should' again!) be done with children and young people. I mention this to emphasize that within the family there are often very strong ideas about exactly how things should be, and that every family sees its way as the best way.

If we are to understand who we are, it is not a bad idea to start by looking at the family. In this way we can avoid repeating mistakes and confusions that may have plagued our parents, and, instead, we can value and build on the good aspects. It needs time and care to do this, and you may need to return to these writing exercises more than once. You may want to do them with your significant other, or with a sibling or friend, and use that as a basis for further discussion.

In this way writing can become part of a process that gives you back to yourself.

Chapter Five

PLAY AND TRANSFORMATION

Some of our best self-discoveries can be made through play, but very few adults take the time to explore play - and certainly we do less of it than children. Somewhere around the age of thirteen or so play becomes taboo, babyish, and many people don't venture there again. Paradoxically such play as does exist beyond that point becomes strangely stylized. Dungeons and Dragons and computer or video games often have a large number of rules (far more than chess, for example) and are usually angled towards destruction of opponents. Sports are 'play' in a form that is highly competitive - often exclusive. Ask any twelve year old who didn't make it into the soccer team. Some of the interactive computer games I've seen stress the reaction of the figures in the drama to the way the player asks questions. For example, if one asks the question too insistently the figure can clam up, or become hostile. This is an approach to 'real' interactions with real people, but it has as yet none of the complexity or subtlety of live conversations, and so is actually inferior to what children do as they play, which is to engage each other socially.

This section is designed to encourage you to play so you can learn at the same time.

EXERCISE 1:

❖ For this exercise you'll need access to one of those booths that sell four passport photos for $2, or better still, a camera or a video camera. Photograph yourself. A polaroid held at arm's length will work. Record your voice on a tape recorder or do both with the camcorder. Play up to the camera. Ask someone else to take your picture. Every drugstore sells disposable cameras, so you don't need any special equipment. Look at the pictures. Then do the exercise again.

The purpose of this exercise is to let yourself see yourself at play. Hamming it up can be a great idea because you get to play roles you might not otherwise even consider. Children do it all the time; as they play dress-up they practice and explore possible future identities, and begin to understand the workings of the adult world. A child can release several 'selves' through fantasy play in this way. Most of us, however, feel a little nervous or inhibited about this. At Halloween parties it's rare to see people who really know, as adults, how to dress up in costume. Most of us fudge something at the last moment and hope we'll get away with it.

We do this exercise twice because the first time we do it many of us will still be inhibited even if we're on our own, and a pause for reflection can help liberate the creativity.

Look at yourself on tape or in the pictures. Do you recognize yourself? Yet, this is who you are or can be. It's these 'other' selves we have to explore.

One woman so enjoyed this exercise that she made a point, she said, of diving into the four-for-a-dollar photo booths whenever she could, usually during her lunch hour, often bringing a friend with her. Sometimes she would rework the images later, using colored pens. Eventually she took some of her favorite sets of pictures and framed them in a sort of collage. It was an eloquent witness to the fun she'd had playing with her image of herself. In an era when women's sense of body image can be so precarious and even dangerous (anorexia and bulimia are the legacies of this) she was able to move beyond that minefield and experience some joy in being who she was, in all the varied forms that involved.

EXERCISE 2:

❖ Eat something sarcastically; timidly; dismissively. Now pretend you're putting money in a parking meter. Do it several ways - arrogantly, reverently, cluelessly, carelessly, furtively, absent-mindedly. Now, do it every time you park your car. Read the instructions to a VCR manual or something equally dry, like the phone book. Do it like a dictator, like a nun, like a prayer, like a whore. Tape or photograph any or all of the above.

The exercise can be as varied as you want to make it. Responses to this have been suitably hilarious, and part of the reason for this exercise is, certainly, to have fun. There's another reason also. When one is doing the actions in the suggested way one is engaged in the action and the feeling rather than the theoretical value of the word that describes the action. We think we know what we mean by 'arrogantly' but until we've done an action or two in that mind frame we may not really feel what that means.

An example may help. When I was first writing short fiction my instructor used to underline all the adverbs I'd used. "Don't tell me that this character did something 'questioningly,'" my instructor would say, "show me what the action is, and I'll know it's questioning..." Her point was that the adverb is weak. It's like a man telling you in a calm voice that he's angry. If he's genuinely angry his emotion will appear, no matter how quiet the voice is. We all know that we're capable of a range of emotions, but we don't often explore them to see how they feel. If we don't know how they feel in practice sessions, how can we recognize them when they emerge for real? That's what play is all about, practice for life, and the awareness of being alive.

Some of those who have responded to this exercise have done so using digital cameras, and they have often been able to manipulate and change the images in interesting ways. The creativity they have brought to this has always impressed me - especially as this exercise is about giving you the chance to play creatively.

Another aspect that I'd like to emphasize here is the truism that play can be fun. If you had fun (and I hope you did), cherish it. Remember how it feels, how your body feels, when you're having a good time. If you do that you'll be able to recognize fun again more easily next time.

This is important - I cannot overstate how important. We can forget what an emotion feels like, just as we can forget what something tastes like. I'm sure we've all eaten something and said, 'I'd almost forgotten how good that is...' In the same way we can get out of the habit of experiencing fun and play, and slide into the habit of expecting to be dulled by life and its pressures. If we let ourselves do that we can lose vital reference points for our psyches. In private work clients have often told me about how they feel lost, or adrift. One of my responses on occasion has been to ask them where their sense of joy is; what lets them feel pleasure? Those who feel most adrift have always had considerable difficulty recalling what things brought them joy. So here is the next exercise:

EXERCISE 3:

❖ What brings you joy?

Often it can take some time for people to recall what it is that energizes and pleases them, and when they do they may preface it with words like 'I used to enjoy...' or 'years ago I used to...' They're out of practice at enjoying being alive. Enjoyment can return, but only if the individual respects it and gives it space in which to grow.

Sometimes I feel that our contemporary culture of counseling and therapy encourages us only to dwell on the negative, on the damage that has been done. I feel it is equally important to honor the delight that one can experience, and to make a point of accessing that. Does it give you joy to feed the ducks in the park? Then give yourself that gift. Joy is not something that is confined to vacations and theme parks (and some of those theme park rides seem to have more to do with fear than pleasure, to me) but is available to us every day. We just have to get back into the habit of identifying it.

EXERCISE 4:

❖ Choose a toy you'd give to someone you know. Choose a toy for your boss; for your mother-in-law.

This exercise is designed to get us to re-engage with what it meant to be a child and unafraid to play. In fact, at Christmas I always note with delight how many dads in business suits are having a whale of a time in toy stores, all the while looking a little self-conscious about it...

Often people will choose toys they themselves enjoyed as children. The more comfortable you are with your playful self, the more likely you'll be to choose something you just happen upon by chance. Choosing a toy for one's boss or one's mother-in-law can also release playful feelings around potentially difficult relationships. Have fun. Be outrageous, if you wish. Be sarcastic if you want. I'm not asking you to act on your choices.

One man described wanting to give his boss a small plastic guillotine, for example. As he spoke about this he laughed. The office tyrant was no longer such a serious threat to him. Remember, the ability to see the humor in things, to play even in the face of serious issues, can help us see alternate ways to react to sets of circumstances we may tend to feel stuck in. Humor diffuses tension; it also allows us to express things that can't easily be stated any other way. Telling someone to 'cheer up' never did much good. Encouraging people to cheer themselves up by finding an alternate way of reacting is more effective.

EXERCISE 5:

❖   Imagine a dream for someone else.

When we wish each other 'sweet dreams,' we have no idea what we mean. In Shakespeare's *The Tempest,* Caliban has such sweet dreams that they become a torture to him, "that I wept to sleep again." Dreams can be powerful communications that act at a level beyond words. One young man described a dream he wanted to send a younger brother who was having a hard time dealing with their grandfather's death. "I wanted him to get a dream that would tell him it was alright," said the young man, and then proceeded to describe a dream he had dreamed, himself, several days after the funeral, in which the grandfather appeared to him and reassured him that he was in "a good place" now. The young man realized that just telling his brother about the dream would never be enough. He wanted him to experience it.

That is what this book is about. We can tell others many things. We can be told what we may need to hear, but in a world of many words and many experiences we sometimes don't manage to feel in our hearts what we need to know. "You'll get over it," we say to the heart-broken friend whose lover has just left. And it's true, he or she will get over it, somehow. The problem is that the distraught individual can only know what he or she is experiencing, which may feel like an infinity of pain stretching ahead. Such a person cannot be consoled by words. Probably the only thing that can console anyone in this situation is the consciousness that others love and care. Saying, "we still love you, old friend," is one thing, but being there so the sufferer can explore the emotion of being loved - well, that's altogether in a different league.

This is why I insist on the experience of these exercises. Many of them may seem silly or frivolous - until you actually do them. By doing them I don't mean sitting in an armchair, reading the exercises and nodding sagely over them while muttering, 'Oh yes, I can see how I'd answer that one.' Whenever we do that we allow the human capacity for avoidance to slip in. We become remote from the real experience. We have to engage in the exercises, or we're like people watching an aerobics video while not doing any of the movements ourselves.

One woman, a teacher, said after she'd done some of these exercises that she'd given her class an assignment that was in some ways similar, but it had never occurred to her to do the assignment herself. "It's a lot more revealing when you actually do it, yourself," she said. And that's my point. We need to do these for ourselves for the transformations to occur.

To explain this further I'll take a few examples from that repository of knowledge, the Bible. Whatever one feels about religion there are usually a number of important human insights to be gained by reading the Scriptures, and they often appear at the least logically explainable junctures. Take, for example, the miracle of the Wedding at Cana, where Jesus turned the water into wine because the guests had run through all the wine that had been brought. As a miracle it seems pointless. Why bother? Shouldn't Jesus be doing something more important? Yet if we take it as a metaphor we can see something entirely different, for whenever two people are truly joined in marriage something transcendent happens, the ordinary becomes miraculous. Just so, the water (which is ordinary, but vital) is transformed into something even more powerful. It's a way of describing the relationship which is transformed from two people who love each other into something far more compelling. If we apply this today to our own society we can think of many people who live together as sexual partners but who don't make the final commitment. There may be many very valid reasons for this - but in one sense they may recognize that marriage really will be a declaration of intent, and so they shy away from the one action that could transform water into wine. Doing these exercises, rather than reading them only, turns the water into wine for you, too.

Here it's worth considering that the New Testament is full of such symbols of transformation. Wine, itself, is grape juice that has fermented to form something better - and more dangerous. Bread is flour and water transformed by yeast. I think it's no coincidence that Jesus took both of these examples of what must have seemed like everyday magical transformation and used them in the Last Supper, where once again, they become transformed into his body and blood. What does this mean? It means the ordinary can become extraordinary when we pay attention to what it really means.

Just think of some of the other transformations that exist in the world. Mud, a mixture of earth and water, the stuff that sticks to our shoes, can be made into ceramics that hold water. We see that as ordinary - but can you imagine what it took to think of that invention in the first place? Archaeologists usually become very excited at the first signs of pottery in cultures, because it represents a leap forward as important as the use of tools, the discovery of fire, and the invention of the wheel. Again, think of the ordinary miracle of thread made into woven fabric. Think of the advance that represented over wearing animal skins. Or, if you prefer, what about the mental jump needed to transform reeds into the first basket. The weak, pliable reed becomes a sturdy basket. This is the transformation that doing these exercises can offer you, but only if you do them, only if you write them.

Often the transformation comes in unexpected ways. In Jesus's miracle of the feeding of the five thousand the disciples ask Jesus how to feed the crowd that has gathered. They only have five loaves and two fish. Jesus orders the food distributed, and not only does everyone eat well, but twelve baskets of leftovers are collected. Peter Richardson in *Four Spiritualities* suggests that what happened was not just a 'miracle' but the miracle of human generosity. Each of those five thousand would have had, he suggests, some food or drink with them, tucked into a fold of clothing perhaps. And each would have been thinking, "I've got just enough for my needs, but I don't want to have to feed anyone extra." Jesus arranged the people in groups, sat them down, and instead of a crowd he transformed them into small groups that could share without being pressured. The miracle is that they did share, and abundantly. The resources are usually there. The problem is getting people to realize it and act accordingly.

In a slightly different way I've been part of this same 'miracle' performed many times by total strangers sitting in train carriage compartments as we've traveled through rural areas of Europe. At around noon everyone pulls out their lunch, and because there are only eight or ten in a compartment everyone shares some of what they have with everyone else. Strangers become, temporarily at least, family. This is the principle of many therapeutic groups, too. When ordinary people gather in that way in order to explore their psyches, each can help the others in ways that can be truly miraculous.

I've written about this at length here because understanding these tranformations is central to the experience this book can offer. The very principle of democracy is based on the idea that weak citizens who band together are in fact stronger than heavily-armed elitist factions, and this principle has proven itself over and over again. Just so with the exercises. Individually they are perhaps not always impressive, but once they are put into action a new dimension emerges. What destroys democracy is the singling out of individuals for victimization, and that is how dictatorships work. Starhawk, the spiritualist, describes how she and many other anti-nuclear activists were once jailed. The police wanted to take each woman out of the over-crowded holding pen - about one hundred and fifty women were under arrest - one at a time, for questioning. Starhawk recognized right away that what was intended was intimidation. One can just imagine five or six burly policemen haranguing a female peace activist half their size, trying to extract the names of the so-called ringleaders. The jailed women responded by refusing to be singled out. They held onto each other - hundreds of hands preventing the isolating move the police intended - and the police eventually gave up. A day later all the women were released. No charges were brought against any of them.

I don't think that what happened that day was a miracle, but something very important did take place. The women refused to be victims and they refused to be isolated from each other. It was a lesson in non-violence that Ghandi would surely have applauded had he been alive. They had claimed back their power, their right to be treated reasonably, and their right to their beliefs. In short, they had claimed their selfhood.

You can do it, too.

Here are two more exercises for you to consider.

EXERCISE 6:

❖ Invent a rule. Invent penalties. Now, invent circumstances in which it's alright to break the rule.

EXERCISE 7:

❖ Invent a secret for someone else. Invent one for yourself.

I've linked these two together because I feel they can complement each other. The rules that people tend to invent have to do with things they feel angry about but powerless to change. One woman invented rules and penalties for those whose dogs defecated on sidewalks, and the only time this was acceptable would be when the sidewalk was outside the house of ex-Nazis hiding out from justice, whereupon it was eminently permissible to get as many dogs as one could and encourage them to foul the lawn, too. The unusual use of the rule she had created served to let her know that although dogs could be a nuisance, in the greater scale of things this was hardly a big issue. Humor transformed anger, and redirected the energy. Many other examples followed the same sort of pattern, and in each case the emphasis was on limits that we routinely come across. For instance, how does one deal with the person who, on a crowded bus, takes up two seats? In considering rules we might wish to enforce we are asking, I feel, to be part of a reasonable, decent world. This is very much a part of claiming back our selfhood from the daily incursions that can leave us feeling diminished.

The exercise that asks us to imagine a secret for someone else can be as playful as you wish. Some people have, however, come up with some very gloomy secrets as they imagine colleagues to be ax-murderers, and so on. This is not to say that this exercise has not worked for them. The purpose of the exercise is to ask what we see behind the daily faces we greet, and to remind us that every person has a secret well of energy that fuels him or her - and that we do, too. The woman who imagined a colleague as having a secret farm on which he bred zebras was engaging in a lively and imaginative leap of creativity. She was, in effect, claiming her creativity and her right to speculate, her right to play. She was also acknowledging that we all have, inside us somewhere, a passion or an enthusiasm that the world tends not to value, or to actively de-value. But it is in that passionate imaginative inner world that our energy resides. So, what were your secrets? What might that tell you about the sources of your energy? Can that energy be liberated, literally brought into 'play'?

A last exercise may be helpful, here.

EXERCISE 8:

❖ Imagine that a postcard arrives for you. It is addressed to you, with your name clearly on it. The message, however, is written in a language that you don't understand, a language that may be unlike any you have ever seen. Write this message.

❖ When you have written it, imagine how it sounds. Then translate the message.

This is an exercise that most people greet with looks of puzzlement whenever I've done it in groups. Sometimes they ask for several extra clarifications. "The language is one we don't know, right?" or, "What do you mean, a postcard?" The uncertainty that some people have displayed is always useful information, because this is, after all, an invitation to play in a way that asks each individual to make up most of the rules. Most adults doing this exercise seem to want to have someone else make up the rules first.

The postcards that have appeared as a result have varied enormously. Some people have drawn the whole card, including the picture on the front, the stamp, and the postmark. Most people do quite well at producing imagined languages, with strange letters. Some have even produced languages that were non-linear, that worked in a spiral, or that moved from the bottom right of the page to the top left, or were composed mainly of pictograms. Most participants have been reluctant to say their new language out loud, however.

When we come to the translation I usually ask each person to read it out and then add a few words. It always astonishes me how much people are able to understand about their messages. Perhaps it is because the twists and turns of doing the exercise have released them from their usual sense of caution, or perhaps because the superego has been kept busy with the demands of the task - for whatever reason this exercise can lead to important insights. A young woman translated her message as "All will be well. Looking forward to seeing you..." What she was able to say was that she was due to see her parents, who had moved to a foreign country, and that she longed to see them. Her worry was that she hoped she'd be able to feel 'at home' in their new place, because she knew the foreign country would feel alien and even threatening to her. She wanted 'home' but was afraid she wouldn't get the reassurance she wanted. She was also afraid because she'd had an unsuccessful and destructive love affair while her parents had been away, and she wanted very much to tell them about it, but was afraid they'd be disappointed in her. Those four words "All will be well", with their somewhat stilted, almost biblical quality, contained a powerful and consoling message that this woman wanted to receive, and needed to hear.

Another example is provided by a woman whose card came from an unknown correspondent inviting her to the tropical island of Saba. On the picture side of the card she had drawn a boat. She pointed to it and said, "And that's me there in the boat!" This was, literally, a card from herself to herself, asking if she would come out to the island and play. The more she thought about this the more excited she became, seeing that she had chosen to communicate with herself in this way, and wondering what to do about it. A vacation was, she admitted, just what she needed, but could she really allow herself to take one? A few weeks later she did, in fact, go on vacation to Saba. A third example was slightly different in that the man who wrote it said the card was from himself in the future to himself now, giving himself advice he needed to take. Considering this he was able to see that he knew what he had to do, but still he felt tempted to do the opposite, even against his better judgement. The exercise had allowed him to access his wisdom. Now, whatever choice he made, it would at least not be done in a state of confusion.

I could multiply examples, here, but the crux of this exercise is that these are messages we want to send to ourselves, and that we are, in one sense, waiting to receive from ourselves. The question to consider, perhaps, is that if these are the messages we want to receive, what are we doing about making our futures come true?

A secondary observation might be that this is a playful exercise. How difficult or easy was it for you to play? Picture postcards are still usually linked in our minds with foreign vacations, with relaxation and play. How easy was it for you to respond to the invitation to be inventive, silly, and playful?

Lastly, it's an exercise about what we feel we deserve, about our 'luck'. Many people have written or said, as they discussed this exercise, that they would like to get a card like this, but know it won't ever happen. The card from the long lost friend, the invitation to an exotic place... no, it'll never happen. So many people assume they don't deserve to be happy, and will make no move to bring it about. This exercise can help to overturn that attitude and lead us to think about our needs in a more productive way.

Chapter Six

SCHOOLDAYS

You can use this chapter several ways. The first way is for you to reflect on your own experiences at school. This is very useful as a way of learning more about some of the forces that helped to shape you. The second way is for you to use that information so you can remind yourself of what your children or relatives may be facing as they go to school.

Going to school is often our first experience of others in mass quantities, and our first time being away from familiar or home-like surroundings. It's also likely to be our first encounter with discipline and rules. It can be a delightful transition or it can be bewildering. For the first time we may meet children who are older and bigger than we are, children we don't know, who look different and behave differently. They may not even speak our language. We may respond to this with delight at the wonderful variety the world offers, or we may feel threatened. This first experience of school is also where we test our expectations. Until now only the family or neighborhood circle made up our world, and we were likely to be seen as 'the child of...' rather than as just a child. The wider world greets us. As such, our experiences may help to shape the rest of our lives as the fragile, emergent 'I' meets 'Them'.

For example, the Vietnamese child who knows no English, or the Russian child in a similar situation, may have mixed emotions about the first confusing days of school. One man reported his fear at going to school. Hungarian-born, he wondered what his new school in the North of England would be like. This apprehension turned to relief when he discovered a number of other Hungarian-speaking children in the playground, all of whom had very little knowledge of English, and they quickly formed their own club. From that point on he loved school.

EXERCISE 1:

❖ Write your first memory of school. How do you think this memory might have related to the rest of your school career?

Most of us have very strong memories of our first day at school. It was, probably, the most exciting time of our lives up until then, because at that point we were big enough to be allowed to take part in the grown-up world of learning and work. One man recalled with delight how on his first day the teacher had all the children make and decorate a brief case - a piece of thick paper folded and stapled to hold the drawings each child had done that day. He recalled his happiness at having a briefcase and papers to put in it too. As he walked across the playground to meet his mother he tucked the briefcase under his arm and announced that tomorrow he was going into the city to his father's office. It's a wonderful memory, full of the sense of enthusiasm and empowerment that children have, the feeling that he'd finally entered the real world of adults. Writing it, he couldn't quite believe he'd ever felt that way, and he wondered how he'd reached the situation where he accepted his own work as drudgery and his daily world as a grind. By accessing this memory, he was able to rediscover the child who was curious and eager and who was not yet jaded. It was one of a series of steps that eventually helped him to get out of his mental rut.

An older man recalled being so excited to go to school that when he was told about it at supper the day before he raced outside to his tricycle and began peddling down the road, only to discover he wasn't entirely sure of the way to school once he'd turned the first corner. It never occurred to him he'd be nearly twelve hours early. School would welcome him, and it's a memory full of optimism. This was all the more remarkable because the man thought of himself as pessimistic, even depressed. The recalled memory let him know he hadn't always been the way he was now, and that he might have reserves of optimism he'd never tapped into since those early days. The memory helped to uncover the strength he had misplaced as he grew up.

A middle aged woman wrote about how excited she was that first day, and then she looked at the desk next to her and saw her neighbor, a little boy, who was fast asleep. She couldn't understand at the time how anyone could sleep on such an important day. Several years later she was able to see what was going on. The little boy came from a violent and alcohol-abusing family. For him school may have been the one place where he felt safe enough not to be shaken awake - a safe place in which he could relax. That first memory impressed itself on her as indicating the little boy's future, and her own quite different path.

EXERCISE 2:

❖ How tall were you when you went to school? Did that make a difference? Write a narrative in which you describe the different body types of your class-mates.

Responses to this vary between the sexes. Boys seem to want to be big more than girls do since that means they are less likely to be victimized or bullied, and more likely to become leaders. In the case of girls, surveys have indicated that big or tall girls are sometimes ignored by teachers in favor of small and pretty girls, who tend to be pampered and given extra attention. Heavy-set and ordinary-looking girls, even if very intelligent, are likely to be treated by teachers and peers in a somewhat cavalier way.

'She'll manage all right; she doesn't need help,' seems to be the refrain recalled in adulthood. In a culture that reveres the ideal of the thin and the pretty, large girls may be thought of as lumpen, slow and lazy even if they are demonstrably intelligent and athletic. Aspects of this way of thinking have been explored by many researchers (Dorothy Binder, M.Ed. thesis, Curry College, 1997 offers a good overview of the field) who have revealed a prejudice against large students that is deeply embedded. Just similarly height can be an important factor. Tall boys are often given credit for being leaders and role models even if they do not have those qualities, and they tend to stand in opposition to the 'nerds' who may be smaller but far more accomplished.

In first grade size is destiny, and alliances ensure success and survival.

At this point you may wish to look at your responses and compare them to other memories of a similar sort. Can you recall your first day in High School? Talking with Junior High children in the Boston area revealed a high level of fear about that prospective first year at High School. The girls were excited by and afraid of the older boys who they knew would pursue them, and yet they prepared to ally themselves to these older boys so they could gain status, invitations to better social events, and access to parties where alcohol was expected. Although they didn't always admit it, it was clear they found their male contemporaries to be less exciting, but also less threatening. Older boys had cars. Older boys knew about sex.

Their male peers felt differently. Many were afraid of being beaten by the older boys. They knew that the previous year's victims would be this coming year's victimizers of new students, and the underlying feeling was that sophomores would move in on the freshman girls, and that meant asserting themselves against the freshman boys. Hearing all of this, one wonders if any school work ever gets done.

Take this one step further. Compare your memories of school to your first days at college, or at work. Similar forces are likely to be present. Can you see any common ground?

EXERCISE 3:

❖   Who were your friends? Write about them. Where are they now?

Friends, alliances, peers, sporting teams, all of these are ways of developing meaningful relationships that will, in a sense, be reflected in many other friendships throughout one's life. Were you popular? With whom? Did you find it easy to make friends? To join teams? A small and frail child may need to have strong friends, or sharp wits, to avoid being a victim of the bullies. Some children buy their way into strategic alliances by supplying candy, or money, or cigarettes, or drugs. Others develop a quick tongue and the art of repartee to put down aggressors, and gain respect. The over-achiever may join with other over-achievers, or may coach others, and so establish status. Often, however, these powerful alliances fade when the individuals graduate, since there is less daily contact and a diminished daily need to band together; yet these are people we shared important aspects of our lives with.

Recall your friends. Rethink what their friendships meant and mean. Value those times. These are the people with whom you went on adventures, with whom you got yourself into trouble. These are the people with whom you talked about parents, school, drinking, drugs, sex. They may have shaped your attitudes to sex and sexuality, even to morality. If you have a picture of any of these people, it may be worth finding it and considering what made these friendships special. What, if any, were the conflicts and compromises you went through?

EXERCISE 4:

❖ This exercise moves the previous one into another realm of enquiry. What were the happiest moments in your schooldays? What were the least happy? Can you recall a time when you felt particularly close to your friends? Can you recall any fights?

School is intensely exciting for most children, most of the time. Although a teenager may claim to be bored and have done 'nothing' during a school day, if we go back a few years and ask the same question of an eight year old we are likely to be regaled with tales, stories, and minor adventures. It's the time when we develop our first strong relationships with those beyond the family circle, and its also the time we are likely to experience our first fights. One man recalled how he could clearly remember his first fight at school. Although he'd often fought physically with his older brother and the neighborhood boys, those seemed to be nothing compared to the horror he felt when he gave an older child a bloody nose. The sense of fear, of wondering if he'd be punished for asserting his rights (the older child had run off with his hat) - all this made the event memorable. The crux here, is that this man began to realize that the fights he'd had with his brother were just squabbles - that the two of them would carry on as before after the disturbance had died down. A fight with a stranger, however, offered no such limits, and as a child he had been afraid of the reprisals he might provoke, afraid he'd made an enemy who would 'come back and get him'.

These early experiences of fighting, both verbal and physical, can be terrifying because they bring emotions that were essentially private to the family group, and make them public. The rules are not the same, the emotions are not the same. An example might be that one could shout an insult at a relative stranger and simply receive a jeering response. If, however, one were to shout an insult at one's father or mother, one could expect some unpleasant sanctions to be applied! It is the contrast between 'home' and 'social' behavior that tends to arise in these examples.

EXERCISE 5:

❖ What gave you a sense of achievement? Write about an event that gave you a feeling of personal accomplishment.

By the time we reach adulthood we've often forgotten the things we enjoyed doing for their own sake because we've become focused on career goals. Even casual conversations about school days tend to turn up statements like, 'I used to be pretty good at that as a kid,' or 'I haven't painted/danced/written stories/run track since...' What this means, usually, is that we have exiled a portion of our creative selves in the desire to follow a career. Claiming back our creativity is important, because that is very often where we can be most authentically ourselves - and if we don't claim it, it can, like an unwatered plant, shrivel and die. Many retirees have spoken to me about how they always thought they would make time one day, and then, when retirement arrived, they found they no longer had the energy, the desire to follow the task, or they found they'd stopped believing in it. If we can recall what gave us delight we can access something that fed our souls, and that can continue to nourish us.

One woman recalled having written a class paper into which she had put her usual verve, but almost no book-learning, since she'd neglected to do it. The teacher returned it to her claiming, 'It was the best paper she'd ever read'. The student was delighted, of course. What she had learned by thinking about this episode was far more important than the initial sense of relief she'd experienced all those years before. What she saw in that tidbit of history was a moment of recognition. She knew then that book learning was not her strength - her strength lay in her energy and her intuitive ability to express what was needed. It was a small moment of recognition, but she had identified valuable skills as well as areas of weakness. As she said: 'Ever since then I've known what I was good at and what I wasn't good at. I've shaped my career as a result.'

Remembering what we are naturally talented at doing is an obvious way of playing our strongest cards. But let's look a little closer: creative self-expression, however it is achieved, is an externalization of abilities and deficits. The painter may feel she has captured on canvas something that could not have reached expression any other way for her. It is a 'success' and a 'failure' at the same time, since not everyone will understand the artist's motivation in producing the painting. Even the artist may be unsure.

We are all capable of this type of deep expression and all of us have different approaches to the challenge. The difficulty is that we sometimes forget about this and a sort of spiritual constipation is the result. This exercise is designed to help you recall some aspects of your creativity and its specific expressions, so you can, if you wish, tap into one of the psyche's most powerful natural coping mechanisms, one that you already have. In a sense, all the exercises are a way of nudging you towards this goal, since writing is a form of creative productivity. And in the end, it doesn't matter if no one else understands what you are doing. What matters is that you find expression for those feelings.

EXERCISE 6:

❖ Think of your school, as you knew it around age eight, and then again at fourteen, perhaps. Draw a picture of it, or a map. Look at the drawing. Is it accurate? What sections did you have difficulty with? What were the 'danger' areas?

Considering how much of our time we spent in school buildings, it always astonishes me how hard this exercise can be, and how much people enjoy trying to puzzle out exactly what went where. This is because as we grow up we do not always think in terms of mathematical precision but in terms of emotional impression. Those items that were impressive to us will appear emphasized, large, in such a sketch. Those parts that have little to do with our personal needs may be very vague indeed. The 'danger areas' where we did not go, at least not willingly, may be somewhat ill-defined. In doing this exercise one man realized something he'd long ago thought he'd forgotten - just how dangerous it was for him to go to the shed in which the bicycles were kept, because his rivals used to meet there, and would give him a difficult time if he appeared. Another man described a long detour to avoid the field house, because of the other students who gathered there to smoke and drink, and who regarded him as a wimp. In their drawings both men made the danger areas far larger than scale - which suggested how important these places were for them.

In this exercise I've suggested ages eight and fourteen as points of reflection partly in order to focus your thoughts (after all, you spent about twelve years in school, so it's easy to lose a firm sense of how things were at any one time!) and because I consider these to be important times of transition. At eight we are beginning to encounter higher expectations such as homework, written work that has to be neat, and so on, and we're expected to be accountable for our actions in a much more definite way than before. At fourteen we are starting to be interested in all sorts of things that we don't have the personal autonomy to pursue yet. We want to drive cars, go to dances, drink beer, go snowboarding, and any number of other things, but on the whole we have to wait for adults to let us do things or make them happen for us. It's the time when what we want collides with what we're able to do, and in that space many important emotions dwell.

As you wrote you may have had many thoughts about these times. If you chose to write about a different age it's likely that this was an important time of your life. Do you know why?

EXERCISE 7:

❖ What would you like to say to your teachers if you met them now? Choose at least one positive statement. Choose a negative comment. Choose a neutral comment. Write about a relationship you may have had with a teacher, or would like to have had.

Many of us feel anger towards at least some of our teachers, and many feel profound gratitude to others. Teachers have the power, often, to devastate with a few words, or to make us feel useful and competent by a gesture. They mold our lives in ways we can hardly comprehend. A teacher who turns us on to a particular subject can lead our destinies in ways we couldn't have predicted. It's an odd, one-way relationship. A successful author recorded that he wrote to one of the teachers he had found most profoundly influential, thanking him, only to discover that the teacher only had a vague memory of him and seemed bemused by the letter he'd received. On a similar level, the teacher who made harmful and destructive comments may just have been having a bad day, and probably forgot all about the event immediately it was over. Yet the hurt stays with the pupil, sometimes for years.

Some people write eloquently about the friendships they would like to have had with teachers, even to the extent of wishing to be adopted by them. Others have written about the wish to have had a romance with a particular teacher. It's worth examining these, since teachers are in loco parentis (Latin for: 'in the place of the parents'). The desire for a friendship may say a great deal about the person's potential future relationships. Does this perhaps reflect a desire to have a permanent guide throughout one's life? What is more important, here: the friendship with the individual or the desire to keep learning? In the same way the desire for a sexual relationship may reflect the student's wish to be 'completed', made intellectually or socially superior by an alliance with an instructor, and may have less to do with sex and love than one might think.

Let's take this exercise a step further.

EXERCISE 8:

❖   What did school give you? What did it deny you?

Responses to these questions are often very strong. No school can nurture every aspect of every pupil. Notice, also, that the question is: 'What did school give you?' This can be seen as the whole experience, not just the classroom lessons. Some people will respond to the word school as meaning the social experience, the process of growing up, because that was to them the most vital part. Your choice in this answer will say right away where your most important relationships were - were they with the subject matter being taught, with the teachers, or with your peers?

"School gave me my best friend and my future husband. It denied me any chance to learn about art. I really love to paint." A reply like this shows both gratitude and regret. In each case there is something to be valued. How wonderful to have shared one's school days with one's spouse! Few of us can claim that level of shared experience. Yet the regret expressed for the lost chance to learn about art is also worth valuing. It's up to the individual how to take that information, value it, and do something about developing that neglected artistic interest.

EXERCISE 9:

❖   What were the family expectations of you at school? Were there any pressures?

All families have some expectations of their children, and sometimes these can be crushing. From the baseball coach who never made it to the majors and who wants his son to be a great player, to the family that wants their daughter to be an attorney, the pressures are on. Sometimes there are negative pressures, also, such as the man who recorded his father as saying that school meant nothing, and the moment he got out he'd put his son in charge of running the store. It is hard for any student to do his or her best under these circumstances. In fact, it's hard for anyone to discover his or her true talents and abilities, if there's a chance that may lead to family conflicts later. This leads to the next exercise.

EXERCISE 10:

❖ How did you respond to rules, and authority figures? Can you describe a time when you were in trouble for breaking the rules? Whose rules were they? If you prefer you can describe a time when you were unjustly accused of something.

Rebellion is often a healthy way of expressing oneself against laws and understandings one does not accept. It is an obvious form of self-assertion. When we grow up we always push the limits, bend the rules, just to see what we can do. Curfew is at 11:00, but what about 11:05? or 11:20? Often it's only by coming up against an extreme sanction or reaction that we learn to respect those arbitrary rules. What will I feel like if I drink a whole bottle of whiskey? We try, we learn from the headache. Most of the time, though, we don't need to test the limits to understand what the likely consequences will be.

Sometimes authority figures have proven to be ogres. A woman of fifty wrote with rage about an alcoholic school principal who criticized her readings during a school assembly, humiliating her in front of the whole school. She had broken no rule, and yet was being punished in this arbitrary way. It was clear that for her this was a terrifying event, one that had genuinely caused her to reshape her life in order to avoid any possibility of being criticized in this way ever again. Much of her subsequent life had been a reaction to this experience. Writing about it allowed her to feel the anger and begin to free herself from its shadow.

EXERCISE 11:

❖ What are your memories of lunchtime? Did you eat school lunch? Did you bring a lunchbox? Describe the experience.

I've left this until last because it's a particularly rich topic. Lunch at school is an emotionally loaded time. Think of it - all those people together, all those cliques, all that jostling as to who gets into line where, who sits with whom, and who sits alone. The food itself is always the focus for many comments (everyone always criticizes institutional food, no matter how good) and who eats what, or who fails to eat what can become stigmas. How someone eats can also become a point of discussion. 'He eats that stuff and he loves it. Look at him slurp it down!' Suddenly we have a whole new vocabulary of criticism with which to judge and be judged. The number of teen films that contain a school lunch-room scene reminds us just how emotionally loaded that half-hour can be, because that's when the bully can find the weak person, when the unwanted admirer can pester the embarrassed beauty. That is the time when everyone can see how we dress. Judgments are freely dispensed at such times.

There's no respite for those who bring their own lunches, either. From the earliest years children compare their lunches, trade sandwiches, admire each others' lunch boxes, and sit near those who habitually have candy or chocolate with their meals. One mother recalled being extra careful to make her son's lunch delicious and to include M&Ms so he could share the candy easily. "My mom used to make me horrible lunches, and I never forgot the fun that was made of me. I didn't want my child to have to go through that," the mother said, as she explained her reasons.

A young man recalled his acute fear of lunchtimes because his family had raised him as a strict vegetarian, but he was aware that this made him different, and left him at risk of being an outsider. He began to eat meat just to conform, and didn't tell his parents. The whole experience left him feeling as though he had to tell white-lies in order to be accepted.

Again, overweight or large-sized children are particularly vulnerable to criticism about food and eating, and the cruelty of comments made by peers and by teachers, on occasion, has emerged with great force in this exercise. Anorexic and bulimic students have written about their sense of disgust at school lunches which they picked at or bolted down, or ignored only to binge on chocolate, in secret, later. They went to lunch only to be with their friends, to appear normal, or because they knew their absence from the lunch table would make them the focus of gossip and criticism.

If you have a history of eating disorders you may find this very hard to write about. In addition, it must be said that eating disorders and food anxieties are potentially very dangerous indeed. If you have ever starved yourself, especially if you have continued to the point at which you've become unwell, or if you have ever found yourself bingeing and purging, that is eating compulsively then forcing yourself to vomit, you may already know how dangerous this can be. If you are currently engaging in any of these behaviors you should not delay in getting professional help. This book may be able to help you through your difficulties - it can certainly be useful as a way of encountering these issues - but it cannot give you the sort of direct help that a counselor can give you. A counselor can move the process of self-discovery along much more rapidly than you can working alone with this book. So if you think you may have an eating disorder you should waste no time. Delay is dangerous.

The examples I have given so far are fairly clear reactions to the social situations involved in eating. The anorexic and the bulimic are also responding to an internal drama or tension. Eating, after all, is a time of some excitement. Think of how loud the baby cries when hungry. Then think of the intent concentration on the baby's face as she sucks from the bottle or breast. This excitement never fully leaves any of us, and so eating can become a focus of many hopes and anxieties. An instance of this would be something I observed several times with disturbed adolescents, mostly young men who had suffered physical and emotional deprivations. I discovered it was often very difficult for these young men to remain calm when being served in a cafeteria or a restaurant, particularly if the waiter was male. The situation would often be very tense as the adolescents became suspicious of the waiter, muttering about how slow the service was (even if it wasn't), and about how they imagined the waiter was removing items from the plate or the server was giving less than full measure. The reactions were less extreme if the wait person happened to be female, young, and reasonably attractive, in which case there was likely to be a similarly exaggerated fondness.

Observing these repeated behaviors over time it seemed highly likely that we were dealing with a food anxiety based in the young men's long-held fears that they would not be fed adequately. This fear was often rooted in the deprived circumstances of the birth family, where food might have been in short supply. The anxiety had now become focused primarily on the male waiters who provided the food by delivering it to the table. This was, quite possibly, a displaced fear of male authority, as well as a deep suspicion that males could never provide for the primary needs involved. Logically this is absurd. A male waiter is as capable as a female waiter, and anyhow that person neither selects the food nor determines the size of the portion. It would seem that a hostility to male figures, perceived as in authority, was playing itself out here in an oblique fashion. Just as it was too risky for these young men to challenge directly the father-figures in their lives, so they simmered in quiet resentment, displaying old angers to the helpless staff. More basic than this, though, was the fear that these young men would not be adequately provided for, that they had been abandoned. Surrounded by food all they could feel was anxiety about being fed. I give this extreme example because aspects of it are to be seen in every school lunch room. Behaviors around food often provide clues as to what was happening for those around us, and for what our own issues might be. There can be no easy diagnosis, of course, but the drama of the lunch room is rich and varied, and deserves attention. Few actions are more basic than eating - the decisions about what we want to take into our bodies, how, and when - and few are more richly symbolic of our response to the outside world. The young man who came to college with dozens of boxes of tinned Spaghetti Os was making a statement about his distrust of new foods and new experiences, and also about his fear of being away from the safe and familiar. It was a strong symbolic statement about his unwillingness to 'take in' anything unfamiliar, including knowledge.

This section is called Schooldays for convenience, but so much happens in those years from five to eighteen, that it could have been called almost anything. In other sections, we will return to specific aspects of school-time that are not covered here. The emphasis in this section has been to ask you to consider these formative years as part of a process in which the personal world and the social world come into conflict. It was a time when we had to make compromises, in order to be allowed to proceed. Because so much goes on for us during these years, we often have trouble making sense of the experiences. You'll notice we haven't spent much time looking at such things as sex, or alcohol and drug use. We'll look at aspects of these in later sections. For now we have more than enough material.

The blur of school days - "the best years of my life" as one man recalled, "the pits" as another put it - needs to be broken down into distinct questions like this so we can begin to understand it. Sitting around with friends telling stories of school may be fun - Bruce

Springsteen's song, 'Glory Days' depicts it well - but it may not help us get to the heart of what it all meant to us, as individuals. That's why we need the privacy of writing, the intimacy of our own thoughts, and the time to reflect rather than to exaggerate for an audience. School made us much of what we are, so we need to understand what happened. Then we can understand how we came to be who we are now, and where we are now.

If you have reached the end of this section and you feel you have only random and disconnected thoughts to show for your efforts, do not despair. Change is not immediate, and it always happens at an unconscious level. We can rarely pinpoint the moment when we became wiser or more aware, but we do know that it is happening, usually at its own pace. By reclaiming your memories and impressions you can help that unconscious process to move forward.

Chapter Seven

RELATIONSHIPS: FRIENDS AND ROMANCE

Who we have as our friends and loved ones has a profound impact on us. How we deal with intimacy and sharing, and how free we feel to take emotional risks can also dictate our fate. Relationships, therefore, is a huge topic especially since relationships will change as we grow and as our needs change. I've divided this section in two: personal relationships and romantic relationships. This is not to say that the two don't overlap. Many people refer to their spouse as their best friend and lover. The split is intended merely to raise a distinction between those things we need and like in our friends and those things we want from our lovers, and to acknowledge that we can accept those things in our friends that we would find very difficult to accept if we wanted that person as a lover. Many heterosexuals, for example, have homosexual friends, and those friendships are strong and enduring. I'd suggest, however, that there might be some obstacles to romantic attachments in such instances. We can love and care about our friends and yet not feel we have to go to bed with them.

So let's start with friends. Many American sitcoms are predicated on the idea of a small neighborhood and a wide range of friends, all of whom know each other and care, to an extent, about each other. I think this is worth noting because neighborhoods and communities have been hit heavily in our mass culture. The images of friends and friendship that come to us from our TVs are, on the whole, atypical of real American life. *Cheers* ran for years based on the idea of a bunch of people who always gathered in the same bar, with the same bar-staff, and enjoyed each others' conversation. See if you can find that at your local bar. For one thing, the bar staff changes, sometimes every day in urban areas, so you may never see the same people working in the place. For another the fact of regular customers is a rarity. Finally, many bars have several loud TVs blaring sports channels, or a juke box, or both, effectively killing conversation. For most of us the typical bar is noisy and filled with people sitting alone or in couples. Rarely is there a table of five or six people talking with each other.

I give you this example of the friendships in one TV show - and I could give you others, from *Seinfeld*, *Friends* (note the name*)*, even *Melrose Place* - to suggest that friendship is lionized in our sitcoms but very different in real life. In fact *The Real World*, that strange program that is neither real nor any world I come from, makes itself attractive because the roommates are always squabbling - a sort of negative engagement with each other. This, too, feels staged. Usually if roommates or housemates don't agree they'll just avoid each other, go their own ways, or maintain a polite distance.

From this we can deduce that friends are something we all like the idea of having, but on the whole we don't do very well at living up to the screen image - the image we may feel ourselves obliged to aspire to, or to judge our lives by. And the screen image is compelling. Hollywood has for years given us the 'buddy' movie - the story in which two people, usually two men who are law enforcement officers, work together and stick to each other through thick and thin. It's a version of friendship, yes, but not one most of us can relate to directly.

When we do these exercises, we may want to consider this, so that we can separate cultural expectations from what we may really prefer our friends to be.

EXERCISE 1:

❖ Who was your first best friend? Write a brief story describing the things you did and enjoyed, together. Who is your current best friend?

❖ If you made a list of all your close friends over the years, what do you think these people would have as shared attributes? Make the list.

Often we choose the same sorts of people over and over. If we come from a family with divorce or some other disruption, we may find ourselves unconsciously choosing friends who have similar backgrounds, because they will understand certain things about us just as we will understand certain things about them, without needing them to be explained. When we are young we may choose friends who are representations of who we want to be. That's why the taller, better-looking, more accomplished children are always so popular. Who did you want to be like? Why?

Making a list of our close friends can be revealing, as well, since it tends to turn up disparities between those friends you chose, and those who chose you. We can all recall those people who wanted to be our friends, when we didn't feel the same way about them. Such imbalances are part of every relationship from time to time. Think about this. Now return to the exercise. What did you need your friends to be? Write a narrative of an occasion when your friend came through with flying colors. Now write about a time you were let down. When you have finished, ask yourself again: what did I expect my friends to be? Do I still expect that?

A surprising number of people - especially men - reply to these questions by saying that they do not feel they have many close friends, let alone a best friend. Sometimes this leads them to reminisce about other friendships. This can be very revealing because often the biggest single component for a friendship is the amount of shared time spent with that person. These days we may relocate for a job not once but several times, we expect to work long hours, and we may live in areas that are geographically removed from our colleagues, causing us not to see them that often outside work. Friendships can often be casualties of this sort of movement. Not so many decades ago most people would expect to spend most of their lives, even those who lived in cities, surrounded by those they knew. We cannot pretend this image of community is true for many of us anymore.

EXERCISE 2:

- ❖ Recall an adventure or a travel situation that you undertook with others. What were the best moments? What were the worst?
- ❖ If you prefer, imagine being on an expedition. Who would you choose as your traveling companion to see you through tough times in foreign lands? You can choose anyone, actual or mythic, alive or dead. Now give reasons for your choices.
- ❖ A variant on this theme is as follows: If you had to be in a space capsule with up to four other people for some period of time, who would they be?

This exercise gives possibilities of response that can be very abstract. One could imagine being in a space capsule with Napoleon, Voltaire, and Charles Dickens for example. It's certain one would have an interesting time, but it's likely the conversations would be different from those one would get with Mickey Mantle, Joe Montana and Michael Jordan. The people you choose can say a huge amount about what you want from relationships, life, the world. However, this kind of thinking may seem too unrealistic, which is why I gave you the option of writing about an actual event you have experienced. In each case the core remains the same - what did you get from the people you traveled with, what did you value about that relationship?   One man who had gone on a sled dog expedition as the photographer, and so had not known anyone beforehand, described his sense of joy at being accepted for who he was, without reservations. He felt privileged, he said, to be taken on to the team, to be treated as an equal, and to know that his team-mates would speak directly about anything and everything. He valued the openness and generosity that demanded only directness in return.

At the most abstract level, one's choice of companion in the space capsule can mirror the needs we may have to understand the world. The person who decides to have Jesus as a traveling partner presumably wants to learn about God, the universe, heaven, and so on. Such a person will, in real life, choose friends who have the same interests. The person who selects George Washington may be fascinated by history, but may value humor less highly. However we respond to this choice 'history' is the way this person has chosen to understand the world, this is the levering point from which he or she prefers to make sense of what goes on. Neither point of view is more valid than the other, but they do give a clue as to the values we hold dear and expect others to respect.

Another exercise extends this series of ideas.

EXERCISE 3:

- ❖ Imagine you are giving a dinner party. You can invite anyone, alive or dead. Who would you place next to whom? What would you serve?

Responses to this have often been hilarious. One man had Karl Marx placed next to Queen Elizabeth II of England just because, as he put it, he "wanted to see sparks fly". Clearly his sense of fun and his attraction to scenes of conflict were the issues here. A woman wanted to invite Antony and Cleopatra, but only if they sat at opposite sides of the table, or divided by someone dull. She felt this would fuel their impatience and their sexual frustration would make compelling watching. Her interests seemed to lie in watching the world around her as a human drama.

Does this sound too vague? If so, think of Judy Chicago's famous installation 'The Dinner Party' in which places are set at a large three-sided table, each place representing a famous feminist. The viewer comes away with a sense of great women thinkers and the possible conversations they could have had. Again, Caryl Churchill's play *Top Girls* starts with a scene in which women from several different countries and centuries are sitting at a lunch table discussing their lives. As you imagine your dinner gathering, think of conversations and disputes your figures would have. In all likelihood, even if you invite famous figures you don't want to be exactly like Thomas Jefferson or Sylvia Plath, and you know that. But you want to learn from them - from some aspect of them - and you want to enjoy them. What do you want to learn from your friends? And what do you want to give them in return? Remember, a dinner is a 'giving' of sorts, an honoring of the guests.

The point here is simple. If we don't know what we're looking for in a friendship, and what we need from our friends, we're likely to make vague alliances with all sorts of people, many of whom we cannot hope to have much deep connection to. The result will be disappointment and loneliness, which may leave us grasping at straws for the next friendship. If we aren't clear about what we want we can waste a lot of time.

ROMANCE

Was ever any topic so laden with potential disaster areas as this? In romance we all make far more mistakes than we achieve successes, and happily-ever-after is not something most of us see around us on a large scale - even though we may find ourselves hoping for it. Romantic relationships need work even after Prince Charming meets Cinderella, and we often have to remind ourselves of this. Unfortunately Hollywood does nothing to help, and popular culture is full of happy endings that, if we were to regard them soberly, we would realize are just the starting point for making the relationships work out in the long years ahead.

Looking at it in this light we can say that much of the disappointment and heartbreak in romantic relationships comes from the tendency that people have to deceive themselves. If we don't know what we want in a partner and we meet someone else who also isn't sure what he or she wants, then we can't be surprised if we end up in a mess. The following exercises are designed to help you spell out what you may be looking for, and what you may want to avoid so you can make reasoned decisions rather than compulsively driven decisions. Obviously I can't guarantee that doing these exercises will save your emotional life. I can only suggest that they could save you some mistakes. For example, if I start a business I'd reasonably expect to research the prospects for my product or service, make sure the market is ready for what I have to offer, and draw up a business plan. The bank will certainly require me to be clear about what my objectives may be, or they won't extend a loan. I'm investing thousands of dollars and years of my life; I owe it to myself to be careful. A romantic relationship, also, is likely to take up years of one's life and huge amounts of money. If there are children, the amount of time and effort and energy and love needed can be staggering. So why is it so few of us seem to think through our romantic relationships as carefully as we'd plan our careers? I'd suggest it's because we assume, with the fairy tales we heard as children, that it'll all just work itself out somehow. I'd contend that it can only work itself out successfully if we take steps to know who we are and what we may be looking for.

An example may help. A young woman was looking for a possible partner or husband and had no success. One of her interests was sailing, and over the preceding two years she'd gone to her sailing club hoping to find a promising man, only to be disappointed. It wasn't until she asked herself what she wanted from a possible partner that she began to realize she wouldn't find many suitable candidates in her sailing club. There were lots of nice men, she explained, but the non-sailing parts of them didn't coincide with her preferences. Once she began to look elsewhere she found more people who were more to her liking. If we don't know what we want we can't expect to find much that fits our needs. Or, as one man wrote, "If you grasp at straws you'll get straws."

Now I do not mean to suggest that romantic partners should share all one's interests. Even if that could be possible it still tends to breed its own tensions. Ask any husband and wife team who run their own business, for example. Sometimes that degree of shared experience can be claustrophobic.

What helped the woman from the sailing club to understand her needs for a partner was an exercise that I have called a 'star chart'. You may want to attempt one yourself. For her the 'star' was something a little like this:

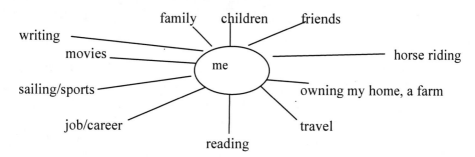

At each of the points of the star (and you can have more than six) she wrote a word that described her interests and things that were important to her such as family, love of movies, sports. Depending on how vital they were to her she put them close to or far away from the central circle, which she called the core self. Then she drew a similar star for the man she was currently dating. The diagrams showed her several things. The first thing it showed her was how few shared interests they had, and that she didn't know how he felt about certain things. There were, in fact, unknown areas that she had forgotten to ask about because she had assumed that because he shared some of her values, he must share them all. Her family was very important to her. She had no idea how he felt about his. She wanted children, eventually, seeing this as part and parcel of her 'family' issue, yet she had no idea how he felt about children.

The result of the star diagram was that the woman began to realize that the central core of a person was what most mattered, and that surface characteristics could confuse the issue. She drew another star in which she listed her faults and failings and those of the man she was dating. What she discovered there was that the annoying little characteristics became manageable. When he was irritable, for example, she recognized that this was not the center of who he was, but a localized phenomenon. If she responded thoughtfully, rather than reacting to the surface behavior, she could allow him to re-contact his core of self and so let his best aspects emerge.

I think it's worth emphasizing, here, that in our core selves we are, almost all of us, loving, kind and caring. The world's treatment of us may cause us to adopt defensive postures, and some of those postures may be unpleasant, causing us to appear mean, or selfish, or callous. These are the surface characteristics that may tempt us to reply to mean-ness by being mean in return. The question this young woman was eventually brought to ask was, is the man she was dating prepared to let his core self emerge so he could be himself, fully, with her?

This star-chart is just one response, but it is a technique you may want to use and adapt for your own needs.

EXERCISE 1:

❖ Take a moment and draw your own star now. When you've done so you might like to write about what you have discovered by putting the information in this form.

Part of the effectiveness of this star exercise is that it is non-linear - it is almost not a writing exercise at all. As such it can cause us, literally, to see familiar information in a whole new way. The picture before us alters our usual way thinking about the situation, and can give us immediate, important, insights. Usually, when we think about the other person, we may tend to make mental lists of shared interests or conflicts. Or perhaps we'll focus on one particular aspect of the relationship, good or bad, and build that up to be the whole discussion. Doing this exercise is like the difference between having a pocket full of objects that we rummage around in hopelessly, relying only on our sense of touch, and choosing to tip all those objects out onto a tray to decide which are important. It's a good idea to write about those insights.

Here is another exercise that can help to uncover some of your unconscious choices about your relationship.

EXERCISE 2:

❖ Who was the first person you had a crush on? If you can't recall the very first, then think of any big crush you can recall. What attracted you?

It is said that our first romance sets the pattern that we will follow in all our subsequent romances. I'd modify that statement so it becomes something like this: our first romance will tend to reflect preferences and behaviors that are deep within us, and which can be very hard to alter. Our courtship patterns tend to be just that - patterns we repeat as we approach the other person. Our earliest crushes are likely to repeat themselves, also. If we can recall those awkward occasions we can begin to identify the origins of our later attractions. How did you behave when you had your early crushes? Do you see any vestiges of that now?

Let's take this further.

EXERCISE 3:

❖ Describe your perfect partner.

Once you've had fun describing the perfect match, you can re-read and be more realistic. One man said he wanted a partner with the mind of Sir Kenneth Clarke, the genius of the philosopher Hegel, the body of Claudia Schiffer and the worldliness of Cleopatra. When he reflected on this impossible (and extraordinary) array of talent he realized straight away how absurdly unrealistic it was, and then he noticed he'd asked for a combination of male genius and female physical attributes. This allowed him to push further and ask why he didn't see women as being able to match what he saw as 'men's ideas'. Once his prejudice was revealed, it was possible for him to stop demanding that women match his absurd standards. Gradually he started to appreciate that many women might have equally fine qualities that he was choosing to ignore. Until he could do that he was blinding himself to the possibilities that did in fact exist.

EXERCISE 4:

❖ List the attributes of significant partners in your life. If it helps you may want to look at pictures of them to freshen your memory. Are there any repeated attributes?

Sometimes the patterns are subtle, sometimes less so. One man recalled that of his first seven girlfriends, only one had been a native English speaker. Although English was his mother tongue, it was not his biological mother's language, for she spoke with a German accent. Another man found that three of the most significant women in his life had mothers who had killed themselves, and the woman with whom he finally settled down had a difficult (but not suicidal) mother. This led him to a number of explorations about what it might be about this mother-daughter relationship that he was tuning into, and why it could be attractive. A young woman wrote about how all the men she was attracted to had what she called 'secrets' that she only uncovered after she was already romantically involved, when the secrets actually threatened the relationship. It was only when she began to look at this that she became fully aware of the secrets in her family, and that she regarded men with concealed inner lives as 'normal' and even as attractive because her father had been such a man.

EXERCISE 5:

❖ Describe your first romance, or, if you prefer, your first sexual encounter.

For some the first sexual encounter is not always linked to love or romance, but it is, on the whole, a rite of passage that we recall and return to in our memories. For some of us it may be disappointing or a source of shame; others may see it as a blissful time of happiness. On the whole, the chances are that we were confused, afraid, anxious, and less sure of ourselves than we would have wished - even if this was a romantic occasion with a loved partner. Sex is something that not many of us are good at right from the start. For many women, the first sexual encounter can be painful, and may include fears of pregnancy. Some women report being relieved it had finally happened. In every case the experience is likely to reflect our then state of mind and form our later expectations of sexuality. "So that was it?" wrote one woman, "What a disappointment. It wasn't until years later that I learned what it could be like." Not everything we do results in our spectacles becoming rose-tinted. If our first love is a disaster we may, in the future, assume that our luck means all love affairs will be disasters, and we may act in ways that make that a self-fulfilling prophecy.

An example may help, here. A disturbed adolescent I worked with spent the first two years of her residential placement kicking and hitting people and objects. The people she hit most often were those close to her, her friends. When she began to explore this she discovered that it was a reflection of the many foster-home placements that had been failures in her, so far, short life. Her earliest memories were of being rejected and then being sent to yet another foster home. After a while the fear that she would yet again be rejected caused her such anxiety that rather than wait in fear, she wanted to hit someone so she would be rejected. It was the only way of dissipating the fear that she could think of, and it was also an act of assertion that said, 'if anyone's going to do the rejecting, it'll be me!' So for two years this young woman hit people, waiting to see if they'd fulfill her expectations and send her away. At the end of that time she was able to verbalize her fears. The result was that it was no longer necessary to be violent, to act out her fear, and she stopped her behavior, much to everyone's relief. At the core of herself she was a loving and kind person, but the presenting behavior, the persona she had adopted, was unpleasant in the extreme. All because of fear. It is the core self that we need to identify.

Certainly I'm not suggesting that any of us should accept violent behavior in others. That is not what I'm intending to convey. I used this example simply as a way of showing that considerable defenses frequently exist, and they can confuse us in our evaluations. Remember, no one should accept physical threats or physical violence from anyone else. If you have a history of violence with your partners, you should not delay in seeking help. No one deserves to live in fear of physical harm.

This young woman had set up certain negative expectations at a very early age, and she then found herself trying to make sure they happened. We can all see in ourselves versions of the same thing, if we are alert. Making these early imprintings conscious can help us to become free of them. This is amply demonstrated in the next example, a man who wrote about his distrust of women and his expectation that they would always betray him. Whenever he found a woman who, it seemed to him, was not about to betray him he became acutely anxious. His thinking was that if she really was loyal then he'd have no reason not to love her; but if he loved her and he was mistaken about her loyalty then he'd be far worse off than before, when he trusted no one. The choice was between repeated neurotic behavior in choosing relationships that would become betrayals, and taking the steps necessary to change the behavior, and his life. When he looked at his relationships the man was able to see that his reaction was a compound of many things - his mother's decision to divorce his father (which the man had seen in his adolescence as a betrayal of himself), and his own first romance in which the girl had left him for one of his friends. These betrayals had affected him so deply that he had chosen to perpetuate them for the next decade.

This leads us to another area of discussion. Any relationship will impose certain restrictions on the individual. At the most basic level, if one is in a sexual relationship it takes time. Even if one spends more time in bed, one may actually spend less time sleeping, so the rest of one's life is effected also. We give up a certain amount of time, and freedom, too. If our mate expects us to be back in time for dinner, we cannot stay out drinking with our buddies from the office without some repercussions. This may be seen as one person cramping the other's style, or threatening his or her freedom - others may see it as simply good manners to stand by an expectation that someone has of us. So here's an exercise:

EXERCISE 6:

❖ Can you write about a time you felt fearful of the demands made by a relationship?

Fear can be seen as physical fear - the terror of being beaten up by one's spouse. This is a serious concern, and as I said in the preceding paragraphs, can be very dangerous, even life-threatening.

Fear can more often mean mental terror. People have written about the mental cruelties inflicted upon them by their lovers. In every case, I would repeat what I have said already - that no one should have to live in fear. The only reasonable response is to leave. Never attempt to make a deal with someone who uses fear as a tactic against you. It's like negotiating with terrorists. It doesn't work.

The types of fear that I have most frequently encountered in the responses to this exercise run as follows: Men tend to be afraid of being tied down for the next thirty years to a mortgage, a boring job and a situation they cannot leave. Many men write about feeling trapped - they have to keep making money to support the family and their own wishes may not be able to be explored. Estimates vary, but to raise a child to adulthood is reckoned to cost parents about $200,000, on average, and that's before college tuition! It's not surprising men fear and can even resent the role they find themselves in. Women are just as anxious, it seems, since child rearing takes them out of the work place to a greater or lesser degree, and can affect professional ambitions. It can leave them feeling trapped in a marriage they can't afford to leave, or they may be afraid of the effect that leaving will have on the children.

Men and women everywhere have written about the fear that their relationships may actually prevent them from being all they can be. Possibly this fear can be turned around, made into something more productive, by rephrasing it. If it is reformulated it can become: 'Will this person help me become all I could be - and will I in turn be able to help him/her?' By revising the problem, the other person ceases to be seen as the major obstacle. We all need relationships and these relationships make demands on us. What we have to decide is whether or not this is a supportive association, one that can move both partners ahead in their ambitions. If we decide it isn't, then we have to acknowledge that we had a part in choosing the relationship.

In this way the mind can play interesting tricks on us. One man wrote of his wife's resentment of his modest successes. He had supported her for several years because she wanted to be a writer, but in that time she had written nothing. In fact she had spent a considerable amount of effort in making him feel it was his treatment of her that was blocking the path to literary success. Writing about his situation he began to see that his wife was using him as an excuse for what was essentially her problem, rather than facing the possibility that she just might not be a writer after all. Her fear, 'will this man let me be a writer?' had blinded her to a more likely reality - that she wanted something she wasn't capable of achieving, at least not yet. Her fear seemed to be that men cramped women. Even though the husband did all he could to be supportive, she was determined to have her fear proven true, and so she had, literally, sabotaged her own situation.

Fears like this, if not confronted, have a way of destroying even the best relationships. The husband, in this case, probably wasn't the 'problem'. The point is that the wife had chosen to blame him as a way of avoiding her own ambivalence. The story that she told herself was that men always cramped women writers - which has so often been the case in the past - and she then believed that story rather than observing how supportive her husband actually was.

This is, I think, a particularly difficult issue in America. In this country, as in few other countries in the world, we are encouraged to believe that we can do anything, we can achieve anything. This is the land of opportunity, and if we don't succeed it is only our own fault. Sometimes this leads to unrealistic dreams, ones that cannot succeed. Hollywood, L.A. and New York City are filled with people who call themselves actors, but who earn their money waiting tables or working in offices. While focusing on getting their big chance many of these people may be unable to see that they may not succeed in their dreams, since statistically so very few ever do. The problem is not lack of talent but too much competition for too little space. I give this example because in relationships one may fear the loss of something one never had, far more than one may fear the loss of something more immediate.

This is a crucial point. The man who quits the rock band, marries and has a fulfilled life may always regret it if the band goes on to sell a million CDs. But this, actually, is an exceptional instance. When you write about your fears, be as exaggerated and fantastic as you wish. Then try to assess coolly what the real fears are, and what the fantasies may be.

EXERCISE 7:

❖ Imagine a really dreadful relationship. Describe it. Be fantastic, if you wish.

Often it is only by describing the opposite of something that we begin to see what we expect and value most highly. People have had a great deal of fun with this, describing drunken brawls, infidelities, scenes in public places. The things you describe will reflect directly what you value. You may be surprised at how many things you do expect, value, and even demand of your relationship. Make a list of the results. Would you add any more items?

If you prefer, you can describe the relationship of some public figure, as you see it to be, and write about why you see it as being a disaster. Re-read what you wrote. You may find you can jot down the things that make that relationship so ghastly. Some lists I've read include the following: shallow people acting selfishly, lack of honesty, no dignity, no pride, mean-spiritedness, hypocrisy, lies... the list goes on. The things you will not accept emphasize what you do expect.

In this section I've encouraged you to use fantasy (i.e. 'the perfect partner' and 'a really dreadful relationship'). Since fantasy often includes desires that are not fully conscious they should be taken seriously. Once we've looked at the extremes we can work back towards differentiating our wishes from our needs. We may wish for Val Kilmer or Sandra Bullock, but would we, in reality, be able to deal with all that it would entail? Probably not. Our need, then, would be for someone attractive, sexy, witty, but that need may have to be moderated in the light of reality. Still, we have identified aspects that we may consider important, since each of us is different. Gradually this allows us to work back towards reality, so we can look at the mass of people out there and chose our life-partners with the sense that we know what we need, and are not prepared to settle for a pale imitation. This is vital. When we settle for second best we diminish our self-esteem, subtly, until we may begin to feel that we only deserve second (or third) best in the rest of our lives, too. And if that's what we feel we deserve, we'll never get what we need. For without a clear idea of what the best is, how can we be sure we've got it? Life is short; failed relationships take up a great deal of time. For our own sakes, we owe it to ourselves to get this aspect of our lives right.

COMMUNICATION BETWEEN THE SEXES

If we're thinking about male-female relationships it's well worth being aware of certain discussions that have come to the surface in recent years that suggest there is a difference in the way men and women communicate. Harvard psychologist Carol Gilligan's *In a Different Voice* (1982) and Jean Baker Miller's *Towards a New Psychology of Women* (1976) have blazed a trail that suggests men and women perceive differently and use different communication techniques. The result is, sometimes, that women have been misunderstood by the dominant male culture, and their observations have been downgraded. The insights that these researchers reveal are vitally important if we are to understand how men and women communicate, or fail to. Men and women actually seem to have different development patterns and so different value systems can result. For example, studies of suicides have shown general trend differences between the sexes. Men are likely to kill themselves because of issues of pride and failure. Women tend to kill themselves for love or relationship reasons. Gilligan's work has shown that women seem to value conversation as a way of creating community and relationship, while men use conversation either to convey information or to 'score points' off others. In this case conversation is more about raising status than about developing friendship. These differences and others like them carry a heavy price. For instance, in our society young girls find themselves caught in a male values world, where intimacy is not prized. This tends to lead them to doubt themselves, to panic and become passive.

Deborah Tannen's *You Just Don't Understand: Men and Women in Conversation* (1990) gives a large amount of mostly anecdotal material that reinforces these ideas. She sees men using conversation to establish social status, and identifies very clearly the different ways the sexes use talk about personal problems. Women, she shows, use 'troubles talk' as a way of establishing closeness, and often no solution is sought for the problem described. Men see the same conversation as a way of asking for advice. By doing so, the man shows his inferiority, and the advisor, by suggesting solutions, shows his superiority. Women, then, talk to establish intimacy. Men seem to want to use talk to re-establish dominance. In this situation it's clear that men don't like to be told what to do. Where a woman may make what she feels is a simple request for collaborative help, a man may feel he's being ordered around, which will cause resentment. Under these circumstances a simple statement like 'can you take out the garbage?' becomes potentially explosive.

Gilligan's study is especially interesting because it is so detailed, and in it she shows that women's moral development may well be quite different from men's. She contends that men are quick to leap on the practical side of moral issues, and have little trouble identifying a hierarchy of moral values. Using Lawrence Kohlberg's tests devised to measure moral development in adolescents, she shows that women are less able (and less eager) than men to reduce human dramas to mathematical equations, and so often have no clear answer to give to questions on the standardized tests. Here is an example of one of Kohlberg's questions: A man must get medication for his sick wife who will die if she doesn't get the drugs. The medication costs $2000, and the man does not have the money. The pharmacist refuses to accept less than the full amount. What should the man do? Should he steal the drugs?

Adolescent boys were quick to make the hierarchical judgment that saving a life is more important than theft. Adolescent girls tended to think about the bigger picture. Stealing is wrong, the man might be sent to jail, and that would hurt his relationship with his wife, possibly leaving her even more unprotected than before. Couldn't he borrow the money? These far more complex responses emphasized relationships, rather than abstracts of what was 'right'. This ability to see both sides of an argument left women, at times, powerless to make a decision because no matter what happened someone would be hurt. Consequently they did less well on the test, which expected a definite answer. Adolescent boys had no such problems, and they saw theft of the medication as the only way forward.

Such stark differences can only lead us to consider how men and women ever manage to communicate at all! The popular series of books by John Gray, *Men are from Mars, Women are from Venus* plays into this, and to judge by the huge sales of the series of books and tapes of this and associated titles, many people see this somewhat basic division to be an accurate enough representation of he way the world works.

With this information in mind, try the following exercise.

EXERCISE 1:

❖ Recall a time when you and your partner felt the same about something. Can you describe that time?

❖ Now recall a disagreement or a misunderstanding. Can you describe a time when you felt misunderstood?

We can all recall misunderstandings and disagreements. I don't want to focus on the negative, however. For many of us the recollections of these occasions are painful and - and this is important - full of surprise. "Why does he think like that?" as one woman put it, surprised that her husband of many years had done something without consulting her. "Why does she always do this to me?" wrote a man trying to understand his girl-friend's decision-making. In each case the individuals felt diminished, unvalued and, yes, surprised. One should value that sense of astonishment, since it indicates how good the rest of the relationship is. After all, if one is constantly at odds with one's partner it's hard to feel that sense of sudden disappointment.

One man put the whole thing rather neatly: "When we discuss any household improvements she wants to talk about it endlessly, while I want to get on and do it; and then when I get tired of the endless round of discussion, she gets upset that I'm not interested. Well, I was interested for the first four days, but enough already!" If we see this through Gilligan's lens we can reassess the situation. The man is simply being the goal-oriented problem-solving male. The woman could be seen as using the discussion not just as a means to an end, but as a way of establishing intimacy with her partner. When he, with his mindset of getting the task done, showed annoyance, she felt he was rejecting her efforts to foster intimacy between them. The disagreement was not the result of one person being unkind, but of fundamentally different ways of approaching the task, which neither had expected.

I give this example as a possible way you can re-assess the argument you have just described, since understanding can lead to less friction in the future. Here's another exercise:

EXERCISE 2:

❖   What don't you know about your partner? What questions do you want to ask him/her? What do you want to be asked? What are you afraid to ask?

In the rush of everyday lives we sometimes forget or avoid asking about aspects of the other's life. Julian Barnes' novel *Before She Met Me* is based on just that anxiety, as a narrator wonders what his wife's previous life and lovers may have involved. Often we're better off not knowing some of those previous events, since they may be painful for both partners to consider. We have, on the whole, more unsuccessful love-affairs than successful ones - but then we only need one successful one to take us through the rest of our lives. Sometimes then, it's not useful to dwell on the failures, but it may well be useful just to know about them. This exercise is based on the assumption that what we don't know about is not the same as a blank space. We know that our partner had a life before we met. Acknowledging that can often prevent the blank spaces from taking on mythic proportions in which our imaginations work against us.

An illustration may help. A man whose partner already had a child when he met her wrote about how he feared his wife stayed with him just because he was steady and made good money, and he feared that she'd sown all her wild oats in her youth, settling for him as second best. This was a real fear and potentially a very destructive one. Writing about it the man was able to get his thoughts clear enough that he could ask her, calmly, about this. The resulting conversation was, he reported, one of the best of his life, since she was able to say that the love she felt for him was altogether different, far deeper, than any she'd felt in her previous relationships. This allowed him to open up aspects of his past for discussion, and both felt that the resulting dialogue had brought them closer. An area of potential anxiety had been transformed, through gentleness, understanding, and courage.

With such very sensitive issues it is vital to be first and foremost clear in one's self as to what one is asking about. That's why a written exercise can be useful. The typical 'male' approach might otherwise be a disaster. We can all imagine the man obsessing about the question, having a few drinks too many, then wanting to talk at the wrong time - late at night after a hard day, for instance. Such a scenario is bound for brutal conflict. And yet the same impulse is there; it's just the potential to reach deeper intimacy that has been lost in this second instance.

If you found this exercise somewhat threatening, here's another you can try. This next exercise is one that appears in a slightly different form in the Play and Transformation section. I include it here because it can work particularly well in examining issues about relationships. Many of the exercises you may see in other chapters can be adapted in this way, although I have purposely kept repetition to an absolute minimum. If you see an exercise that you want to use in a way other than that in which I'm asking you to use it, go right ahead. Feel free to use the material as you see fit!

EXERCISE 3:

❖ Invent a secret for someone else. Invent a secret for yourself. What would happen if the secrets were shared?

This is a fantasy exercise at the core of which lies the expectation that revealing one's secrets may cause an extreme reaction. If we can indulge this fantasy we can return to reality and know that, actually, most of our secrets won't shock or upset anyone. Since these are invented secrets they can do no harm anyway. If, however, you do have potentially damaging secrets, such as you are having an affair behind your partner's back, you may want to ask yourself why you need to do this. This exercise can be used to explore what sort of reaction it would provoke. As one man wrote, "If I'd known she'd be so upset by the affair I'd never have had it." The reply to this has to be that he should have been able to imagine the potential for disaster, and that his failure to do so is partly what caused the damage.

This exercise can help us project possible scenarios. There cannot be many people who haven't been tempted to stray from the spousal bed. Whether or not one acts on that impulse must depend on how clearly one sees one's present circumstances. Having a secret, a secret life, or a secret affair is often just another way of signaling that there's something one wants that one wishes the other would guess. It's not fair to expect one's partner to be a mind reader. A huge number of people with secret lives have felt only relief at being able to let those secrets out. Often they may have diaries and journals which, it would seem, are kept in the expectation that they will be discovered and used as evidence. On the whole, people want their secrets to be heard, so that they can become authentic to themselves and in the public world, too.

The following poem seems to express some important aspects of secret-keeping.

Please Hear What I'm Not Saying

Don't be fooled by me,
Don't be fooled by the face I wear,
For I wear a mask, I wear a thousand masks,
Masks that I'm afraid to take off,
And none of them are me.
Pretending is an art that's second nature with me
But don't be fooled, for God's sake don't be fooled.
I give you the impression that I am secure,
That all is sunny and unruffled with me,
Within as well as without,
That confidence is my name and coolness my game,
That the water's calm and I'm in command,
And that I need no one.
But please don't believe me.
Please.

My surface may seem smooth, but my surface is my mask,
My ever-varying and ever-concealing mask.
Beneath lies no smugness, no complacence.
Beneath swells the real me in confusion, in fear, in aloneness.
But I hide this.
I don't want anybody to know it.
I panic at the thought of my weakness and fear being exposed.
That's why I frantically create a mask to hide behind,
A nonchalant, sophisticated facade, to help me pretend,
To shield me from the glance that knows.
But such a glance is precisely my salvation. My only salvation.
And I know it.
That is if it's followed by acceptance, if it's followed by love.
It's the only thing that can liberate me, from myself,
From my own self-guilt prison walls,
From the barriers that I so painstakingly erect.
It's the only thing that will assure me of what I can't assure myself,
That I'm really worth something.
But I don't tell you this, I don't dare. I'm afraid to.
I'm afraid you'll think less of me, that you'll laugh,
And your laugh would kill me.
I'm afraid that deep down I'm nothing, that I'm just no good,
And that you will see this and reject me.
So I play my game, my desperate pretending game,
With a facade of assurance without, and a trembling child within.
And so begins the parade of masks
And my life becomes a front.
I idly chatter to you in the suave tones of surface talk,
I tell you everything that's really nothing,
And nothing of what's everything, of what's crying within me.
So when I'm going through my routine do not be fooled by what I'm saying.

                                                              Anonymous

The theme is clear, isn't it? Sometimes we have secrets that we want, with all our hearts, to have pried out of us. Fear prevents us. It keeps us from doing what we long to do, from being real. Some secrets are too damaging to reveal, sometimes, but most are not. Professional, legal and military secrets may best be left as secrets, but much of what we conceal may not hurt anyone. Revealing it may even help us get closer to those we care about.

Another poem may help to clarify the point here. The theme is the masks we wear out of fear.

        To show your emotions
        Is to be weak.

People think you don't care,
But deep inside your soul
You are crying
            and it hurts
Behind your eyes there is no feeling.

Why, why is it so hard to show yourself?
You are crying
            inside,
Yelling for someone to hear you
But you put on a mask of confidence
And all the fear
            and sorrow
is covered

And you are left to decide,
To wear a mask
Or show yourself.

                                                                    M. Munson

I've quoted both these poems at length because they reflect the fear that so many of us have about whether or not we will be acceptable to others if we really allow ourselves to emerge. The fear that we will not be understood is so great that we *become* our own secrets. Many of my clients have said things like, "I don't think my wife/husband would understand..." and they're not talking about aberrant behavior but about things they care about which their partner does not seem to be interested in. There is a double sorrow in knowing that something cannot be adequately communicated, and in having to keep that part of themselves to themselves - a secret by default.

Here's another exercise that may give you a different approach.

EXERCISE 4:

❖ What things annoy you about your partner? Make a list or describe one thing in particular.

Notice the word 'annoy'. I'm asking about the little things that get on your nerves, for often it's those things that cause tension. In *The Road to Wigan Pier* George Orwell recounts sharing rooms in a lodging house with three other men, but the one he found himself disliking most intensely was the one who had halitosis. He could have forgiven that man many things, he wrote, even a completely different moral and political outlook, but the bad breath was more than he could bear. The same sort of thing is likely to happen to us. One man couldn't stand his partner's habit of walking around the house without shoes or socks because he imagined (rightly or wrongly) that her feet would carry dust and germs into bed. It's a minor item, but it gave him great grief and produced a huge amount of anger in him. The question has to be, why such a strong reaction?

There are several aspects to this, the first is that these annoyances may well be very deep seated. If they simmer until they burst out in rage, they can lead to the kind of irrational arguments from which few of us can emerge with any positive gains. Here is a clue. One man wrote about how he found himself seething with anger at the way his partner piled dishes in the sink and didn't rinse them properly before placing them in the draining rack. It was a small detail, but it made him rage. By writing it out he was able to see that what he was responding to was an inner expectation of how a kitchen 'should' be run, something he'd never really spelled out to himself or anyone else. He had, in fact, internalized his mother's slightly obsessive attitude towards a clean kitchen. Although he didn't like his mother's standards much - he thought they were too strict - he still found himself judging his partner by those standards. In effect, he was saying to himself, 'What would my mother think of this? She wouldn't approve!' This made him angry.

Once he realized this the way forward was relatively easy. He asked himself how he felt about the dishes and then did two things. He asked his partner if he could be the one to do the dishes and if she'd take over one of his chores. Then he put a light near the sink so that he could see whether or not the dishes were clean - since part of the problem had been the poor light and his partner's eyeglasses, which tended to steam up when she washed dishes. No wonder the poor woman neither liked dish-washing nor was good at it!

This example may help us to look behind the annoyance and ask where our reactions really stem from. The danger of any internalized standard like the one described is that the person who has it may not even like the standard much. The man in question found his partner attractive, he said, partly because she *wasn't* obsessive in the kitchen, the way his mother had been. Yet here we had a situation that could be directly related to the mother's viewpoint, a version of the Internal Critic - that internal voice we may sometimes find ourselves responding to that says that something is not good enough, that we ourselves are not good enough. It can be crippling, and it can destroy a relationship unless it is acknowledged and dealt with.

I'll give a few examples of the Internal Critic to explain. I've mentioned this figure in other sections, but it's information that we do well to remind ourselves of. The Internal Critic is what we hear when we realize we haven't done something correctly. "Oh, I'm such a fool!' we may say. This is us calling ourselves stupid - doing the job of an external commentator before anyone else can do it. It usually comes about because we expect criticism, from a parent or a sibling, and so we've taken those values into our psyches and provided our own feedback. The problems arise when we begin applying the criticisms to ourselves before we've given ourselves a chance to do anything. 'It'll never work, I'm always such a failure,' we may say, and it paralyses us, before we've made a move.

To neutralize such potentially damaging behavior we have to deduce who first implanted these messages in us, and then try to change the message. A good way of doing this is to write a dialogue between yourself and the 'critic', and keep doing it until the critic shuts up. In Federico Fellini's movie *8 1/2* the central character, a film director, can't make his movie partly because he's followed around by the figure of the press critic who keeps telling him how bad his ideas are. The central character doesn't want to listen, but he always does anyhow, and so feels he can't make his film project work. Fellini's own answer to this is to have the critic led to a scaffold and, still criticizing as the rope goes around his neck, he is finally silenced. Then the movie can get made.

Others' values, if internalized, can stifle us. In Iran currently, I am informed, an interesting variant of this is in place. Anyone can write what he or she wishes, but if it offends the religious leaders, then the book or magazine has to be withdrawn from the shelves. The catch is this - the censorship doesn't occur until after the entire print run has been produced. The effect of this is that publishers and printers don't want to risk losing an entire print run, so they only print what they can be sure will be acceptable, and so avoid losing money. This means they play safe and apply stricter standards than the religious leaders. Authors, in their turn, see how cautious the publishers are and, because they want to earn their livelihood and see their books in print, they write even more cautiously. What had been a vague standard of not offending the spirit of Islam has, as a result, become a strict personal policing, probably much stricter than anything the religious councils ever intended. Authors have effectively censored themselves. That's how the Internal Critic can function.

Which brings us back to those 'annoyances'. To what extent are they really important? Would you leave your partner on the strength of these items? Probably not. Yet if you do not face these areas of tension and arrange to talk them through calmly, they can be destructive. Why? Simply because the person who feels the annoyance is probably at war with his or her own Internal Critic. A person at war with him or herself is under stress, and that person may find it easier to walk away from the perceived stress than to deal with the truly central issues. Although we may love and respect the core personality of our partner, we cannot under-estimate what annoyances may do if we fail to face them. This exercise is a first step, but an important one.

EXERCISE 5:

❖ Now that you've read the preceding paragraphs, how do you feel about your spouse's or partner's annoying habits? Can you imagine a scenario in which you begin to talk about this with him or her? Write about this imagined discussion, or about an actual one you may have had.

Writing beforehand can get one clear about what one wishes to say and so can help us to keep calm, relaxed, and non-confrontational. It may also help us to see what we hope to gain. Do we want to change our partner's behavior? Is it feasible? A small habit may be easily changed by a comment: 'Please hang your coat up rather than putting it on the couch.' A larger habit, such as a spouse who spends a lot of time on a sports activity, or not enough effort helping around the house, may need to be negotiated over a period of time until a new balance is reached. Occasionally we may just have to accept that some things probably won't change much, but we can help ourselves by seeing that these are just one aspect of our partner. If she always goes out with the girls on Tuesdays, it is, after all, only on Tuesdays, and one can make one's own plans. Sometimes compromise is noble, it's an acceptance that all is not perfect, but that one loves one's partner anyhow. Compromise, if given in such a way that both partners recognize it, is a gift that shows love and caring. Such gifts deserve to be graciously given and honored by the recipient, which leads to the next exercise.

EXERCISE 6:

❖ Make a list of all the things your partner does for you. Make a list of all the things you do for your partner. Which things go unacknowledged?

I call this exercise 'checking in'. The woman who has come to think the meals appear by themselves, or the man who assumes the car gets fixed of its own volition - both these figures shortchange themselves. If someone does something for you it is always a life-enhancing experience to stop and be aware of it. Sometimes doing this exercise can bring to light just how much more one person is doing than the other, which is why it's sometimes a good idea to do this one as a couple and compare results. Most of us will willingly do a great deal for someone we love as long as we know that our efforts are noticed. It's the fear that we've not been acknowledged that leads to strife.

In this section we've covered just some of the issues couples face. More are covered in 'Couples: Problem Solving' and even in 'Divorce', which I'd advise you to read also. The aim, in each of those two sections, is to understand how communication can fail and to face the real problems involved so that each person can make reasonable decisions and move ahead to a productive future, whether that be alone or as a couple. Before you do that, however, it might be well worth your while to reflect on what sort of writer and thinker you may be, which is what the next section asks you to consider.

Chapter Eight

REREADING YOUR WRITING -
RECLAIMING YOUR SPIRIT

I want to use this section to examine what happens when we write responses to the exercises in these chapters, and to spell out why it is important to write, and not just think, our reactions. I also want to take the time for you to reflect on where you are now, and what the exercises may feel like.

We all know what it means to be dis-spirited—we're downcast, we feel defeated, we've temporarily lost our 'fighting spirit.' When we have our energy back we may well hear people using phrases with the word spirit in them, phrases like 'a spirited response', and we may notice that in such cases the very idea of spirit is of something that is somehow a tad embarrassing. More often than not we'll hear people talk about 'high spirits' - usually a euphemism for drunken and rowdy behavior - or we'll read of a sports team making a 'spirited defense,' where the clear hint is that they had more guts than ability, and lost anyway.

Spirit is a word that has slipped into the doldrums. These days we either tend to think of the spiritual as something practiced by Tibetan mystics on mountain-tops, or as something New Age and, perhaps, slightly suspect. Yet not so long ago spirit, which is related directly to the word inspiration, had to do with the breath of life and energy. Respiration - the word commonly used for the breathing process - has the same Latin root. During the Romantic period of literature in the early 19th century the poets openly equated the breath of life with creative inspiration. For a while there were brisk sales of an instrument called the Aeolian Harp, which was a harp that fitted into a window frame and was activated by the movement of the air - the divine creative force of the earth. Whatever we think of this, the connection was not questioned at the time, and the same idea still exists in the use of wind-chimes, and perhaps even in the raising of flags. Inspiration, creativity, the Spirit, and breathing were all seen as interlinked. Spirit is our vital creative self, the energy of who we are, our life force, and it is my contention that it deserves a little more respect than we've been giving it recently.

In these days when energy is so often equated with cups of coffee and power bars, or vitamin pills, or pumping iron in the gym, I'd like to suggest that we all have 'spirit' but that it gets pushed aside in the rush of activity. We take our inner life-force for granted until one day it is no longer there and we burn out. Burning out is what happens to a fire that isn't fed fuel. Is that what's happening to us?

I can only say that we have a record number of Americans suffering from all sorts of mental crises, today. The accepted statistic is that at any one time there are 9 million Americans suffering from depression. Depression has many causes, and many of these people recover, but there's always someone to take the place of each person who finds his or her way back to a happier existence. Prozac and its derivatives are now the biggest selling of U.S. pharmaceuticals. One in four women will suffer some sort of depression-linked episode in her lifetime. And what about the huge number of people who give up, turn to drink or drugs, or who die early from *them*?

I suspect the problem, the loss of spirit that hits so many people so hard, is a vast problem, amounting to a national disease that has many different symptoms and expressions. It's ironic that this country, so famous for its 'can-do' enterprise and for its ability to be innovative and creative should suffer in this way. I can only suggest that we are, to an extent, like runners in a relay race. For a while each of us is in the forefront, racing the others, then we hand the baton to someone else and collapse, fighting for breath, paying off that oxygen debt that our heroic dash has engendered. We are, in effect, using up our energy capital, and when it's all gone, we slump, each of us individually. We're not fuelling ourselves, our spirits, along the way, and we only notice this as we lie, panting, on the ground.

So how do we feed the spirit?

I'll answer by telling a story. Long ago when I first came to the U.S. a friend loaned me his huge old Chevy Malibu. He told me it would work fine as long as I remembered to fill up the oil from time to time. The first time I pulled into a gas station it was one of those ones where the attendant sits behind bullet-proof glass, and so I paid for gas and said, "And a quart of oil for my Chevy Malibu." "What sort of oil does it use?" came the reply. "I don't know," I replied. "Well, what year and what size engine is it?" The attendant was beginning to sound as if he was dealing with an idiot. Flustered, I said, "Oh, just let me have the ordinary sort." "Yeah, well, we have seven different sorts of oil," said the attendant, "and I don't know which one you want..."

It took a while to locate the right oil, and then a little longer while I raised the Chevy's hood, realized this engine was nothing like what I was used to back in England, and wondered where to pour the stuff. The point of this anecdote is that most of us don't know how to feed our spirits, what to feed them, or where the food is meant to go, simply because we're not acquainted with our own spirits. The exercises in this book have all been tested over the years in classes, small groups, and private counseling sessions, and all of them can be successful in meeting ourselves, perhaps for the first time. Once we've met ourselves, really met ourselves so we know who we may be, then we can determine how we need to be fed. Just like that old Chevy Malibu, which I hope is still plugging along somewhere, we need certain things and without them we'll stop in our tracks. And unlike that car, what we'll find is that every time we discover something about ourselves, we've engaged in a form of creativity that actually does feed us.

I say this because as you write in response to the exercises you may at times find yourself asking why you are doing it. After all, some of the things you'll be asked to write about may not be very pleasant. What you write may even make you feel gloomy as you recall the events, and so you may well be tempted to give up, to remain in the realm of unacknowledged feelings. It's a real challenge for you. Therapists have often noted that some clients, after a few weeks, are tempted to give up. The pain of unearthing the past can seem to some to be a step back to a less-healthy mental state. I would argue the exact opposite. We have to acknowledge what happened, feel the emotions, and then find the wisdom that the events have to convey to us. Until we do that we cannot move on.

Writing about events that have happened, or about thoughts that you have, can be very helpful for psychic health. At the most straightforward level when one writes out one's thoughts and feelings one accepts that one has those thoughts or feelings. This is an important step towards the vital task of self-acceptance. It's often all too easy to have a feeling and then, in the rush of other events of the day, push it aside. Like food left in the back of a refrigerator, it will decay until we accept it's there and deal with it.

Without this self-acceptance we cannot hope to change, grow, or develop, since we cannot be expected to believe in changing things whose existence we have not yet acknowledged, or which we wish to deny. Just similarly, when we recall an event which troubled us, we rescue it from the abyss of denial and we open the door to self-forgiveness. It may in fact be easier to do this than we think, since if we do not try to deal with these issues we may find that every day we have to invest fresh energy in continuing to blank that information out.

This denial increases the likelihood that we will repeat the actions that we wish to deny. If it wasn't a problem the first time I did it, because I denied it, then how can I take it seriously as a problem the next time? If I am unkind to a friend, or hurtful to a loved one, I may feel shame and choose to blank out that memory and the memory of the hurt I caused. I cannot expect to be able to learn from an error if I don't accept that I've made it, and I cannot expect to forgive myself for doing something if I don't see that I did it. Each time I do something similar I'll use more and more energy as I try to blank out yet another unfortunate occurrence. Pretty soon my friends won't speak to me and I'm likely to ask, "What's wrong with *them*?" rather than changing my behavior. All this takes more energy than anyone can spare, and still doesn't save the friendships.

Forgiveness is the center here. If I can't admit my actions, own to my actions, I can never look at them in a non-blaming way and ask myself why I did them. When I begin to do this I can start a process of understanding that allows me to think about ways to avoid doing the same hurtful things.

A young man of twenty-four wrote about this in terms of his lack of time management. He was always late for everything, but he always said it wasn't his fault because ... The excuses were endless. It finally reached the point that he'd agree to meet people at certain times, knowing even as he made the arrangement that he had little hope of arriving at the right time. He had effectively given up hope for planning his days, and he couldn't see the infuriating aspect of this for others. "Eventually someone said to me, 'When you say yes you'll be there it means maybe you will. When you say you'll be late it means you won't be there at all!' It wasn't until she said it that I realized what I was doing. Once I saw how I was alienating people I began to take charge. I made a point of being on time, of not putting too many events into the day. And I began to look at why I was trying to please everyone by not saying 'no' at the time, but by saying 'no' whenever I failed to appear... "

When we begin to accept what we've done we become more real to ourselves and we can feel our emotions. As Nathaniel Branden puts it:

Experiencing our feelings has direct healing powers. (p.92)

One of the things to recall, as you look at what you have written, is that there is a special value, an intrinsic power in writing out the stories of events - the events of your life and experience. Certainly one can analyze these stories as if they were raw data about one's life. This can be very revealing, and it is often the basis of insights of extraordinary value, as I'm sure you will have seen. I would suggest there may be another level to consider in addition to this one. When we tell stories about our lives they are, inevitably, colored by personal viewpoints. In fact, the very choice of examples is highly personalized. What one family member recalls as being typical of us may seem to be absurd when we hear it. A forty two year old man argued with his mother because she loved to tell stories about the family and yet she never seemed to refer to any event he could recall - or if she did she gave a different aspect of it. Behind his annoyance lay an important fact. The mother was making her mythology of the family, choosing the tales she would tell, and he held on to a different series of stories. He saw the mother's view as inaccurate and silly. She saw his as absurd.

The point I wish to make is that reality is always subjective, and the memories we cherish or that haunt us are part of the reality we create for ourselves. I'm not suggesting that traumatic events are not deeply disturbing. Some memories are hard to come to terms with and cannot be eradicated. I'm only suggesting that the memories we have are like the language we choose to describe our lives - they confirm our inmost prejudices about what our lives involve. They become personal myths. Thomas Moore, the philosopher, certainly suggests as much in his book *Care of the Soul* (1992), and he goes on to argue the persuasive power of these personal myths for each individual. In the preceding section on *Play and Transformation* (chapter 5) I spent some time discussing the stories that our culture tells us, its citizens, and how some of them can distort our reality. I would like here to suggest that we also make our own stories within that series of cultural myths. Re-reading what we have written may help us to unravel those stories, and even to recast them.

Clearly this is not a straightforward challenge, and there can be no easy answers. For now it would be useful, however, if you bear this in mind and think about how you worded your responses, and what role you seem to place yourself in as you re-tell your experiences. Then ask yourself if you could have chosen other responses. If you are working with others in a group it will be fairly straightforward to compare your responses to others'. If you are working alone allow yourself to think about some of the examples I have included from my own work with individuals and groups. A good question to ask yourself is: Could I have responded differently? Re-read your responses. How do you feel about them now?

EXERCISE 1:

❖ Choose two or three of your written responses, ones that seem to you to be especially memorable or important, and write about them.

Often we're surprised at what we wrote in haste and how it exposes feelings we might not be prepared to acknowledge at other times. The responses can help us vent our feelings - which is always useful - and when we re-read we can reassess our mood. Did we really feel like that? Well, yes, we did. The words on the page let us know that. But all that resentment? Yes, that's what you felt then, perhaps. It deserves to be acknowledged, and also to be placed in context. You probably don't feel like that all the time. For instance, the person who gets angry in traffic really is angry, sometimes to the point of being homicidal. I've witnessed upset drivers trying to force other cars off the road; I've seen those annoyed by someone else's lane-changing slam on brakes in the clear desire to have the other smash into the back of their own car. We've all seen it. We all discount it. That's just some nut; I'd never do that, we say. Really? We may not act on our feelings as these other people do, but we still have them. If we can't accept that we have those moments of irrational emotion, how can we ever learn not to be the victims of our own feelings? So, please, don't discount the feelings you have written about. Listen to what they are saying just as you'd listen to anyone you love.

In re-reading we must also remember to ask ourselves the next question: what lies behind this? Every act, everything we do exists on at least two levels. The first is the act itself. The second is how that act fits into an overall pattern. A person may write copious complaints about her mother, and this may correspond to some real perceptions. All well and good. But if the complaint is always about the mother one is entitled to ask where father appears in all this. Perhaps the mother is the target because the feelings about the father are too difficult and complex to emerge easily.

A third level exists, which is the hardest to describe because its power resides in its very inability to be rendered in analytic terms. As we write we are presenting to ourselves the poetry, the story of our lives, and this poetry exists in ways that have to do with the act of bringing it into existence. What do I mean? I mean that one aspect of writing is the pleasure it affords in doing it, or in having done it and looking back on the page we've brought into existence. A comparison may help to show what I mean. If we dance with someone and we find we dance well with that other person, whereas we usually don't think of ourselves as dancers at all, how do we describe that experience? It's hard. And in the end our ability to describe it matters far less than what we felt, what we experienced. Saying, 'you have to experience it to know what I mean' is not necessarily an evasion. It can be an honoring of the experience, a profound acceptance of something that exists where words can't easily go. As I write this page I feel a deep satisfaction in the act of writing. This satisfaction has nothing to do with the quality of what I write. I will revise this page, and many, perhaps all of the original words may wind up in the trash can. The pleasure I feel is that as I write I am approaching a deeper apprehension of something that has emotional importance and truth for me. Of course, I'm delighted if my words can guide someone else. But more important, in some ways, is that my words reach out to touch the truth however imperfectly. In this, there is satisfaction. Andre Dubus, describing the daunting task of writing about the car accident that shattered his body and confined him to a wheelchair, wrote about his struggle to write as follows:

> I may as well plunge into it, write it, not just to rid myself of it, because writing does not rid me of anything, but just to go there, to wherever the woman [who had reminded him of the accident] had taken me, to go there and find the music for it, and see if in that place there was any light. [....] Everything I have written here seems flat: the horns dissonant, the drums lagging, the piano choppy. Today the light came: *I'm here*.
>
> (Best American Essays, 1998)

Sometimes, with writing, we don't know how it works its magic on us. All we know is that we've arrived.

This was said just as poignantly by Hong Ying, writing about her life and struggles in China. At the end of her book *Daughter of the River: An Autobiography* she makes an extraordinary, haunting, statement that, to me, sums up so much of what we are doing in these pages.

> After finishing this book I know that nobody can save me apart from myself. Writing is the only way I can cure myself.

At this point I'd like to show you a technique that you can use to respond to the questions asked in these exercises, and one that you can also use to help you link ideas that have been awakened in the process. In this sense the technique can work in the particular instances of individual thoughts that may spin off from exercises, and in the understanding of whole chapters.

For example, I'm sure that at times you've found it difficult to respond to some of the individual questions. They may seem too mechanical, or too difficult. "O God, he wants me to write about *that*!" is the way you may find yourself reacting from time to time. This is only natural, especially if you're dealing with difficult memories. And yet that reluctance to write may cause you to by pass the very thing that is most worth looking at. The can of worms that turns you off might just have gold in the bottom. One way of getting to that gold is the technique of Webbing.

It's a technique that has been used for some years now. I learned it from Dr. Gertrude Webb many years ago, but many other people, notably Gabriele Rico, have also used versions of it. It goes like this: the question may be something like: 'write about your first grade class'. If you're not sure what to write, this is what you can do. Take the words 'First Grade' and write them in the middle of a blank sheet of paper. Draw a circle around the words. Now write down ideas or memories that occur to you, in one word form, as you let your mind free associate about the first grade. The name of your teacher may appear, perhaps, and the names of your friends; possibly the things you recall about the room, too. Jot these single words or short phrases down around the central words 'First Grade'. If the added words spark memories or ideas write those in as well, with connecting lines. Don't worry about neatness. After a while your page will look a little like this:

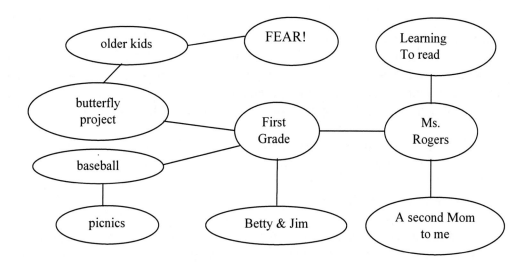

Don't edit anything out. Write it all down.

After about three minutes of this you'll find things occurring to you that you hadn't expected. You may have drifted to a different topic altogether, and you may find that you're becoming more interested in some of those ideas. This is a hint that you're reaching what it is you truly want to write about. In the sample given above the writer discovered a level of fear around the experience, and then chose to write about that, contrasting it to the fondness he felt for his teacher, Ms. Rogers. In this way Webbing can lead us to what it is we most want to explore.

Try Webbing at the end of each chapter, if you wish, putting in the key word that seems to you to sum up your situation or feeling. It can be a wonderful way of getting all the ideas out onto a page so you can sort out the ones that feel most important to you. You can also try using it in response to individual questions. Many people have said that working this way has helped them to identify what they really felt they wanted to write about when the topic at first seemed barren to them.

The method works, according to theories of brain function, because it encourages us as writers to think in a non-linear fashion, thus allowing the right side of the brain to dominate. The right hemisphere is the part of the brain that is responsible for creativity, for the perception of patterns, and for intuitive leaps of connection, whereas the left side of the brain (which controls the right side of the body) is stronger in logical sequencing and ordering. The two halves of the brain are linked by the corpus callosum, and messages zip back and forth from one hemisphere to the other constantly, so it is never correct to say that one is only using one side of the brain. All we can do is allow one side to be dominant for a while, which is why some of the exercises in the book have included such things as star diagrams, photographs, and drawings of postcards. Webbing draws on the same resources. The aim is that if we can get away from our familiar thinking patterns we can, often, see with new eyes and hear with new ears.

If you allow yourself to reach whatever it is that feels important to you, you'll let yourself contact the most authentic part of you, which is what this whole book is aiming to do. For in finding that truthful, essential you, you will be claiming back the person who was forced to be quiet and cope with the situation.

Leslie Newman in *Writing From The Heart* puts it beautifully: "Your writing, if you let it, will lead you to new places deep inside yourself." We can give this gift to ourselves if we choose to, and Webbing may help you get there.

Perhaps Emerson said it best in his 'Address to the Harvard Divinity School' in 1838:

But speak the truth, and all nature and all spirits will help you
with unexpected furtherance. Speak the truth, and all things alive
or brute are vouchers, and the very roots of the grass underground
there, do seem to stir and move to bear you witness.

This may seem like a large claim to make, that the world will help you if you express what is your truth. I don't know that there's any objective way that it can be statistically proven. But I do know that again and again my clients, people I've spoken with, and sometimes even casual acquaintances have said much the same thing. Perhaps it could be because when we speak our truth - the truth we've always known but been unable to admit - we come back into harmony with ourselves. When we do that we re-establish a harmony with the rest of creation, too, in the way Emerson suggests, and we reclaim our spirit.

Chapter Nine

STRESS

I'd like to start this section by considering stress and then lead into a discussion of career and job-related issues. This is not to say that stress only occurs at work, far from it. The home can often be stressful. If you are specifically looking for exercises and comments about home-life and its stresses I'll refer you to the chapters that deal directly with them. If children are part of the stress you may want to turn directly to the section on *Parenting*, chapter 10. If one's relationship is one of the factors, look at the chapter on *Relationships*, chapter 7, which is divided into romantic and other relationships, and also look at chapter 11, *Couples Problem-Solving*. If your home is stressful because of ailing or aging parents you'll want to look at the sections on *Care-Taking* in Chapter 16. Having said that, I'd advise you to read at least the opening pages of this chapter, since you'll find a great deal that can be of use.

Stress is hard to define but easy to recognize. Sometimes it seems as if the difference between a pleasant day and a stress-filled one is about ten minutes. Imagine arriving at work ten minutes late and just not being able to catch up all day. Ten minutes is not much, but if you're late for all your meetings it can be very anxiety-provoking. Then, on the way home, you're ten minutes late to pick your child up from school and you find her in tears, afraid you'd never come. One stress after another. Yet it's only ten minutes. One aspect of stress can be seen, therefore, as the attempt to put more into the available time than is possible, and the resulting feeling of frustration.

Some people claim they like stress. They get so much more done when they're under pressure, they say. This introduces us to a different concept - that we may choose to have stress in our lives. We may actually like a small amount of it. However, even that can turn to dislike if we have too much for too long. Still, we may feel we need a little stress. It makes us feel as if we have a lot to do, as if our tasks are important, and consequently, that we are important. That's a nice feeling. So we fall into the stress-habit. Descartes reasoned in his famous saying, "I think, therefore I am." We may choose to rephrase that in our own lives by saying to ourselves, 'I run around in circles a lot, therefore my life has meaning.' Unfortunately, that may not be true. What it may reveal is the mildly obsessive or even the workaholic personality. The workaholic uses work as an excuse to avoid asking what he or she really wants from life. In fact, such a person may be unable to know what he or she wants, at a profound level. 'I want my business to prosper,' or 'I want to be rich' may be the answers such people will give. These are good, valid answers. I would only question them when I see a situation in which a father has no time for his family and is ruining his health working long hours. Is the business really that important? More important than personal relationships? More important than one's spouse? 'But I'm making this money for them!' comes the reply, which fails to acknowledge that a real presence may be what is needed, not just money.

This is the extreme example, of course, and we can all claim to be familiar with it because examples are all around us, every day.

EXERCISE 1:

❖ Can you think of an example like the one just given? Were you raised in a family with an over-achiever? Could you be one? How do you feel you balance your family/personal life and your work?

We can see all around us people who have chosen the stressful life, even if we ourselves have chosen otherwise. Each morning the roads are clogged with people desperate to get to work, driving while using the car phone, coffee mug on the dashboard, and no time to have a decent breakfast. We accept this, and yet it's not healthy. We accept that every day someone will die on his way to work, because of a car accident. We drive past the EMT vehicles and the wreck and say, 'there goes another one.' We accept what is, actually, unacceptable and we still drive to work too fast.

EXERCISE 2:

❖ Think of your day. Do you often find yourself rushing? Describe a situation when you felt pressured.

When we're rushed we tend to make mistakes, and if we drive cars, those mistakes can be dangerous; sometimes fatal. This exercise is designed to help you recapture moments of stress so you can identify them as potentially dangerous. At the moment we probably see them as being normal. One man related how he always took a short-cut even though it involved a dangerous turn across a heavily-trafficked road. It wasn't until his car was hit by a motorcycle coming round the blind bend that he realized the danger to his own life if anything larger had been coming along. The motorcyclist was crippled for life; the motorist spent weeks of his life dealing with insurance companies and a sense of guilt. He now thinks very differently about his daily commute. He has re-assessed what is 'normal' and what isn't.

Another insight might be gleaned by comparing the experience of Robert Graves in his autobiography *Good-bye to All That*. Graves describes his time as an officer in World War I, and how he'd move along dangerous sections of trench giving odds on the exposed sections such as a one-in-three chance of being killed when crossing a gap. He'd take a breath, mutter one-in-three (or whatever) and run. He was quite at home with this until the day he was shot through the chest. It wasn't until much later that he realized how easily he'd accepted this terrible logic and then came to confront the enormous stress he'd been under. How often do we catch ourselves thinking something like that? 'I've done it before,' we may say, or something similar.

We all think we know what stress is, but the probability is that we have clichés in mind rather than an actual sense of what it means. We watch the TV news and see footage of the traders at Wall Street, bustling around like crazed insects, and we say, "Wow, that's high stress!" Yet if one talks to those same traders many will admit that this life is exciting even if exhausting. They enjoy it. Place a New York Stock Exchange trader in - say - a first grade classroom and the trader may well find the constant demand of five-year olds to be more than he or she can bear. Stress is not what you do, but who you are when you do it.

If we enjoy the pressures we put ourselves under they still may not be good for us in a purely physical sense. Heart disease has been linked for many years now to high-stress tasks and careers, and heart disease is the biggest single killer in America today. Almost all stress is self-inflicted. We choose to accept it, even though it is avoidable, even though it may kill us. Robert Graves was under considerable stress but he was in a war, whereas we seem to have created war-zones in our own lives.

The objective of this section is to begin to identify areas of stress in our lives so that we can make sense of those experiences. Understanding them will help us to make meaningful choices about how we can adapt ourselves and choose less-stressed lives.

EXERCISE 3:

❖ Complete the sentence: "What drives me crazy…" Do about ten of these.

When you have your list, select several you consider to be key that you want to explore more fully. If you have an item that you really do not want to explore this is a likely indication that it is a major crisis area. You may not feel like writing about that topic today or even this month, but you must be aware of it, because sooner or later it'll need to be addressed. Usually sooner.

The sorts of lists that this question generates are always very varied. What surprises most people is that sometimes it is the small things that can cause the most anguish. "People who drive in to my lane in rush hour traffic (lane changers)," wrote one man. This immediately caught my eye, since one's reactions to commuting may have something to do with the way one feels about the job itself and how much personal sacrifice it demands to keep doing that job. In fact by writing more about this issue of job and home the man was able to spell out that he felt he was unappreciated by his family. He felt he was just a person who left home every day and came back late at night, whose wages kept everyone but himself in leisurely comfort. The anger he felt at this perceived imbalance tended to get expressed at other drivers. Once he noticed this pattern he was able to ask himself whether his image of how the family ran was accurate. Not surprisingly he saw that it wasn't. What he had seen as 'leisurely comfort' was in reality the family's attempt to make him feel loved and valued, because they saw only too clearly how distressed he was.

Other responses to this question are more global in their scope. "What drives me crazy is the way the Iraqis mess with the UN and always seem to win." Thus wrote one man. There's not much any one of us can do about this, of course, unless we are very highly placed in political circles. Even then it seems to be a difficult struggle. So why should a middle-class man find this to be enough to drive him crazy? I'd suggest the real issue may be with the idea of justice. A person who sees injustice everywhere may be reliving a childhood which was confused and marred by erratic or unjust parent figures, for example.

I give these two examples because often it is the more outlandish - or the easily discarded - items on the list that can have important clues. In each of these two cases the complaint is seemingly unfixable. Or is it? If one really wants to avoid traffic one can go to work before rush hour, and that may provide the necessary sense of calm that allows the individual to deal with the family issues that lie behind it. Similarly, the man who complained about the UN could stop reading the news and look at the real, personal, issues behind the feeling.

One of the things that emerges most fully from these lists is that often stress is not just a case of having too much to do, but of having to do those tasks, and keep on doing them in a certain fashion, even though one can see better ways to complete them. Stress comes about not when three people have to do the work of five, but when three people know that normally this is a job for five but the management refuses to hire two extra people and at the same time uses the money saved to boost executive bonuses. It is when we are expected to pretend something is fine that stress becomes most acute. Again, a diligent quality inspector who finds his job is a sham because of a company policy is likely to feel under tremendous stress because of the false position he feels himself to be in. Or there is the situation of the teacher I worked with who one day realized that a large part of her daily task was not educational but simply to keep the adolescents in her charge off the streets until they were old enough to leave. Concluding that this was in great measure the true nature of her work caused her huge amounts of stress. The conflict between her idealistic belief in education, and the task she actually had to do, often with inadequate resources, was heartbreaking.

In short, the things that may cause stress are those situations in which we are actually helpless but for which we are likely to be held responsible: lose-lose situations. These are the most stress-filled of all, and they are not a recent phenomenon. They have been commented on for centuries. Perhaps the classic example would be *Hamlet*. I mention it because the play is probably one of the best known and most widely-mentioned in all of literature. Everyone knows something about the story. The extent of its appeal may say something about the validity of what it has to convey to us still. As you may recall, Hamlet has to avenge his father and the ghost of his father comes to tell him to do so. In order to do this he will have kill his step-father, his mother's new husband, his own uncle. This would be bad enough, but how can he trust the ghost? Is it a devil come to tempt him to do a terrible sin, namely, to kill the king who is God's deputy on earth? Hamlet's feigned madness is his only refuge from this stress. It's a good example of how any one can feel trapped by circumstances that place one in a lose-lose situation, and how this can cause us to feel crazy. Stress, and craziness, come from situations in which we feel we cannot win. Can you identify any of those in your life? I'm sure you can. From the man who says he just can't do anything right for his wife, to the woman whose boss always criticizes everything she does, the examples are endless.

Notice that the exercise asks you to list the things that "drive you crazy", rather than just "stress". Stress as in "stress-reduction planning" is a buzz word for so many things and so many approaches that it can become almost meaningless as an idea. Many of the programs are certainly good, as they urge us to exercise, eat well, meditate and give up destructive habits. All this is admirable, but it tends to be outer directed or use behavior modification only. I'm suggesting we need to look inward at some of the causes of the behaviors so we can be free of them.

So what does this give us? I'd suggest that stressors arise principally from levels of helplessness. Being trapped in one's life is certainly a feeling many have, and feeling trapped is often a result of such things as not being able to change jobs, of having a mortgage or family payments to make, or of feeling caught in a marriage with an unsympathetic spouse, perhaps. In the First World War soldiers who had suffered 'shell shock' developed a bizarre array of symptoms that made them unable to fight. They, in effect, allowed their bodies to express a mutiny that their minds could not consciously allow. This was one of the first occasions in history that such behavior had been seen in such large quantities. Each successive war has produced its own crop of behaviors, each more complex than before.

Today the man caught in a situation he sees is impossible may run away, or he may fall ill, thus avoiding the situation. In war-time of course, running away would get you shot, so it wasn't a real option, hence the upsurge of ailments that incapacitated the soldiers while being involuntary in the same way as a physical wound. Stress, then, is really linked to fear, and it can cause a disturbing array of physical ailments.

EXERCISE 4:

❖ "I'm afraid when… " Write about eight of these. More if you can.

Answers to this have been almost always very candid. "I'm afraid I'll kill this kid" ; "I'm afraid I'll strangle one of these children one day"; "I'm afraid I'm the only one that's ever felt this way"; "I'm afraid I'll fail." Look at your list. Are these real fears? If they are, and you have found yourself about to throttle someone, for example, then you need to ask the next question: "What must I do to deal with this fear?" If that means going to the local hospital or health center to ask for help, then do it. If it means calling a friend, or a contact, then pick up the phone. Remember, fear has a way of defending itself with such excuses as, "I'd do it but… " Write out a couple of those excuses now.

"I'd do it but I'm afraid they'll tell me I'm wasting their time…" This is a fairly common response, and it's understandable. We've all felt that way at some point. There's only one thing worse than feeling bad, and for many people that exists in being told they're wasting someone else's time, or that their feelings don't count. It confirms the sense of trapped-ness, and increases the levels of fear and anxiety. What keeps people trapped in their fear is, paradoxically, the fear that others will tell them something that will make them feel more trapped.

The usefulness of this exercise is that it shows us that certain emotions are natural. What can turn the situation into a nightmare is the sense that one is not permitted to have such feelings. What is necessary is to identify the fear, see it plainly, and then decide what options are available. Options provide freedom and empowerment.

EXERCISE 5:

- ❖ Think of a metaphor or a simile for your present situation. "My situation is like ..."
- ❖ When you've done a half dozen of these, see if you can find a simile or a metaphor for what fear means to you. If you wish, you can draw this.

Out of many striking examples that arose from this exercise comes one from a young man who described his fear as, "like a wild dog running loose through the house." He spoke movingly about how the house was himself and fear seemed to run through his veins, yet he was in the house, running from the dog. I asked him to stay with that image and consider what he had to do to calm the dog - what did the dog want? He replied that the dog needed to be fed. Once we had made this connection he was able to ask what the dog actually was to him, and amongst the answers we came up with he felt that in one sense, his fear was that his creativity would not be fulfilled and this was torturing him in his daily life. Some of his life, and his plans for the future, became clearer to him as he contemplated this.

This may seem like a dramatic example, but I use it because it is not that uncommon. Stress is usually about fear, and if we can get a handle on our fear, through the use of metaphor, it will give us all the clues we need to deal with it and turn it into a productive future. The man trapped in traffic, trapped in his job, in his family problems, is crying out surely, for his larger needs to be met and his wider aspirations to be enlisted. He can see there is more to life than this, but he doesn't know how to get there.

We should certainly take this feeling of being trapped very seriously. Amongst long-term prisoners many of the ailments reported, such as ulcers, are exactly what we think they are, stress-related as a result of being trapped in a place full of violent and often anti-social companions. Duodenal ulcers. of course, used to be the occupational hazard of high powered executives, too... The comparison says it all.

EXERCISE 6:

- ❖ List the things you have to do in an average day, and, if you can, the amount of time you are allowed for each one. Then list the amount of time you'd like to spend on each one.

When you've created your list, first observe how much you do in a day. Are you doing more than your share, do you think? Remember - stress can come from doing things you enjoy, but having to do them in a hurried fashion. A wonderful meal eaten on the run stops being wonderful and starts being a recipe for indigestion. Now put into your list the interruptions you can expect. The person who pops his head round your office door to chat could be a friend - but if it turns into a whining session, or a poor-me session, then it could add to your already over-loaded day. Stress can turn even good human contacts into things one shies away from. In the various colleges I've worked at over the years I have noticed that at busy times of the semester faculty will often avoid walking along certain routes to their teaching rooms, often taking elaborate detours to avoid crowded areas. At the start of the semester they may have walked those routes happily, greeting students and colleagues. Stress hasn't made them dislike others, or become anti-social. Instead they seem simply to be protecting themselves from too much of a good thing.

This leads to the next exercise:

EXERCISE 7:

❖ Create the "Day from Hell." If you wish you can do this as a fantasy, or you can write about an actual day you have experienced.

One woman responded to this with a huge collage that consisted of pictures ripped from magazines, plastered on a piece of card. An angry face was labeled "Boss," and the number of pieces of paper attached to the card literally spilled over the edge, taped and stapled two and three deep. They included a picture of a car, ripped in half, to symbolize her car-repairs, and drawings of open mouths wanting to be fed, heard, soothed, when she came home. When she had finished the collage she looked at it, admitted how angry she'd felt doing it, and how hard it would have been to say or write her feelings out. It was like looking in a mirror, she said later, "No wonder I'm so frazzled all the time. Just putting it down like this helps me see it differently."

When once we truly allow ourselves to see what we do we can ask if there is another way to do things. Often there is. My local newspaper, *The Boston Globe* has frequent articles about people who left the rat-race and - so the writers claim - found fulfillment in doing less, living more simply. Indeed, the *Utne Reader* (Sept-Oct 1996) devoted a whole issue to just this phenomenon. Some of it was humorous, of course, but there were some valuable lessons to be learned also.

In this vein writer Bo Lozoff chose to take issue with the Ten Commandments, and observes that they are pretty much all "Thou shall not" statements, which we usually identify as being "forbidding statements." Lozoff prefers to think of them as "quit lists" that ask us to stop acting destructively, or as he says it, "identify what you do, and quit." He argues that wisdom comes from being on the losing side, since winners have no need to reflect. Why should they? They're clearly doing everything right, or so they think. "Thou shall not kill" is therefore transformed from a moral imperative to get even with others to a realization that we don't need to do that in order to live. "Thou shall not covet..." is similarly releasing. Stop envying the Joneses. Who cares if their house is bigger? Coveting will lose you sleep and gain you very little. Lozoff even goes so far as to purpose writing our own commandments, ones that are people-friendly.

EXERCISE 8:

❖   Write your own commandments.

Many people have a lot of fun with this. For example, "Thou shalt not force thine offspring to eat spinach." This is one I enjoyed very much. It certainly reminds me of what therapist Dr. Margaret Frank did with her own family - she challenged the old adage of 'no desert unless you eat your vegetables' by serving desert first. She observed that usually her children ate the same amount of main course when this happened or, in some cases, they actually ate more, since they hadn't been forced into a defensive posture by the threat of broccoli. They would proceed to the main course in a much better frame of mind, more relaxed, and would sometimes make a dent in the green beans just out of curiosity.

After you've created your new commandments, try some of them out.

Tom Hodgkinson has a similar attitude to the 'oughts' of our civilization, and he quotes J.B. Priestley to support his views:

> If, in July of 1914, everybody had been smitten with an intense desire to do nothing, just to hang about in the sunshine and consume tobacco, then we all should have been much better off than we are now.

Its hard to argue against this: sometimes laziness can be a virtue. In fact Hodgkinson goes on to list of the "Seven Deadly Virtues" and their antidotes. The list goes something like this, although I have adapted it somewhat for my purposes here.

1.   Vigilance:
     This is praised as a virtue by those who want to stamp out change before it can happen, since one is vigilant for any change at all in the status quo. Vigilance therefore promotes stagnation - and in a changing world that can be disastrous. We should, instead, embrace laxity.

2.   Silence:
     Silence is a way of denying one's true expressive nature. Noise and good cheer, its opposites, are far more vital. As the old AIDS-awareness campaign used to say, "Silence = Death."

3.   Order:
     Like vigilance, this can never promote real growth or creativity. We would do better to embrace Chaos.

4.   Consistency:
     This is synonymous with inflexibility and the inability to change one's view. Inconsistency is to be preferred.

5. Resolution:

   This can be seen as wedding oneself to a fixed idea, no matter whether it be right or wrong. Procrastination looks attractive beside it.

6. Moderation:

   How does this make sense in a world that seems built on excess? How do we know what 'moderate' is? Excess, like mistakes, can lead us to wisdom.

7. Industry:

   Jesus and Gandhi both preached idleness as a salutary state - Jesus' words to the sisters Mary and Martha surely come to mind, in which he tells the industrious sister to leave her tasks.

Those are somewhat tongue-in-cheek, of course; chaos is rarely preferable to a relaxed and reasonably orderly situation, but Hodgkinson makes his points through this comic exaggeration. Whenever we live by fixed, abstract, standards we are likely to place ourselves in stressful situations. "I should work harder," is, in essence, self-flagellation, and self-black-mail, too. Compare it to: "I could work harder,' Yes, we all could do that. We may choose not to, because that would take away time from other things we value, such as our family life. "Could" represents possibility, not judgment. In our high-speed world where cars have phones and e-mail connections are instantaneous and if not, we rush out and buy faster computers, we could learn from the Spanish concept of *Mañana* (tomorrow…) and the Italian idea of *dolce far-niente* - sweet idleness.

EXERCISE 9:

❖ Produce your own list of Seven Deadly Virtues. What were the 'virtues' that ruled your home when you were growing up? Your School?

The lists of virtues, and the reasons for rejecting them, are often heart-rending. A middle-aged man wrote about the modesty he was expected to show in his schooling. "The first thing I learned in class was never to show you were intelligent. The other kids would tease you for that. And the teachers thought you were showing off and were bratty. So the first thing I learned was how to be duplicitous. I was eager to learn. I loved it; but the price I'd have to pay was too great, so I had to adapt … hypocrisy came to me early."

A different response came from another man. "I learned that if I was good at table, and finished up all my mashed potatoes which I hate to this day, I'd get praise - and another portion of mash! Then if I didn't eat the mash Mom'd be upset that I didn't like her cooking, or she'd think I was sick. I couldn't win!" This man began to recognize, as he wrote more, that he'd spent his childhood constantly trying to second-guess his mother, attempting to find out what she really wanted him to do. Honesty was never the best policy, since the mother, it seemed, wasn't interested in what he wanted but only in her own sense of what 'should' have been the case. He recorded this dialogue from his young adult years, when visiting his mother.

"Have some more peas."
"No thank you, I've had enough to eat."
"So you don't like them cooked like that? It's a new recipe."
"They're good, but I don't want any more."
"If you like them, why not have some more!"
"No thanks. I'm full."
"Ah, you don't really like them…"
"Yes I do…"
"Well then, you can finish up the dish…"

Years later he recalled the stresses of a world in which no was taken to mean yes and yes meant almost anything. His situation was not unusual, I can assure you.

When things are this confusing we sometimes need to recall that there is another, more stable world.

This brings us to the next exercise

EXERCISE 10:

❖ Create a quiet place, a place of peace. Write about it, draw it, imagine it. When you've created this space, consider how you could turn it into actuality. Can you make it happen in your life?

I've had many encounters with these 'bliss-spaces' to use Joseph Campbell's phrase. Some cultures have them built into each home - a small meditation room, a prayer room, a shrine room. These were once common in China and Japan in wealthy homes. Poorer homes might have had to make do with a shrine in a corner and a set time each day which was given over to quiet contemplation. Indeed, the college at which I teach has a meditation room which is set up at certain times of the week, is available for those who wish to have some quiet time, and is packed up at the end of each session. Chapels and shrines have long been the bliss places of those who have no quiet space in their own homes. And look at the time and effort spent decorating some of those chapels, especially in medieval Europe!

We all need that quiet space. Do you have one you can go to? Too often we confuse this need for quiet with 'vegging out in front of the TV'. Unfortunately the TV may tend to occupy our minds just enough to prevent us from reaching that calm quiet place we really crave, which exists at a different level. So much of today's TV is of such poor quality that it's hard to find much that's positive to say about it, especially since it often gives the illusion of relaxation rather than the real thing. In one case I can think of a man in his thirties who used to come to therapy and simply remain quiet for the whole fifty minutes. Sometimes he'd sleep. When this was pointed out to him, he nodded and said that he really valued this quiet time - so much so that he was happy to pay the fees to do, ostensibly, nothing.

We need this time. Do you make space for it in your life?

EXERCISE 11:

❖ Imagine a freak snowstorm has descended on your town during the night, and you cannot get to work. The phones are out. Your children are safe with their grandparents or friends. You have plenty of food. What would you do?

The over-achievers amongst us would, I suspect, immediately set to work repainting the living room or drafting a report for work. However, such people probably haven't read this far in the book. Notice I've chosen a snowstorm that confines you to your home. I could have suggested that you were at the beach in Barbados, perhaps, but there are too many cultural expectations surrounding that situation, expectations that have to do with being social and having fun. This situation means you can't do that sort of thing.

Some people have responded to this exercise with relief, writing about how much they'd like to do drawings, or write poems, or just laze about, and how rarely this actually happens for them. Others have found the prospect boring. Some have felt frightened. My response to that would be - are you frightened about who you may be when you are not engaged in external tasks? If you are, it may be an idea to think about.

EXERCISE 12:

❖ Make up an excuse. You can do this as a fantasy or you could describe an excuse you once used. Who is the person to whom you will give this excuse? Possibly you could give an example of an excuse that was true but that no one believed. You could even describe a situation where someone else's excuse made your life difficult.

We've all had excuses thrown at us from 'the check's in the mail' to 'my dog ate it,' and we've all been infuriated. Often we've wanted to call the person a liar, but because of the situation we were perhaps not able to do that. Now's your chance for revenge. Be outrageous if you wish.

Responses to this exercise have often been hilarious, and often angry. One woman described how she couldn't finish the report because her boss had insisted she run a silly errand for him, even though her car wasn't in good condition, and she had to take it from the brake-repair place before they'd had a chance to fix it, and so she'd had an accident, and was now in the hospital ... The anger was clear to see. What she learned, reading over her response, was that she was angry at herself for not saying no, for placing herself in a potentially dangerous situation (the response was true, except for the accident) and for allowing situations like that to develop with this particular supervisor. In realizing how she had been taken advantage of she was able to reduce her anger and stress and subsequently to make her life a little better and a little safer. Stress, she learned, is something we do to ourselves twice. The first time is when we take on extra work, the second time is when we realize we're being exploited or abused.

EXERCISE 13:

❖ Describe deliberately wasting someone else's time, either as something you'd like to do, or as something you've already done.

Again, this is a wonderful chance for revenge. Think of all those people who have wasted your time, and now you have the upper hand! Doing this exercise an administrative assistant to a busy office described how she took the fuse out of the Xerox machine and made a sign saying 'broken' for it. Several things happened. The first was that people stopped coming up to her desk, dumping heaps of paper in her lap, saying, "I need it now". Instead they took their copies to the other end of the building where there were other machines. After she'd done the fuse trick a few times and the machine had a reputation for unreliability, people either went elsewhere as a matter of course or allowed sufficient lead time so the repairman could fix the so-called fault. After two weeks of this the manager ordered a newer, better copier, placed it in another room, and told employees to do their own copying. Reducing one's stress level means educating others, sometimes tacitly, on how to do their own work. I'd recommend a more direct action than this one described by the administrative assistant, but whatever works is not to be underplayed!

Stress, then, depends upon many things. It is something we choose, sometimes. At other times it is something we allow others to choose for us. That, too, is a form of choosing. The thing to remember is that no one can reduce your stress for you. Only you can do that. First, however, you'll have to recognize what you are doing to yourself. Some situations are forced upon us; it would be foolish to pretend otherwise. But we do have choices in how we react, and with practice we can differentiate between long term stress, such as being in the wrong job, and short term stress, which comes under the 'bad day' category. In each case we can form strategies to help us through, whether it be the creation of a quiet place we can retreat to or some deep breathing before we react to something. By choosing our responses we are choosing whether or not we want to accept the stress.

Another aspect of stress that is worth noting is that the greatest stress is often associated with the possibility of good things happening to us. How many of us have lost sleep over whether to buy a Chevrolet or a Ford, a Honda or a Mazda? Students graduating college report the most stressful time to be when they are thinking about what to do after college. One would like to think that this would be a time of joyous empowerment. Instead it's often a time of some desperation. The feelings may be of comparatively brief duration, but they are acutely felt. We are, on the whole, far more anxious when going to interview for a new job than we are at almost any other time, even if we have nothing to lose. This is short-term stress that we choose in order, we hope, to reduce long-term dissatisfaction; but we've still chosen it.

And here is a purely subjective observation. I've noticed that people tend to select as much stress as they choose to. The person who decides she can fit in just one more social event, just one more errand, is choosing that route. Those who simply refuse the extra duties refuse the stress. Of course, we could reply to that by saying that such people never get anything done, but on the whole that's probably not true. Writers that I know regularly refuse to do certain things so that they can do their writing. W.H. Auden, the poet, used to have his day arranged so carefully that he always went to bed at the same time, 9:30. On one occasion, much to everyone's surprise, he politely excused himself and walked out of a live TV interview just so he could stick to his regimen.

If we wish to reduce stress in our lives we may have to reorganize how we do things. Children may have to be encouraged to do their own laundry, help with the shopping, and so on, so that the household can run effectively. Some parents would regard that as horrifying, perhaps. I would tend to see it as reflecting a possibility that all of us could embrace. Having an idle teenager in front of a TV screen while mother runs twenty errands an hour is not healthy. The teenager merely thinks all adults are crazy, the parent tends to feel resentful, and meaningful communication is unlikely to be happening. How can you simplify your life? What can you give up doing? Who can you ask for help? You may want to write about these topics. Take a moment now to do so.

STRESS IN THE WORKPLACE

I'd like now to move to a different aspect of stress, this time specifically to do with the nature of doing one's job. I'll focus my examples on work situations for clarity, but they can be equally applied to many other situations. Stand in any bar on a Friday evening and the chances are you'll hear people complain about their work. Better still, stand next to the water cooler at work (or a similar strategic place) and listen to the comments about work problems. Everyone has a complaint, and many people are genuinely very upset by the situations. Anger and depression are the usual responses, both of which send people to therapists and counselors in droves. Here is an exercise that may help to clarify the situation for you.

EXERCISE 1:

- ❖ Take a piece of paper and draw three vertical lines, producing four columns. In the first column write down the four or five things that are in your view impossible to change in your work situation.
- ❖ When you've done that move to the next column. Next to each entry in column one, list what it would take to change the situation. So, column one might have 'poor productivity' written in it, and next to this, in column two you could write 'fire the boss'.

❖ When you're finished with column 2, move to column 3. In this column ask yourself what it would mean for you if the situation magically did change. If the boss really were replaced, and productivity were to be enhanced, what would that mean for you personally? Write something in column 3 next to each entry that appears in column 2.

❖ Now move to column 4. Here I'd like you to write down what the advantages might be, for you, of things remaining unchanged.

This exercise can be used for many different situations and I urge you to consider it as a re-usable resource. The pay-off is frequently to be found in column 4 or column 3. What many people discover is that if things really were to change in their company, then they, too, would have to change. In many cases this would be disruptive and might well involve a lot of extra work. The attraction of leaving things unchanged, therefore, could be as basic as the fact that it would be a familiar, easy rut to remain in.

What the exercise tends to show is that even though we may talk about change, frequently we may have motivations we don't even realize that stop us from accepting change. If we don't see how we ourselves contribute to the problem it's unlikely we'll ever solve it satisfactorily. We may prefer to complain rather than do anything about it. Others' inefficiency may make our own jobs easier. As one man said, talking of his teaching colleagues, "I know they're lousy teachers, but that means that with almost no effort I can look really good beside them." The more he complained about his colleagues, the better he appeared, so the last thing he really wanted was change. He needed things to stay the same so his status would not be threatened.

An exercise like this can help us see what's really at issue rather than what we think is the case, and in that clarity we can reduce our stress.

A more localized stress reliever (but just as important!) is this:

EXERCISE 2:

❖ 'I wish I'd said that...' What do you wish you'd said, and to whom?

Every day on my commute to work I look at other drivers. I notice that some of them are talking to themselves. Specifically, they seem to be rehearsing arguments with other people. I've done it myself. I suspect that these people are re-running confrontations they didn't feel they won at the time. These are the things that keep us awake at night, that fill our idle hours, and that can poison the remains of our day. Writing these things down can help to free our minds.

Why do I suggest this? The most bitter arguments I've come across in the work place are between those who simply cannot see things the way their opponents see things. As a result it is all but impossible to convince those one may be arguing against, since they do not accept the validity of one's discussion. We may find ourselves wondering how we could possibly be victorious in argument, but it cannot happen, because those people may be speaking a different language of values. An example may help, here. At the time of writing Senator Helms has been campaigning to slash budgets for the humanities, and has been successful. I do not find Senator Helms a sympathetic individual, but he has a right to his opinion, and his opinion is that money goes to the arts and humanities and there is nothing to show for it but projects and art he cannot understand. Therefore he cannot see any gain in this activity. He wants to be able to see something he can call 'value for money'. Meanwhile, I believe that the effects of art and the humanities upon people are that they become more aware, more enlightened, and more humane, and these are unfortunately not things that can be measured or demonstrated easily. A military budget takes X many billions and produces Y many soldiers, tanks and guns. We can all see whether or not there is a measurable return on outlay. The same equation does not exist in the same demonstrable way for those who believe in the arts. Those who support the humanities will never convince people like Helms until they can demonstrate that humanities-educated citizens save the country money by being better, more productive people. This is, of course, very hard to prove in statistical terms, although many people would take it as self-evident. Senator Helms, however, does not see this and so cannot be convinced.

This example can show us how useless certain confrontations can be, and how exhausting. By writing about what you wish you'd said you may be able to clear your mind and so move beyond your rage. Is it really worth rehashing those arguments from work? Perhaps not. The question now becomes: How do I relieve the frustrations I feel? And that leads us to another exercise.

EXERCISE 3:

❖ Imagine an argument. Tell someone to shut up. Keep writing until that person does shut up.

This is a version of Exercise 2, except that this time you get to win. Go on, have fun. Enjoy the fantasy. When you have finished you'll have written down all those things you always wanted to say, but they'll be safely on paper where they cannot cause hurt. You'll have got it all out by the time you finish, and then you can reflect on the fact that this is only a fantasy. In reality you'll probably never get to do this, and even if you did you'd not persuade the other person of your point of view. This is a venting exercise. Venting is necessary so you can move to the next stage, which is the next exercise.

EXERCISE 4:

❖ 'Just let go...' If you could let go, what would you let go of? What would happen?

I suggest this exercise because, by now, you may want to let go of the angry discussions in Exercises 2 and 3. Disengaging can be very useful. A clear example is provided by a man who struggled to chair an academic department and found that he had become the focus of the group's anger. After much heartache he decided to step aside and let his chief rival take over the position as chair. What he learned was that his rival, so fierce in destructive criticism, had no idea of what constructive things were necessary, and he floundered in the job he'd so eagerly fought for. The strategic retreat of the previous chairperson therefore made it plain to everyone else where the problem really lay and that it was up to the members themselves to sort this out. The retiring chair had feared that his retreat would mean chaos in the department. Indeed, he was correct. But once he stopped cleaning up after everyone else he discovered they quickly learned to do their own work of keeping things running. By refusing to keep on working in a stressful no-win situation the retiring chair had helped himself and others to become more mentally healthy.

This exercise can help us contemplate what may feel to be impossible, and perhaps help us to reassess our situation. If your work situation is causing you great stress, could you quit your job? Many people have written about how this 'unthinkable' situation actually became quite a useful consideration. Rather than gritting their teeth and hanging on, it motivated several people I worked with to explore other possibilities that were ultimately to prove fruitful, and they made the transition to other jobs. This is a better tactic than resigning in disgust with no idea of where to go next. Not only does it avoid a spell of unemployment, but it avoids the negative effects of a resignation. By this I mean that most people resign at the point at which they feel defeated, un-empowered, and desperate. This is not the best frame of mind in which to look for another job. Nobody wants to hire someone who seems burned out and angry. By using these writing exercises we can avoid such dire situations as we work through our frustrations prior to moving ahead.

This brings me to the next exercise, which builds on all we have discussed so far.

EXERCISE 5:

❖ Imagine a new job, a new career. You're doing what you want in the place you'd like to be. Perhaps you already have an idea what this is.

❖ Now take a large piece of paper. At the far right place the words 'new job'. At the far left write the words 'I am here'. How will you get from 'here' to the 'new job'? What are the steps you must take? If you wish you can attach pictures to this chart to show the stages you'll have to go through.

The exercise can take a few minutes or be spread over several days, as you wish. I'd recommend doing it for a few minutes and then returning to it each day for a week. Certainly you'll want to return to your chart. A useful way to do this exercise is to pin the chart to a wall where you can see it every day, and add words or pictures to it as you feel it to be appropriate.

One young man wanted his new job to be his perfect work situation: he'd own his own restaurant in Colorado. This seemed impossible since he was working as a waiter in New York - until he divided his chart into stages. First he put postcards of Colorado around the 'new job' section, so he was able to visualize his future as possible, in a real place, not as just a fantasy. This is important, for all of us. If we don't believe our future ambitions are possible we'll never make real strides to get there. Having made his objective real he began to think of what he'd need to do to make it happen. He'd need to get more training in restaurant management. This was step one, and he wrote it in. Step two was he'd have to go to Colorado, find a place, get a job, rearrange his life... It all seemed too overwhelming. But putting it on the chart made him think seriously about it. He decided he could go to Colorado, be a waiter, take classes at night and help to make his ambitions reality. He attached pictures to his chart showing a classroom, an airplane, and a restaurant table. But there were problems: how could he get the airfare? Where would he live? These were important questions. He decided to drive, (a picture of his car appeared on the chart) and stay a few days with a college friend (snapshot) until he could get a house-share (picture taken from magazine).

Using pictures or diagrams in this exercise is vital. If we are to make real changes in our lives we have to enlist the help of the Unconscious. The Unconscious operates at a surprisingly basic level in terms of needing concrete images. The Unconscious, for all its power, doesn't seem to be able to grasp abstract concepts. Phrases like 'a meaningful life' mean nothing to the Unconscious; indeed, I doubt that many people would know what that meant without a good deal of clarification. What motivates the Unconscious is an awareness of the particular attributes of that life. So words like satisfaction don't have any meaning to the Unconscious, although it understands perfectly the sense of satisfaction that comes from a completed task, a kind word, an ice-cream cone, or winning an election. Sometimes that can also cause the Unconscious to lead us astray. It doesn't understand what our larger unhappiness may be, but it knows what can make us happy now. This can result in the person who has just broken up with a partner becoming a compulsive shopper, perhaps. The concrete gratification is seized upon when the larger comfort is missing.

The pictures and details of this exercise are important for another reason, too. It is only when we break down a big task into manageable sections that it can become possible for us to make changes and treat the project as a reality. In addition, when we visualize things in a definite way - perhaps by making a chart - we can feel them to be real enough to act upon. In this example the chart helped to take a scary idea of change and turn it into something less stressful. The young man was able, as a result, to leave a job that wasn't what he wanted, and was therefore a source of stress and tension - and take charge of his life.

You can do that, too. I don't guarantee success; no one can do that. I can only tell you that if you do agree to take your aspirations seriously you'll be living your life and not some restricted version of who you could be.

STRESS AND BURN-OUT

One of the things I think it's worth mentioning here is burn-out. We may be so depleted and discouraged in our work that we feel it is impossible to turn up for even one more day. This is a crisis and under circumstances such as these it may be very hard for the individual to see any way forward at all. How can we feel anything but a sense of failure when this happens? The first thing to realize is that burn-out - if it is the real thing - is an extreme reaction caused when doing a task we loved and valued suddenly becomes repugnant to us. If one is bored with working at a menial job one is not, genuinely, burned-out. Burn-out (as its name implies) suggests that there once was a fire of enthusiasm that has now been exhausted. It occurs when we believe in the importance of the task we have taken on, when we really believe we can be of benefit to a small portion of the world, and when that inspiration cannot be sustained. Burn-out, then, can be seen as a moment of wisdom when the fantasy is assailed by grim reality.

What does this mean? I have observed true burn-out and it seems to me that it occurs when idealism is unsupported in its struggle against difficult situations. For example, a young teacher really wants to be a good and effective educator, but because she is junior in rank, there's a strong chance that the first assignment may be to a class that no one else wants. After a few years of attempting to educate those who are already alienated from school, with upheavals in their home life or bad experiences in other classes, the young teacher may become overwhelmed at the seeming impossibility of the task. The high hopes and enthusiasm have run aground on the rocks of an all-but-impossible situation. It is this rapid descent from idealism to depression and hopelessness that is at the center of burn-out.

In one form or another we'll all experience it.

The question is, how does one get anything positive from this?

I would contend that most of us can deal with burn-out quite successfully if we are prepared to see it as a stage towards wisdom rather than as a defeat. It is but one battle in a long campaign. A typical scenario of burn-out is that the person in crisis reaches a perceived deadlock and then gives up. The perceived deadlock for the teacher might be that the educational system pretends to care, but in fact, is under-funded by those who claim to care the most. This piece of political hypocrisy is only too familiar to most of us in one form or another. Observation seems to suggest that if the teachers know this, consciously, from the start, then they are less likely to become upset and disillusioned later, since they've already accepted the real parameters of their work situation. For the person working in industry the disillusionment might come from the company selling goods that are not really marketable. Few companies can be entirely innocent of this all the time. Whether it be sub-standard software, or unsafe cars, we're familiar with the situation. The bargain price home appliance that breaks after a month is an annoyance, but we don't as a rule, give up our jobs because of it. We wise up, buy quality next time, and accept the ways of our world. Put another way, we only become distressed by such things if we've invested a lot emotionally in them. In that sense burn out is very like heartbreak, because we are most hurt by those in whom we have invested love who do not return that love in equal measure.

EXERCISE 6:

❖ Think of a time when you were disillusioned and disappointed in a job, possibly your current job.
❖ How did you feel about your work after that?

A man of sixty recorded being disciplined by his supervisor because he was not soldering enough circuits in the time available. But as he told the supervisor, it couldn't be done properly in the time prescribed. The supervisor replied that he didn't care if the job was done properly, he wanted it done in the time available. Disturbed, the man made some inquiries, since the circuits were to be used in defense systems used by the U.S. Navy, and he began to realize that in order for the company to meets its bid price it had to send out what were, in effect, non-functioning circuits. Although the story was resolved happily, the man related it as a tale from which wisdom could be learned, since he had begun to see things in a different light. He then began to take steps to change his employment.

Another example comes from a business woman who recalled her disgust when her boss told her to lie on the phone to important clients. It was a point of crisis for her, one she felt was the end of the 'innocent' period of her life, as she called it. As a result of this experience she began to re-think her career aims. How did she want to spend her working life, really? Both of these events were turning points for the people concerned. They were experiences that provided a flash of insight, of wisdom, that caused those concerned to make important adjustments. This brings us to the next exercise.

EXERCISE 7:

❖ What does your job give you besides money? What do you look for in your 'ideal' job?

Replies to these questions are often poignant. Many people expect their jobs to give them status, self-respect, even a mission in life. One woman described her job as "a crusade to save others", another wrote that she wanted her job to be an important contribution to the world that would "save her soul". A journalist wrote that he'd started as a "crusader, a man on a mission" and had ended up as "a hack".

In our status-conscious world many people want to define themselves first and foremost through their jobs. The trouble is that if we rely on our jobs to complete our identity, to 'save our souls' as the woman suggested, then we are expecting rather too much. That road leads only to disappointment. Very few of us will win public recognition or prizes, and even those who do may find their work less wide-reaching than they'd hoped. When William Faulkner accepted the Nobel prize for literature he already knew that many of his more acclaimed books were actually out of print, because there was so little popular demand for them.

A job that is in tune with who you are will certainly help you live a fulfilled and meaningful life, but it's not the only way. In fact, it's not even an essential. Saving our souls takes a lot of effort over a long time and is accomplished in any one of many ways, all of which are to do with inner self-examination. If we expect our jobs to make us whole, we are setting ourselves up for failure and a huge amount of stress. This is important. Stress that we do not realize we have imposed on ourselves is the most damaging of all. Unexamined, unrealistic, expectations cannot be met, and the results are devastating. So, ask yourself:

EXERCISE 8:

❖ What is my purpose on this earth? What am I here to do?

Return to the question from time to time. The clearer you can be about this, the less you will be stressed and made anxious by the little things of life. If you can accept that you have a purpose, and that part of the purpose might be to learn as fully as possible who you are (for without self-knowledge it can be very hard to know how to proceed) then you will be less likely to seek total fulfillment in external things. A good job, or a good relationship, can certainly help you reach your full potential, but in and of themselves they cannot get you there. Only you can do that.

Perhaps we can only ever ask what it is we're here to do, since we'll all come to slightly different answers, ones that seem right for us. One of the possible answers, I like to think, is that we are here to be as aware as possible of who we are so that we can let our own individual talents shine clear. Another purpose might be to leave the world a little better than we found it. The Dalai Lama has a response to this question that I believe many of us might find helpful, and it seems to embrace the previous two possibilities:

> I believe that the very purpose of our life is to seek happiness.
> That is clear. Whether one believes in religion or not, whether one believes in this religion or that religion, we are all seeking something better in life. So I think that the very motion of our life is towards happiness.

On a lighter note, here's an exercise that may give you a chance to reassess your work situation.

EXERCISE 9:

❖ Who do you like at work? What do you like about your work? Who do you dislike?

Work is social. Even if you do not care for the work itself, you may enjoy many of your co-workers. What do you like about them? One woman wrote that she liked a colleague because, "she didn't give a damn; she didn't take it all so seriously, and she didn't let anyone push her around." Just knowing this person seemed to make everything more bearable: in other words, to reduce stress. Those you dislike will be those who make you feel tense and anxious - the stress creators. It could be useful to look carefully at those people and deduce what characteristics these stress creators share, so you'll know how to recognize and avoid them in the future. I mention this because it's not always obvious. One man wrote about an administrative aide who always seemed cheerful and friendly. When he examined this woman's behavior he saw her friendliness was expressed in the re-telling of inter-departmental rumors. She was being open, but she was being open only in the way she retold gossip. Although the woman intended to be chatty and friendly, the effect of the stories she told was that the man began to feel depressed about the squabbling in his office. In this way a generous impulse of friendliness had, in fact, become highly stressful.

EXERCISE 10:

❖ What do you fear might happen at work?

Fear is always greater in anticipation that the event itself. If we can face up to the fear in our own time and space, we can do a great deal to avoid stress. For most people, the main fear in the workplace is of being fired, or replaced by a new system. This is a real fear. Sometimes there's very little we can do about it. Management decisions may eliminate our department with little or no warning. If, on the other hand, we're not doing well in our work and we're afraid of being fired it may be sensible to deduce that, for one reason or another, this is not a compatible environment. Rather than gearing up for a showdown with the boss, we may be better advised to calm down and think of what to do next, or of a way to get a half-way decent reference from the management. Fears like this, when faced, are never as monumental as they seem when we're fleeing them. Losing one's job is a serious situation, but it is, after all, only a job. It is not life itself.

In this section we've worked towards the identification of stress, and this can allow us to see it more clearly, and take control. Just as a shopping list enables us to break down the task of buying food into manageable chunks, so these exercises have been designed to examine stressful areas of living with a view to seeing them as they are. We are all capable of getting into a panic. We may run around saying things like, 'Oh dear, I'll never get it all done in time!' Stating it like this to ourselves is almost a guarantee that we will not be able to take charge. A more successful way to proceed would be to make a list of all that has to be done, prioritize it so that must-do items are attended to first, and then be prepared to abandon a few less vital tasks. We can choose which method we prefer. We can choose to have stress control us, or not.

EXERCISE 11:

❖ Can you think of the positive aspects of your job? What satisfaction does it give you? Can you describe an occasion when you felt proud to be doing your job, or when someone else praised you?

If it seems that up to this point I have been somewhat negative and critical of the situations work can produce, I want, now to value work. Many people get immense satisfaction from their work. People in the armed services, for example, write about the pride they feel in what they do, and the sense of purpose it gives - they are serving their country in a meaningful way. Those who retire from the forces have frequently written about how much they miss the life, and how their existences are less vital, less energized as a result. Teachers, social workers, policemen, and others in the human services branches have reported feeling good about what they do, that they are contributing to the good of the world. A car mechanic wrote about how he loved his work - he loved repairing things, he felt it was his duty to give people good value, and he enjoyed the fact that he was well-liked because of this. He felt he'd earned a place in his community and had earned respect. On one occasion I read in *The Boston Globe* the obituary of a manufacturer of cat litter. For forty years he had dedicated himself to the goal of finding the best product he could and of selling it at a reasonable price. It had made him a millionaire, and until he died he maintained his search for high quality cat litter products. It was clear that this man was highly thought of in the local community. Respect is not necessarily intrinsic to the task one does, but in the way one approaches it.

Freud was very clear about the redeeming quality of work. When asked what people needed to be happy he replied 'Arbeit und Leben' - work and love. One can certainly love one's work, although one probably should take Freud's hint and see that work cannot substitute for love. If we have any doubt about the power of work, talk to any unemployed person. Many will recount a sense of being adrift, of having no reason to get up each morning - a sense of not really mattering in this world. For Mohandas Gandhi all work, even the most humble, had value as a social contract that could improve everyone's lot. As he said, 'What we can do may feel infinitesimally small, but it is vitally important that we do it.' In such a light, there is no such thing as humble work. It's all important, because every bit counts towards the common good.

Work can provide us with a sense of belonging, also. We have friends and colleagues we work with. People often date and marry those they know through their work, and work will always plug us in to a network of other people, one way or another.

Work can also help us to feel competent in this difficult world. Advertising has a tendency to make us feel not very good about ourselves - the famous nurturing of dissatisfaction that is said to make us want to buy something to perk ourselves up again. This may help retail sales, but it's often not good for our sense of effectiveness. Our jobs can provide that. We know when we've done something well, and this feeling is to be treasured. One man put it very simply when he wrote: "I work hard, I do good work, and I pay my taxes." He said this with pride. If that sounds humble, I'd remind you that no less a person than Nathan Rothschild put it like this: "I don't play cards, I don't go to the theatre; all I do is business." He was proud of his work ethic and of his success, and he recognized how central they were to his sense of self.

Even those of us who don't particularly like our jobs can see the benefits if we think about the work. A teacher related that she didn't feel she was the best teacher on earth, but it gave her time off during the summers when she could work on writing her fiction, which she felt was what she needed to do for herself. Work gave her money and freedom.

And this really is the center of the exercise. Work can give us a great deal, as long as we bear in mind that it, alone, cannot complete our lives in every way. If we realize what it can do for us, what it does for us already, we are less likely to find ourselves expecting too much. If you drive a Ford, you can't expect it to be a Ferrari; and if you have a Ferrari, you'll probably be frustrated by the way it has to be used in traffic, and the small amount of space for groceries. Don't expect your job to be everything. America tends to want to define people by the work they do and the money they make. 'Oh, he's a doctor, he makes $200 thousand a year'; 'He's a lawyer in the corporate world. Very wealthy.' Just because the rest of the world uses this as shorthand for who a person is, it should not delude us as to what's really at stake. Having a title is nothing if you cannot be at peace with what it means to be that person.

COPING WITH WORK

Before you change your job you may want to take further stock of what your current work is like, so you can decide whether or not you really want to change. Sometimes a little humor can help change jaded perspectives.

EXERCISE 1:

❖ Write the weather report for your place of work.

"A stormy front forming over the manager's office will dissipate by the time it reaches the high ground of senior management, although there will be floods (of tears) and chaos in the lower lying districts..."

It's often hard to know how we feel about work because those feelings can be so volatile. Most people who quit their jobs do so within a few days of returning from vacation, according to surveys printed in *Time* and *Newsweek*, and I think this has to do with the shock of finding oneself back in the same old place after taking time off. If one asks people, directly, what they feel about their work and work mates, they tend very quickly to get embroiled in the details of office squabbles and personality clashes. Such disclosing, I've found, can be very lengthy and ultimately just feed the anger it describes, rather than being able to move to a better understanding of it. I like this exercise because it can encourage each of us to be slightly more humorous, less passionately engaged, and so allow us to see the typical workplace patterns in a new way. Work, just like the weather, is pretty much always with us, and we'll have to get used to it. We can observe, marvel, and watch out for the rain showers.

Writing the weather report can help us keep a healthy distance on the problems that might otherwise infuriate us, and it can remind us that the situation will change, just like the weather. It can also remind us that, contrary to what employment agencies promise, there is no perfect job, just as there is no perfect climate. Some are better than others, true, but hankering after a perfect job will only breed discontent. Even the best task has some downside. The important thing is to know what you can hope for, and what you can change. Which brings us to the next exercise.

EXERCISE 2:

❖ Design your preferred work space.

Could you rearrange your workspace? Sometimes that's not easy. Is there anything you can do that would make you more comfortable in your physical environment? Too often we accept that we have to arrange our space in a certain way. We don't. We can import plants, pictures, rugs. We have freedom, if we choose to use it. How would you change the lighting, for example? Light is one of the most important elements in terms of how mood is affected. Dim red works in romantic restaurants, but flickering florescent drives everyone to distraction. Can you get 'full-range' natural light bulbs fitted? Natural light and natural light equivalents have been demonstrated again and again to reduce fatigue, stress, and even depression. If you want to change the way you feel about your work you could do worse than start with your office.

This exercise can lead on to another, further-reaching exercise. If you are thinking of leaving your job you will need a vision to help you with the next step.

EXERCISE 3:

❖ Design your dream job. Write about what you would do, where, and with whom. A good way to do this is to find images in magazines and stick them on to a sheet of card. Add to this sheet over the next few days or weeks.

This exercise has proved useful to many people who have wished to reshape their lives but didn't quite know how. The trouble is that it's very hard to know what one wants when all one can think of is what one *doesn't* want. The exercise can give specific visual images that the mind can hold, and so move us from an abstraction like 'a fulfilling job' to an actuality we can see. What does a fulfilling job *feel* like? One woman put it very directly: "It's a job where I don't have to wear pantyhose!" Working from this very specific idea, and others, she was able to shape her life anew. She put together her own business, set up an office in the country, and arranged to wear jeans as often as possible. It was a bold move, even a risky one, and there are some drawbacks. She has to travel long distances to get to her clients' offices sometimes. On the whole, though, she is far happier because the disadvantages are those that are part of her larger choice to change her life, and so they are far less onerous to her.

Once we can visualize a change it's much easier to begin to take the steps necessary to make our vision come true. If your vision includes an office that overlooks the ocean, for example, and that feels important to you, it may prompt you to think in terms of moving to a place that is actually near the ocean, or at least to start looking in trade publications that advertise jobs in the preferred location. Once we start thinking this way we can make our futures happen. Although it may sound basic, it always astounds me just how liberating this exercise can be for many people. Above all, think in specific, concrete terms, and the task will become more manageable. What will your place of work look like? What will be outside the window? What will you have around you? What will it smell like? Will it smell like gourmet coffee from the espresso bar downstairs, or will it be the scent of wildflowers wafted on the breeze? The Unconscious and the imagination do not work in abstract terms, as I have already suggested, and if we wish to enlist their considerable energies we'll need to be specific in this way. For without their help no real change will occur.

For those of us who prefer to stay employed by others, however, the next exercise may prove a useful coping tactic.

EXERCISE 4:

❖ Design an evaluation form for your superiors, or an award.

This can be a splendid chance to let off some steam. Our superiors are often called on to evaluate us. How about reversing the power imbalance?

One man, responding to this, described how he would set up an award. The prize would be two weeks vacation in a first class hotel in the Caribbean, airfare and expenses paid for two, and $5,000 spending money. The award would be for the most efficient, compassionate, and effective administrator, he said, and then smiled. "Every year I'd get to announce the prize," he said, "and every year I'd get to say that no administrator had yet qualified." Behind the fantasy lay a dissatisfaction with the administrators, whom he saw as constantly giving themselves awards and pay raises, whilst being out of touch with what was really needed. Instead of just frustration, though, the humor in his response allowed him to see that he himself was doing good work, but that it wasn't recognized. A potentially angry, negative emotion was able to provide enough spark so that he could see his own worth, and value it.

Others have responded to this exercise by designing awards for those whom they felt to be under-recognized, and whose efforts deserved appreciation. The advantage of these exercises is they reach a little deeper than a simple 'how do you feel about your work?' Such a question tends to move the respondents into set answers of anger, or denial, or silent gloom. By approaching the topic from a slightly different angle we can engage our creativity, and even our sense of fun. Whenever we do that we can make discoveries about ourselves. Here's another.

EXERCISE 5:

❖ Draw a map of heaven and hell. Who would you place where, and why?

This exercise can work well in many settings, not just work. It's produced some extraordinarily detailed suggestions, and sometimes the maps produced have been very large.

When one moves beyond the basic reward-those-I-like and damn-those-I-don't paradigm it's possible to see deeper insights emerging. Most people are actually very merciful to those they don't like. Being placed in the position of ultimate judge seems to moderate the destructive impulse. After all, if one is the judge, then one has nothing to fear from these poor souls. In this way the exercise can move us beyond the petty issues that are often so much part of our lives, and ask us to see people with all their frailties.

One man refused to draw hell at all, even though he made an elaborate map of heaven. He simply placed the figures he disliked outside heaven, behind a fence, and suggested that being excluded was punishment enough. Another man had a similar vision, and he left his unfavored figures in a far corner of heaven, all of them isolated from each other. "Those guys are in hell already," he said, "because they're alone with themselves. They can come join us whenever they feel like it."

It's the kindness that comes out of this exercise that I wish to emphasize. When we begin to see others as they are, aside from their ability to annoy us, we can begin to think of them in new ways. These ways may help us to deal with them a little better in the future - and will certainly lessen our fear and stress levels.

One of the other aspects this exercise can show us is what we really feel is important in human terms, and what we feel deserves rewarding. One man drew heaven with different areas for poets, philosophers, and writers. In doing so he identified values he held very dear which did not routinely appear in his work, and which he believed were genuinely 'higher' values. My question to him was straightforward: How are you going to incorporate more of those values into your everyday life?

Another man drew heaven as a spacious landscape, and in the foreground a number of people chatting at a table. Hell, directly below, was a huge crowd, elbow to elbow, all walking on a vast treadmill, unable to see out of the tiny windows on each side, and all unable to see each others' faces. The theme seemed very clear. For him working together, cooperating, and trusting eye-contact were important. I thought this very interesting as he was a shy man who might have been expected to avoid others, yet here he was asking for more direct contact. When he thought about this he was able to respond that this was in fact exactly what he craved in his work, but it was something that didn't seem possible - yet. And the challenge was not to wait until he was actually in heaven before he tried to make it happen!

CHANGING JOBS

I've given this heading a separate section even though it's not realistic to divide it from the preceding section, since so many of us dream of changing our jobs even when we make no move to act on that impulse.

I'd suggest that thoughts about changing jobs are always optimistic. Dissatisfaction often has behind it the urge to do better and be better. Even if you're satisfied with where you currently are professionally it's never a bad idea to keep that creative and questioning thinking alive since it will help to keep you fully engaged in the work you are doing. The danger of contentment is complacency, of falling into a rut. And ruts are always self-limiting.

Even if you are not happy with your work it is still possible to fall into that same rut. Some people expend a vast amount of energy complaining about their work while making no move to improve anything at all. This is all too familiar. We've all seen people like this. Most of us have been in that situation ourselves. The complaining becomes a substitute for action and in time we fall in love with our own discontent. This can be paralyzing.

I use the word paralyzing for a very good reason, since this mind set can render us unable to move. When we complain about our work without wishing to act on our impulses we send a message to ourselves that we do not deserve anything better than a job that annoys us. As a result we disempower ourselves in a most insidious way. Imagine the scene: Jo, at 34, is bored with her job, and so is no longer the lively person she used to be with her colleagues. She decides she has to get another job, because this one is too dull; but because she's lost her spark she can't think of any other type of work she can do. Her thinking might be, 'Hey, it's not much of a job, but I've done this kind of thing for the last twelve years, so I guess that's what I have to do.' She has already decided that she's doomed to that sort of job, and she's given up thinking of creative possibilities. So she applies for another job that is very similar to the one she already has. She tries to appear alert and enthusiastic at the interview. She gets the job. A few months later the boredom has returned, and she's convinced that there's something wrong with her. At this point she may begin buying lottery tickets, hoping for an overnight fix. Or she may begin an affair with a colleague, perhaps. Or she may even seek help for depression, and whilst she's depressed she knows she can't change her job, because no one would hire a depressive, right?

This is what I mean by self-limiting. We may limit ourselves because we want security. A job, no matter that it's not perfect, can offer security - especially if we know it takes less than our full abilities to hold it down. And security is highly important to most people. In some cases, like Jo's, it becomes so valuable that she's prepared to pay a heavy price for it.

Any job we want to leave has the capacity to keep us stuck. Like remaining on a sinking ship, there's always a chance that a rescue vessel will appear, but if you wait too long there's a danger that the undertow from the sinking vessel will suck you down with it. When we stay in work we don't like we tend not to do it well, so we lose sight of our real skills, because we're not using or developing them. In the process we lose sight of our creativity, of our genius, of ourselves.

EXERCISE 1:

❖ Write about the lives you have not had, or lives you may once have wanted. You can make a list, or paste pictures onto a page. Alternately, can you recall the things that, as a child, you wanted to be?

Writing about the lives you haven't had can be a delight. The jazz pianist you might have been, the world traveler you didn't become - whatever it was you had a yearning for deserves some space in this exercise.

Contrary to what one might expect the replies to this are rarely sorrowful. The man who wrote about the water-colorist he'd never become, the woman who had never become a pilot, and so many others like them seemed to be valuing something other than an opportunity missed. Instead they were choosing to reclaim their dreams and fantasies. And it is in our dreams and imaginings that so much of our energy lies, whether or not we ever live those dreams.

This is comparable, perhaps, to those people who go on vacation, have a wonderful time, and then sigh about 'if only I could live there..' What with one thing and another we rarely do manage to live there, for all the good reasons in the world, and sometimes for no reasons at all. The point is that it is the act of asking 'What if...' - it is the possibility - that really gives us pleasure.

This exercise can reclaim the pleasure of creative thinking and re-value dreams without torturing us with regret. For we will always have more dreams and desires than any one lifetime can contain. Regret punishes us for not having lived all our desires, and so it can always hurt us. What this exercise can do is change regret into a valuing of the inner imaginative life we so seldom get to express, and it can encourage us to see ourselves as more richly creative than we thought we were. Creativity and imagination have to be sought out daily or they cannot energize us or fuel our decision making.

Now, look down your list of 'lives' and see if there are any themes or elements that echo each other. One young man produced a list that included such items as fire-fighter, olympic oarsman, first division rugby player, and so on. For him what seemed to matter most in this list was the attachment to teams and a cooperative spirit in an environment that was accomplishing something definite. Since belonging was so important to him - interestingly he was an only child - the question that had to be asked was whether or not his current job was giving him this. The answer was no.

Again, a woman who was just about to take a 'sideways promotion' as an Administrative Assistant in a different branch of the same college she had been part of for some years noted that most of her suggested lives involved being either a lone performer or a director of others. She pointed to the items on her list which she had underlined, and they included the words Actor, Stand-Up Comedian, Orchestra conductor, and so on. It seemed strange that she was seriously considering a job in which she would not be the one making important policy decisions, nor would she be at the forefront. Instead she'd be, literally, behind the scenes, facilitating others to 'perform' as lecturers and academics. As she read over her list she kept referring to her possible job change, saying that she'd told the interviewers she enjoyed organizing when the truth was that she could do it but hated having to. The crux here seemed to be that she was a woman who really could organize and direct, but she could do it effectively only if she felt in charge of the project. Captains do not always make good foot soldiers, and racehorses don't do well harnessed to ploughs. This woman was tired of doing other peoples' tasks. What she needed was to be in control of her own decisions. Working for someone else, going back into a familiar rut, would not be the best choice for her.

Look down your list. What elements are repeated? This list can be an indication of where your energy lies. How you incorporate it into your life is the challenge you now face. Write about this. What stops you following your dreams?

Often there are very good reasons that stop us. We have children to raise. We may have relatives to care for. We may decide that other possible lives will have to remain pipe-dreams. On the other hand we may elect to find ways we can include aspects of these dreams in our present lives. The office worker who wanted to be a college teacher began by doing volunteer literacy work. Emboldened by this she offered a class in basic computing at her local Adult Education Center. Now she teaches one class a semester at a nearby community college. Gradually she's making that aspect of her dream come true, without any drastic changes that would upset her financial situation.

EXERCISE 2:

❖ Draw three circles large enough to use as pie-charts.
❖ Divide the first circle into sections to show the amount of time and energy you put into your work a year or more ago. How much of the circle was work? How much was leisure? What about time spent with friends, or other activities? Now, repeat this with the second circle, except that this circle is now. Put today's date under it. When you've done that move to the third circle. How do you envision the future? What is the balance like?

Compare the results. What can you say about the balance of your life? Is there anything you missed out? A hobby, perhaps? Did you allow enough time for your non-work interests? If you have a large portion of your today pie-chart devoted to non-work pursuits you may want to think about work that will allow you to combine these interests with your work, since it's clear where you'd rather be. Perhaps you love movies and talking about them. It might be an idea to try and find work in some branch of movie production or distribution, somewhere you can give your energies more scope to develop.

Doing both these exercises in tandem can be helpful, especially if you ask yourself the next question:

EXERCISE 3:

❖ Do I want a job or do I want to create my own job?

Perhaps you may want to think in the long term, of moving to a job that will become a stepping stone to the creation of your own work situation. This may sound horrifyingly risky. If it does, write about the risks you see in taking such a step. It's certainly not a step to be taken lightly. On the other hand, unless we take the time to consider it - even to reject it in favor of something else - we may never be able to free ourselves enough from our present concerns to be able to reshape our lives. And please remember, many people who do these exercises come to the end of them and realize for perhaps the first time how much they value their existing work - the same work they've moaned and groaned about for years. Doing these writing exercises can quite literally bring us back to our starting point but with a new appreciation of where we are. And that is not an achievement to be taken lightly.

Chapter Ten

PARENTING

Very few of us are fully ready to become parents. Even those who have had several children already, and who think that one more will hardly be a great shock, have confessed that every new child presents unique challenges. Quite literally, one can never be sure what sort of child one will get. We all imagine that our offspring will have some aspects of ourselves and some aspects of our partner, but we can never be sure of the resulting mix. Children do not emerge from the womb as blank pages upon which the world inscribes what it wants. Children arrive with highly specific genetic coding and, as many mothers will tell you, a character already in place.

An anecdote about the playwright George Bernard Shaw will show what I mean. A celebrated wit, Shaw was approached by the dancer Isadora Duncan, then at her professional peak and a well-known beauty. 'Mr. Shaw,' she is supposed to have cooed, 'I want to have a child by you. With your brains and my beauty what a gift to the world that would be.' The aging Shaw didn't hesitate in his reply. 'Yes, dear lady; but what if it has *my* beauty and *your* brains?' We can't guarantee how children will be when they are born, and neither can we predict with any certainty how they may develop later. So how do we know how to deal with them when they arrive?

One of the saddest things about our culture is that our pervasive sense of uncertainty has been immeasurably augmented by a different kind of doubt - the doubt about how one should raise one's child. Two hundred years ago almost everywhere in the west there was considerable agreement within communities, and within the individual sections of those communities, as to how children were to be raised. The aristocrats' children were to be raised one way, and the middle-classes had their own regimen fitted to their expectations. Everything from clothing styles to schooling was done according to a socially agreed pattern.

In our times vestiges of this still remain, but the huge quantities of books about parenting from Dr. Spock on have served to tell us that we don't know how to raise children and so we need help. Christopher Lasch's *The Culture of Narcissism* makes his point eloquently and in great detail. Socialized health and child care, the welter of self-help books, even the daytime talk shows - all have combined to tell us we're not able, on our own, to be good parents, that we somehow need the skills of specialists to help us manage our children. It begs the question as to how our grandparents managed. Quite well, is the answer to that one!

I'm not trying to criticize all those wonderful self-help books. Society has changed from 200 years ago. There are far fewer agreements today about what parenting involves. Now that society is changing even faster, the essential role that used to be played by the community's validation of child-rearing methods is no longer available to us. However, the effect of all this advice is to make us doubt whatever feelings of competence we might have. Bruno Bettelheim's *A Good Enough Parent* is persuasive in its title - it's reassuring to know we only have to be good enough and not perfect. Parenting also has limits in its effectiveness. Nathaniel Branden, in *Six Pillars of Self-Esteem* makes the point succinctly:

> There are people who appear to have been raised superbly by the standards indicated... and yet are insecure, self-doubting adults. And there are people who have emerged from appalling backgrounds, raised by adults who did everything wrong, and yet they do well in school, form stable and satisfying relationships, have a powerful sense of their value and dignity, and as adults satisfy any rational criterion of good self-esteem. (p.62)

Although there are no guarantees, as Branden suggests, it's probably worth adding that good parenting is always a plus, and that for every child who triumphs over a poor parenting experience, there must be many who are crushed. This concept, known as resilience, has only just begun to be explored. About the only thing we can say at this point is that resilience doesn't seem to have any obvious cause, and that children may well either have it from birth, or not.

I give this background because it may help you to do the exercises that follow. Parents often carry a sense of self-blaming. If you are reading this section it's most likely that you've already experienced how hard parenting can be, and how easy it is to get confused, do things less well than you had hoped, and feel somehow that you have failed to be the model parent. We all make mistakes. The question really is, what can we do to understand these mistakes so we can stop doing them and even correct them?

EXERCISE 1:

❖   What mistakes do you feel you made in parenting?

Sometimes people write reams about this, enumerating every single event. This can help as a first step, after which I ask them to see if they can categorize the results in some way. A forty one year old lawyer produced a list of mistakes ranging from using the wrong kind of talcum powder to failing to monitor the child's TV viewing. When she began to look down the list she was able to see that many of the initial errors were due to her sense of panic about how she was going to deal with this baby. When the panic passed, and the child was a little older, exhaustion was a key factor, and the TV was a useful baby-sitter that allowed her a few quiet moments in the next room, with a book. This sort of response leads to the next part of the exercise, which is to ask: given who you were, could you have done things any differently? Seeing things in this way can help us not to feel bad about our mistakes. Remember - a mistake is something we do when we don't know any better. It is an error, not a moral failing. If we blame ourselves for mistakes we do ourselves a grave disservice. Even saints make mistakes, and that's why I used the word in the question, rather than asking what you feel you did wrong.

Listing one's mistakes can make one see that the errors themselves may be part of a larger pattern. "I should have spent more time with my boys when they were growing up," wrote a seventy year old former military man, who then went on to describe how his life kept him away from his family. In fact, writing this reply allowed him to reflect on the distance that had occurred in the family, and that the only way to correct this mistake would be, even at this late stage, to try to be mindful of what happened and talk with his children about it. As it turned out, he wasn't comfortable talking this out, and he gave his sons a list of these 'should have done' items for them to read. It allowed him to acknowledge his mistakes - in a sense to apologize - and it gave the opportunity for them all to discuss what their early years together had been like. This is the way towards healing.

One interesting thing emerges from situations like this: often the parent will remember something seen as a failure and recall it in fear and pain. When this is presented to the child for discussion (when the child is usually older) I'm sometimes surprised by how often the event that seemed so disastrous to the adult may be barely recalled, if at all, by the now grown child. It's ironic to think we may be feeling guilty about something that has been long forgotten by those we fear we've hurt.

The reverse can also be true, of course. Children grow up and recall injuries that parents may have no conscious awareness of having inflicted. In most healthy families, however, children are only too ready to point out parental failings.

Drawing up this list can tame our formless anxieties. We may feel relief at being able to put our guilty feelings down in a list, and even more relief to see that the list is fairly short, or that, if long, some of the items are very minor. If indeed we have been poor at parenting, if we were absent, unsupportive or unhelpful, it's worth remembering that acknowledgment of our own role can be the first step towards self-acceptance and self-forgiveness. "I've been a lousy father," wrote an incarcerated man, doing life for murder, "but I realize that my kids need a father. I'm behind bars, but I can still help them. If I'm honest with them." This brave statement was, for this man, the start of a new commitment to his family. Even though his wife had divorced him some years ago, he saw his children needed to know who their father was. They visited him in prison and he was able to give them substantial love and support. As far as I know, he still is. It's never too late to do the work of parenting.

The next exercise builds on what has gone before:

EXERCISE 2:

❖ Write about what you feel you did right as a parent.

Some people have trouble acknowledging they did do things well. "The camping trip we took when Jake was eight was a good thing," wrote a forty five year old engineer who had often spent his time away from home at his various work sites. The single camping trip might well have been more important to the developing father-son relationship than any amount of other activities. This is not to say that the day-to-day contact of parenting is not vital. It is, and few things are more important. But when this is not possible, or not as frequent as one would wish, then a shared vacation certainly can help to rebuild the relationship in highly significant ways.

Parents have also written about things they did that they felt were right which were not always easy to insist upon. For instance, visits to the dentist are certainly correct things to do, although few people really enjoy them. The result, in terms of healthy teeth and gums, and a brilliant smile perhaps, are rewards in themselves. A woman of thirty five was proud of having brought up her children with a strict sense of morals and duty. A single mother, she didn't always find this easy, but she knew that she had given them something very valuable, a moral sense.

And this is the whole point of this exercise: by focusing on what you did 'right' you allow yourself to see what you were able to give you children, spiritually and emotionally. If I'd phrased the exercise as 'what do you consider to be the spiritual and emotional support you give your children?' most of us would not know what to say. Most of us wouldn't even want to respond. But when you did something that you felt was right you responded from your core, from your authentic self, and you acted effectively on that feeling. At that point you were, certainly, being a genuine parent, not just someone who was doing what the textbook suggested.

We should value moments like that. A woman of fifty wrote in very emphatic terms about spanking her young son for being dishonest. "I hated doing it. I hate any kind of physical violence. But I know what I did was right, and I'm glad I had the guts to do it." By writing this event out, years later, she was able to validate herself as a strong loving parent. She was aware that the outside world might disapprove of her actions (and I certainly don't advocate corporal punishment, as a general rule) but she was also aware that she had taken charge of the situation according to her best judgment and beliefs. In some ways one could ask for nothing more from any parent.

EXERCISE 3:

❖ Write about moments of doubt you felt as a parent.

All parents feel doubts about what they do, and about what they allow their children to do. Whether it be doubts about the child signing up for football practice or doubts about the wisdom of letting the young adult borrow the car, doubt is always a major constituent of parenting. Doubt can also extend a little further to that sense one may have of not being adequate to fulfill the role of parent, that most demanding of tasks. Whatever the nature of your doubts, you should certainly face them, in writing, so you can be aware of the sorts of things that make you uneasy, and so attempt to come to terms with them.

In the instances you chose to write about, were your doubts proven true? Did the child fail to meet the expectation? Is that because the expectation was too high? You see, doubt has several facets. There is self-doubt ('Am I being a good parent to allow this?'); there is also uncertainty about a situation ('How do I know it's safe?'); and then there is the doubt one may feel in the child's competence to deal with challenges the world provides ('Can my child handle this?'). Where were your doubts? You may find they are grouped mostly in one area. Did you doubt the conditions that existed in the world at large or did you think about what the results may say about you? If you doubt your child's competence, is that a justifiable feeling? Has he or she made many mistakes? Does the child deserve to be doubted? And for yourself, did you often worry unnecessarily?

Whatever your responses, I'd like to draw attention to one thing, and that is that doubt is useful because it envisions an alternate way of doing things. Did I do the right thing? Is the first question in a series that lets us consider future possibilities in which we do things differently, perhaps even better. Doubt is healthy. Only the rigid thinker has no doubts whatsoever. Conversely, the neurotic is plagued with doubts to the extent that they can inhibit all actions, good or bad. We need to see that doubts are healthy, and that often they reflect the love and concern we feel for the child. In addition, since children develop so rapidly, doubt is going to be part of our mental landscape for years to come, since every time a child does something new he or she leaves us wondering (if only for a moment) if the child can manage this new task. Were we wise to let him or her attempt it? If he or she fails, are we to blame for not having been informative/helpful/supportive enough? Such doubts are normal and help to keep us aware of the situation.

EXERCISE 4:

❖ Write about moments of pride and joy you felt as a parent.

Writing about these aspects can help parents to re-value their children, see their qualities. It's also a good idea to save the responses - you might want to share them with the child at some point sooner or later. This tactic has often proved valuable when the child is older, perhaps even adult, and lines of communication feel blocked.

What every child wants is to feel valued and visible to the parent. When we write about pride and joy, we should be aware we are dealing with a possible conflict of values. Are we proud because the child has done something praiseworthy that is the result of the child's effort, or are we happy because he or she is doing what we want? Is this a display of initiative, or is it the action of a robot?

For example, many parents respond that joy was their emotion on first holding their baby. This is, of course, wonderful, but the child hasn't actually earned that response through any action of its own. On the other hand, a father recorded his deep sense of satisfaction when his eleven year old refused to buy a toy and instead gave the money to a beggar. I give this example to demonstrate that there are many types of pride one can feel in one's children. As the child grows, we value the pleasant surprises he or she can give us even when those actions are not perfectly accomplished. The faltering attempt to make a snack and bring it to you, the imperfectly made cookies - pride in these accomplishments does not always have much to do with the quality of the product.

Pride felt by a parent sometimes is in response to things the child may not value so highly. A father wrote about how impressed he was by his adult son's decision to do a parachute jump for charity, even though he hadn't much love of aircraft. When the father shared this piece of writing with his son, the younger man was surprised. He'd never thought much about his father's thoughts concerning the jump. In fact he had hoped his father might have been proud of him for some other, quite different, reasons that were not mentioned at all. He began to realize he didn't have to try so hard to impress his father.

This is an exercise that can usefully be shared.

Pride in our children is a double-edged emotion. We tend to feel pride or joy when the child does something that brings him or her closer to independence - something that will inevitably lead to separation from the parent. It is paradoxical, in fact. The more the child comes into possession of his or her personal power, the less the parent is needed, and so the bond is weakened, in one sense. Pride is potentially sad for parents who want their children to remain as they were - and what parent doesn't recall the baby, the toddler, with fondness? The child needs to see the parent's pride to help validate a growing sense of self, and the parent feels the emotion and feels he or she did a good job raising the child. Although this seems like a moment of closeness, with hugs and congratulations, it is in fact more akin to the departure of a liner on a transatlantic voyage, with one's loved one on aboard. It is a celebration of separation.

EXERCISE 5:

❖ Can you recall how you felt when you first knew you were going to be a parent? Can you recall that for each child?

Most people respond the way one would expect from those in a happy relationship. They are thrilled, excited, scared perhaps, daunted, or stunned. Not all pregnancies occur when expected, for many reasons. The child who was the result of complex fertility treatments for an older couple will perhaps carry with her a heavier weight of parental expectations and longings than other children might.

Some parents have freely confessed that they might not have particularly wanted a child at the time. They may have made other plans - for travel, for a career. Or perhaps the accidental death of another child led the couple to conceive the new baby. All these circumstances can change the soil in which parental love will grow, and so they deserve acknowledgement. It is said, for example, that every successful adoption holds both love and a double sorrow - the sorrow of the mother who must give up the child and the sorrow of the adoptive parents who could not have their own child. What we see as the joy of the adoptive parents may be a far from straightforward emotion, in actuality. Similar factors may well be present for all parents.

And that's exactly the point of asking this question. When a child is born he or she is introduced to a set of circumstances that inevitably shape the emotional atmosphere, and some of those factors will play themselves out in the years ahead. The unexpected pregnancy may turn out to be the best thing that ever happened to the parents, but it may not evoke the same feelings as the carefully-planned family. We may not always be consciously aware of the difference, but it will always have an impact on what the family feels.

If you wish, you can turn this exercise in another direction and write about what you know of your own conception. Often people know a surprising amount. One woman recorded that she had been conceived during a snowstorm when the car in which her parents were travelling became stuck in a snowdrift, and they huddled together in the back seat to keep warm. Whether or not this was true mattered less than that she believed it to be true, and she had allowed it to shape some of her feelings for her parents and their complex relationship.

Inquiring into the circumstances of conception of one's children leads inevitably to the next question, which may be difficult to face: Do you find you prefer one child over another? Although we may want to say we love all our children equally, I suspect that we'll always like some of them more than others. "Some kids you just take a shine to," says the dying Arletta in *Cool Hand Luke*, admitting that she always preferred her son Luke over his law-abiding brother.

EXERCISE 6:

- ❖ Consider what you don't think your children understand that you want them to.
- ❖ Write several short answers. Then go on to answer:

EXERCISE 7:

- ❖ Consider what you don't understand about them.

I want you to tackle these two exercises together, because for some parents the balance only seems to tip one way. We want our children to understand many things: how dangerous drugs are; how dangerous drinking and driving is; how they should be careful in sexual matters, practice safe sex... the list goes on. The trouble is that it becomes a rather forbidding litany, a list of 'thou shalt nots'. Each item, of course, reflects your caring. You want them to be safe. You may want them to understand the reasons behind something, perhaps a divorce, so you can assure them of your love and keep the doors open for their love. In each situation *we* want *them* to do the understanding, and that can be a heavy expectation. Because of this it's always a good idea to leave enough room for them to ask you about things they feel they need to understand. As a former teacher once told me, "Tell them and perhaps they'll remember. Get them to ask you and they *will* remember." It's a good tactic to recall, but it doesn't get around the fact that sometimes children do have to be told about things, because if one waits for them to ask it may already be too late.

Sometimes we shrink from talking with children about serious topics. We're not comfortable asking them about sex or drugs. On occasion responses to this exercise have spurred parents into action as they have come to realize how much they have left unsaid that needed to be acknowledged. Often a good course is to raise the topic and, instead of telling the child what you feel needs to be said, rather take the time to ask what the child understands about these things. Frequently that can lead to an important opening of dialogue that will not sound, to the child, like a lecture or a levying of blame.

If we reverse this situation and ask ourselves what we don't understand about the child and his or her world, we may surprise ourselves with the hidden insights. "I don't understand why he has to play that rap music," complained a mother, a professional woman in her forties, born in Switzerland. "I don't understand why he dresses like that," - a very frequent complaint, this one, as is: "I don't know what happened to the sweet little kid she used to be."

Perhaps a clue to all this lies in a response given by a thirty eight year old designer: "I don't understand why she has to keep saying to me, Mom, you just don't understand!" Teenagers, in particular, like to insist that their parents not only don't understand but are incapable of understanding. This is sometimes the case, certainly; but what is most important to a child of this age is to be able to say that he or she is different from the parents. This is a way of finding an individual identity. If I don't know who I am it's easier to define myself by what I'm not than by what I am. 'I am not my parents' is a formulation of individual identity, and it's quickly followed by: 'if my parents can understand me then I'm clearly not different enough!' This stage often brings grief to parents who mourn what they fear may be the loss of their child. If, instead, we see it as part of a phase in which the child is seeking an individual identity, then the loss becomes a gain. We want our children to have a strong sense of who they are so they can make their own decisions.

This leads to the next exercise. As children mature we inevitably tend to find ourselves feeling that we have lost contact with them. So much of their experience excludes us. We can't go and sit with them in the schoolroom, and the school experience we recall is likely to be quite different from theirs. And anyhow, we have our own work to do.

EXERCISE 8:

* If you are a working parent, write about what that means in terms of demands on you.

This is almost a trick question, since we're all working parents! Running a home has always been just as demanding as a full-time job. It is a valid exercise, however, because the dictates of life always make demands on us. What are yours?

A woman of forty-four, formerly a teacher and now aspiring to be a novelist, wrote movingly about how she had to struggle to make time that was quiet enough to allow her to concentrate on her writing. She could only do this when she felt free from interruptions, and with three children that meant she could get in two hours early in the morning, before they got up, and three hours during the day before the first child came home. To many this schedule may seem ideally relaxed, but the woman wrote with feeling about how she found herself just beginning to make progress in her writing each day and then she was forced to stop.

A different response, and a more common one, is from those who find themselves exhausted at the end of a long day, sitting in front of a TV with the children, or, and this is very common, eating alone while the rest of the family all sit in front of individual TV sets watching different programs.

What parents report in response to this exercise is a level of frustration with their lifestyles and how hard it is to change the facts of existence. A contractor of forty-five put it this way. "You do all this work, you get contracts, you get the money, you do the shopping and the laundry, you spend a few years with diapers, and what do you produce? This small creature who watches TV." Many parents feel under-appreciated, taken for granted, stressed and unhappy, at least some of the time. For them just being able to write about all they had to do was a huge release. Husbands and wives have found it useful on occasion to compare these accounts of their frustrations. As a result they are less likely to resent the other's imagined freedom.

This leads to the second part of this exercise: could you imagine ways to reduce the demands on you? A single mother of two described how she'd reduced laundry and cleaning to the acceptable minimum, streamlined cooking, and curtailed her social life, yet the work-load still had the effect of leaving her mentally exhausted. She regretted that although she was physically present she wasn't fulfilling her own ideal of nurturing motherhood. She couldn't comprehend how other mothers had time to bake cakes and go on excursions with their children.

The point here is that it is not so much the time-value of the demand that matters, as the amount of mental space it takes up. The question is not just one of time management but of being able to separate from the working world, or even wanting to separate. Those who find their jobs mentally exhausting are likely to respond to their families the same way, on the principle that when one is tired, one is tired even if fun appears. The question that might be asked at this point is, what can be done about an exhausting job? Unsatisfying work is always the most exhausting. If this is the case for you, you may want to take a look at the section on stress and work, in chapter 9.

Another avenue that's worth exploring is anger.

EXERCISE 9:

❖   When do you feel anger as a parent?

Write as many responses as you can as rapidly as possible - six to ten is a good number. Then stop, take a look at your responses, and see if there's any pattern there. A professor of forty-one noted that his list included a large number of references to the amount of cleaning-up he felt he was expected to do for his children. A man of patience and restraint, he resented the "thoughtlessness" as he called it, that "reduced him to the level" of one who "had to clean up everyone else's mess." Notice here, first of all, the language he chose to express his anger. As his exploration continued what he discovered was that his anger stemmed from his inability to impress on his children that he had expectations of tidiness. He was more angry at himself and his failings than he was at them, although some of his anger was directed at his wife, whom he felt never helped enforce his expectations - expectations that he began to realize he had never made clear.

A school-teacher in her thirties wrote that she felt most angry when her children didn't listen to her advice. The advice was often very good advice, she felt, but it was rejected, all too quickly. "I have people calling me up all the time, begging me for advice and direction. But my own kids won't listen!" This example is only too common, and all I can say in response is that there are some people in one's family situation from whom is hard to take advice, or whose advice is never taken seriously. Possibly that's why we need therapists, consultants, and outside advisors - not because they say anything new but because it comes from a new source.

Imagine it, a typical scene of a young man being told off by his mother for being messy. The young man ignores the complaint. He goes to a college class and the professor complains his papers are messy. He shrugs and ignores the complaint. Then in the cafeteria he sees a classmate he knows slightly. He decides to ask her out on a date. Her reply? 'I'm sure you're a really nice person, but I don't want to go out with someone who's so messy.' That's when the young man might finally hear the advice that has been directed at him from so many other sources. So, why do children resist advice that's obviously good? The answer can be surprisingly straightforward: if the child is to feel him or herself as an independent adult or adolescent then that means not giving in to dependency, not accepting another's take on things, especially not the parental take. The parent may even feel hurt by this apparent rejection, but for the child it is something far deeper and more vital that is at stake and that is the sense of self as an independent person who can make choices, even bad ones.

Many people have responded to this exercise in a quite different way. They have reported feeling anger at the waste of food, at lights left on, at rudeness, at hysterical behavior ("Everything's such a goddamn drama to that kid!"), at being ignored or taken for granted. I'd like to focus on this anger so we can find the pearl at the center of this irritation. Anger is rarely vicious in these cases. We may say we feel like killing the person, but in fact the irritation is minor. When something big does happen - say the child steals our credit cards and runs off - the response is usually sadness, not anger, at least at first.

Anger is a useful signal because it tells the person that he or she deserves to be treated better; it's a confirmation of wounded self-esteem. There are other aspects to it as well. For example the mother who reported being angry at the waste of food was able to ask herself why she was so upset about this in particular. She realized the waste was, in itself, not significant, but that since she had been brought up in a household in which waste of any sort was a crime she had internalized her own mother's criticisms and was reproducing them thirty years later. When the woman began to see that she was viewing and judging her domestic life through her mother's eyes, she was able to ask herself why she was allowing this to happen, and to understand that her anger was not even her own. I like to think of this as one of those occasions when the child's actions served to educate the parent.

It's a good idea to return to this exercise from time to time. Some anger is often beneficial in a family since it helps to set and enforce limits which are vital if the child is to feel secure and firmly guided. Anger doesn't have to blaze out. If it does it probably means we've allowed the emotion to take us over more than is necessary, and the result may be dramatic but it's likely to be confusing to the child. Children and young adults test everything and every limit. From the infant who places every object in her mouth as a way of finding out what it is, to the two year old who says no just to see what will happen, to the adolescent who does things for a dare, the child is always testing limits. Adults who do this successfully may become brilliant investors or inventors, and they may well try to find out what can be done when others have given up trying. Limit-testing can, therefore, be productive.

Criminals, of course, have tested other limits in their refusal to accept orthodox standards of behavior, and no one would pretend that this is personally constructive. I give these examples because, in one sense, testing the parent is part of the child's job as she tries to find out what's allowable in the world and how society works. We've all witnessed the look in a two year old's eyes when mother says, 'Do that one more time and you're in trouble.' To the two year old that's almost too good to resist. What sort of trouble? What does trouble mean, anyway? Does mother really mean it? Let's find out...

One doesn't have to be enraged at the child when this happens. A sanction or punishment coolly applied will certainly convey the message of action and effect. Bad behavior causes a sanction. We may call this discipline, or whatever we like. It is in fact the productive use of anger.

EXERCISE 10:

❖   When did you feel satisfied as a parent?

This is a challenging exercise for some parents. What does satisfied mean? If we look at its Latin derivation *satis* means enough. Today the word satisfaction tends to suggest being oversupplied with food and drink. I want to return to the original meaning of 'enough'. Satisfaction is not necessarily the culmination of everything good. 'I won't be satisfied until I have a million dollars...' This is not satisfaction. It's wishful fantasy, and may never come true. I'd like to try to bring satisfaction back into our world and ask you to focus on when you felt you did something well.

It's by recalling the times when we did a good enough job that we can remind ourselves of our competence as parents and as human beings. Since children continually throw new tests and challenges at us it's never a bad idea to recall a few successes in what is a constantly-changing struggle, one in which a successful strategy may not show it self to have been a good move until years later. Despite all our care and love in a healthy family situation, the child will eventually move away, and will focus his or her life on a spouse, a partner, or a family. Parenting is, therefore, always a losing battle since the healthy child is moving towards successful independence rather than remaining within the birth family. It is one of the few occasions when we 'win' as parents by 'losing' the child to another attachment, one that makes us much less central than before. We would do well to remember that one of the dominant myths of America is that children and parents remain best friends. The soaps seems to enshrine it, and the villains in TV dramas seem to be those figures who offend against this bond. From Norman Rockwell's gentle emphasis on the traditional values reflected in his illustrations to the Republican Party's slogans about 'family values' the illusion has grown. It is a view that Mark Twain and George Washington - both great rebels - would have found bizarre. All I'm suggesting here is that the older idea, that children are destined inevitably to grow away from their parents as part of their self-development, may help us re-evaluate how we are doing as parents. It's not until children have grown away that they can begin to renegotiate the relationship with their parents. Out of that real trust and love can grow.

The next exercise builds on this.

EXERCISE 11:

❖ What do you feel when you meet your child's friends? Can you recall how you felt when you were a child in that situation?

Responses to this have been energetic, indeed. Parents have reported feelings of horror, despair, disgust, suspicion, and occasionally, even pleasure. Possibly the largest single reaction is fear. The fear seems to be based in the fact that these are companions the child has chosen and who may have an enormous influence over the child - more than the parent, perhaps. The most common way that parents gauge where their children are is by the perceived quality of the friends they have, which may have more to do with the parents' perception of the friend's parents.

It's worth remembering that people choose friends in response to aspects of themselves, rather than as reflections of the totality of their sense of self. So a man can have a friend with whom he shares, say, a love of art, while not sharing his friend's sexual orientation. Sometimes we choose friends because those people represent lives and aspirations or a sense of curiosity we do not have the ability or courage to pursue. I have a friend who raced motorcycles for many years, and though I admire his successes I do not wish myself to race anything. I like and admire his approach to life, one which found expression in motorcycle racing. Children most certainly do the same sort of things with their friends. I've seen many Caucasian children who have chosen black children as friends in part because they have perceived black culture to be more exciting than their own; and I've seen American children be wildly successful in European schools because of their association with the glamorous lifestyle the European children have seen only on their TV sets. Friendships are in sometimes a way of trying out another type of life.

The fear that parents have is that their child will fall in with a bad crowd. This is a very real danger. The question to ask is why the parent feels the child is so much at risk from casual influences. Ironically, the over-protected child is the one who has had fewer chances to find out who he or she really is because of limited interaction with the outside world, and so is likely to be very vulnerable to casual invitations. For instance, Nancy Reagan's overly simplistic advice to children 'Just say no!' was not a great success in the war against drugs - although it contained within it the seed of a great idea. If children can feel strong enough to resist peer pressure they can refuse drugs and other evils. Unfortunately, one needs to have a robust sense of self first. A sense of self is developed in opposition to others, which is another way of saying the 'disobedient' child may well be better prepared for life's dangerous choices. The obedient, good child, may well be so used to conforming that peer pressure is accepted more readily.

When we see our child's friends we may want to bear some of this in mind. As we look at those friends we're asking ourselves how strong our child is.

It's a fine line. If we show that we think the child can't make decisions in selecting friends we may undermine that emerging skill. And if we react to the child with suspicion - and the desire to protect can turn easily into suspicion - the child will not feel trust, and so may stop trusting or confiding in the parent. Since every child is different there can be no set answers. What I'm at pains to emphasize here is that asking questions about our responses is always going to be more productive than a knee-jerk reaction.

EXERCISE 12:

❖ Can you think of an instance when your parents treated you as if you were much younger and less competent than you actually were?

The amount that has been written and spoken in reply to this question is almost overwhelming. From the woman who, aged twenty-six, visited her parents and felt herself regressing to the age of ten, and watched as her siblings did the same thing, to the woman of thirty three who was visited by her mother and was unable to do the cooking in her own home - the examples multiply. Rather than give endless examples I'd ask a second question: Is there anything to be gained by adult children regressing in this way? Who gains what?

"Sure," wrote a man in his forties, "it's always nice to be pampered by your Mom." "She likes it when her kids come home. She gets to be Mom again," wrote another. The gain for the offspring is that Mother, or Father, takes control. The gain for the parent is to feel once more the power and pleasure of being in charge, of being necessary. Each side wins, each side wants to show love and be accepting, and they do so by slipping into a relationship that may be more appropriate for a parent with pre-adolescent children rather than for the group of adults that actually is gathered. "I'll never be equal," as one man put it. "To them I'll always be a kid."

Perhaps your family is not like this. On the whole the chances are that it is, simply because parents and children have a tendency to adopt specific roles towards each other rather than seeing who the other person is. Thus the father may give advice to the son or daughter, meaning to be helpful, doing it out of care and concern, and the response in the grown child may be, 'Why is he telling me all this? I know this already!' Since the adult child may not want to seem ungracious, however, he or she may smile, say something soothing, and go ahead with his or her life. Out of kindness the role is not challenged and so the situation perpetuates itself.

What is happening in such cases owes a great deal to transference. Transference occurs when an individual wants another person to be a certain way. So, for example, a man is attracted to a woman and he wants her to be a certain sort of person, so he creates in his mind an idea of who the woman is that has more to do with his hopes than her character. Later he may find she's very different, become disillusioned, and blame her for not being the person he first met. Another example would be the man who goes to a therapist and wants her to be wise, good, and all-knowing. He projects these attributes onto the therapist, who cannot be all those things (none of us is all-knowing...) since she is only human. This is transference. Counter-transference is what happens when the therapist, or the woman in the earlier example, starts trying to be what the other person wants. An example of that might be the man who thinks he wants a wife, whereas what he really wants is a woman who will mother him. The woman is happy to do this. Each meets the other's expectations, perhaps. And there is nothing wrong with this. Many people make happy lives in this way. The problems only arise when the transference becomes too marked, when the man perhaps allows himself to be infantilized and rendered less capable than he truly is by his 'mothering' spouse.

The reverse situation might be characterized by men who so desire to be manly and dominant that they ally themselves with women who are meek, small in stature, and act immaturely. In this instance we could say the man is being the father-protector to the child-like woman. Not for nothing do such men tend to call their women by child-linked or diminutive names, like "Babe" or "Kid". That could be called transference, or role-adoption. This is the point at which the distinction blurs.

I mention this because in all the cases I have given the tendency is to see the other as a construct - what the individual wants to see rather than who the person is. And this is precisely what the exercise is about. What roles do your parents ask you to adopt? And what does that tell you about the roles you might ask your children to assume for you?

With this in mind I'll venture briefly into the world of Eric Berne and Transactional Analysis. Berne's work has been widely discussed in various forms, since he developed the ideas that were popularized as the inner child, inner adult, and inner parent. Some of his best ideas may be unfamiliar to you, however, and can be very useful here. Berne suggested that whenever we interact with another person we can choose which part of ourselves to use. We can respond to a child by mobilizing our child-self, in which case we may be on all fours on the living room carpet with toys everywhere. We can also choose to be the adult, in which case we're more likely to continue doing what interests us. Finally we can take the role of parent, which may mean taking responsibility, being directive, and making judgements about the child's play. Berne symbolized this by using three circles to stand for each aspect of the total person.

This diagram symbolizes two adults who meet. Ideally, adults will interact as adults, and line AA has arrows at both ends to show mutual and equal adult behavior. What can happen in the family situation, however, is that two adults can relate as parent and child, as in lines BB. This is an unbalanced relationship, forcing one to be in charge while the other remains diminished. This is fine if the child is still young, but if the child is twenty five years old we have the situation described in this exercise. The challenge, then, if we see this in Berne's terms, is for both parties to progress to the adult level so they can become fully real, fully themselves, with each other.

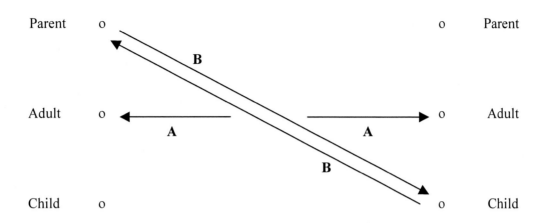

It is the healthy balancing that is important. I know plenty of adults who can relate well to each other as long as they stay in the child domain. They play and have fun. But sometimes they cannot be serious or sensitive to each other if the adult needs are more complex. Likewise, many people choose to respond by remaining in parental mode, in which case they may be rigid, judgmental, distant, and even bigoted. That's hardly an ideal response. In fact we need to access all three domains at times, but we choose to live in one, and our society tends to reward those who choose the adult domain.

Obviously the negotiations of adolescence are all about the clash of these three aspects as the teenager discovers and uses them, and the parent tries to come to terms with this sudden growth and change of behavior. Berne's ideas can help us to visualize what is happening. Draw one of his charts now, and label it with your name and your child's name. How do you relate best? How do you relate less well? What do you think needs work?

I'd venture that a huge amount of teenage distress comes from imbalances that can be charted in this way. An adolescent is frequently unsure as to who he or she is. If we add to that peer pressure, school pressure, expectations of teachers, and so on, we have a powerful assault on the fragile sense of self. Then, at the end of the day, the child comes home, hoping to be able to relax, and the parents have their own expectations, some of which may have little to do with who the child actually is. It should not surprise us, therefore, that so many children and adolescents choose to abuse various substances in an effort to escape. For the escape from all roles is a tempting alternative to having to deal with the complexity of one's emerging identity.

Berne's theories are more extensive than I have been able to outline here, but for our purposes this will be more than adequate. If you need to know more I'd recommend his *Games People Play* as a good introduction.

I want to end this section on parenting by saying there are no easy answers and that we do well to remind ourselves of this. The exercises are intended to help you make more conscious what may be going on, and the ways you can respond. Some of them overlap, in that they will tend to bring up the same issues for you in different ways. This is intentional, and I hope you have noted when issues seem to repeat themselves in your responses. It's a good idea, now, to take the time to think about the chapter as a whole before writing more.

When you have had a chance to think things through before hand - and this includes writing about them in detail - you can speak with your child about your concerns, and do so more successfully. The more conscious you can be, the more vital the connection will remain between the child and yourself. It's the reactive, knee-jerk response to a situation that will tend to leave the child feeling distant and misunderstood. Remember, the child is always moving into new territory, whereas you have been through most of it at least once in your life. You're the veteran, here.

Indeed, often the child doesn't know what is happening at a purely biological level. At puberty the hormones will cause mood swings that may be disconcerting to you - and how much more so for the child! Sometimes this may cause the child to behave in ways that are hard to comprehend. In these circumstances asking a child why he or she did something is sometimes not helpful. Asking the question "why?" presupposes that the child knows what he or she has done. If the action was based in the emotions the child may not know with any clarity. "Why did you have a party in our house over the weekend?" will not get much of a response, apart possibly from a contrite, "I don't really know..." A better question might be: "*How* did you come to have a party this weekend?" The young adolescent has a much clearer idea of *how* it happened and *what* happened, but perhaps no clear idea of *why*. You may already have encountered situations like this, in which case it would be a good idea to write about them.

In the end, there are no golden rules for parenting, just a few basic guidelines. The first is to be yourself. Children spot insincerity easily, and it confuses them. A word of caution is needed here. Being yourself, if you are an angry or violent person, does not give you the right to hit or mistreat your children. Child abuse is a symptom of an emotional upset within you. Giving in to that upset is you *failing* to be yourself, and becoming the disease. You should seek professional help without delay. There is plenty available. Substance abuse and violent behavior are things you may have taken on that are stopping you from being fully yourself.

The second guideline is to respect the child's individuality. Just because you were in the Marines does not necessarily mean your child is going to want to be. If you respect who the child is you help him or her to recognize his or her own strengths and weaknesses. I cannot stress too much how important this is. The child who feels personally authentic is going to grow to be an effective adult.

In respecting the child's individuality one also has to respect one's own selfhood, and that means imposing appropriate limits when necessary. The parent who gives up everything for the child's sake is modelling for the child a very unhealthy dependence. Children need to see their parent figures as happy, fulfilled, self-directed, and as having lives of their own which they are not afraid to pursue. They will internalize this, and use it to nurture their own adult selves. Model what you teach.

Chapter Eleven

COUPLES PROBLEM-SOLVING

Opposites attract, or so conventional wisdom would have it. And it's true that there is often something very attractive about those who are not like us. Various theorists have explained this as the genetically programmed desire for exogamy. This wish to marry outside one's social group or tribe is actually good for strengthening the gene-pool, and so creatures with this desire will tend to be more successful in the wider world. So, through natural selection the attraction for those who are different from ourselves has been carried into the genetic structure of most successful species, especially ours.

Whether or not this is the whole explanation, I can certainly vouch for the fact that many people do choose mates who are in some ways surprisingly not like them. I am not simply thinking of marriages which unite people from different religions and races. I can think of many very successful marriages of that sort. What I'd like you to consider is those unions, for example, in which the only child marries into the extensive Italian, Greek, or Irish family perhaps, to mention just three cultures that value the family highly; or the moneyed aristocrat who marries the workman - a favorite plot line of Hollywood, this one. To what extent can we see people hoping to complete themselves by allying themselves with what they may not have had in their birth-families?

Adam Philips has an interesting idea about this in his book, *On Kissing, Tickling and Being Bored*. Writing about how what we desire is often defined by what obstacles we need to overcome in order to gain it, he makes the tantalizing suggestion that in love the obstacle to be overcome is the loved person him or herself. It is, in fact, the differences that demand to be dealt with that elicit our desires.

The point is that if we form an intimate relationship with someone who is different in background, beliefs, expectations, and experiences, or who thinks very differently, then the things that may have seemed attractive at first might cause anxiety later in the relationship. The quiet man falls in love with the spontaneous woman. He loves her energy. She loves his steadiness. Ten years later he has come to dread her 'flightiness' and she sees him as stolid and dull.

In previous centuries these difficulties were solved by placing one or other as head of the union, traditionally the man. This was, of course, reinforced by religious and social expectations, and usually the woman's way of doing and being was sacrificed to the man's. The model was frequently perpetuated, however, even in same-sex unions. One person might become the 'strong' one, forcing the other into the weaker role. The system worked, but at disastrous cost to at least one partner, who had to give up power or resort to subterfuge, and certainly the cost was also shared by the dominator in so far as he or she was impoverished by not being free to access the wisdom of the other.

Our parents' generation often shows this. Men were expected to be the breadwinners and make the major decisions - a situation of some loneliness and stress. In the British movie *The Full Monty* (1997) the middle-aged businessman played by actor Tom Wilkinson is terrified to tell his wife he's lost his job because he fears she'll see him as a failure. The loneliness and strain upon him are appalling. When she does find out she leaves him - not because he's failed to provide for her but because he failed to tell her the truth. It's a sad vignette in a movie that is otherwise a comedy, and it shows the polarization of roles and the sense of one's spouse as being 'other' rather than a partner.

But this imbalance does not exist only in the past. In our mercenary world many women still are overwhelmingly attracted to men who have power, or money, or prestige. The differences are still with us. Women who already have those attributes are somewhat scarce - after all, it's a male-dominated world - so one could conclude that many women are attracted by what is the opposite of what they usually would expect to experience in their lives.

If I write at length about this it is because on the whole we do not seem to fall in love with those who are like ourselves. Hollywood has made decades of movies on this premise. Difference attracts. By difference I mean differences in how we think, process, and express information. Someone who is too different can often become too challenging for comfort, but initially we relish those slight differences. Later they may be problematic.

An example may help. A couple I know in a twenty year relationship are normally very happy together. They come from similar backgrounds in terms of family structure, education, income and class, and geographical location. In many ways they are very much alike. Yet, they always seemed to argue whenever they bought a new product and read the instructions. He would read carefully and match what he read to the product (a mixer or a juicer, for instance). She would be less patient, would not read the instructions, but would put it all together and so was frequently ready to use the appliance straight away. She followed her intuition. Sometimes she was right and the device was self-explanatory. He, however, doubted intuition and so double-checked the instructions. Sometimes it turned out that his approach was more appropriate. And this was the danger point for both of them. "Don't do that!" he would say. "Stop being so fussy," she would reply - or words to that effect, and an argument was imminent. What was to be done?

The man's solution to this situation is now to leave the room while she follows her intuition. Then if the device doesn't function he will come back (only when asked) and sort out what more needs to be done. Sounds familiar?

How about this: another couple always argue when they attempt a major project in their home. He thinks in terms of simple, practical, durable projects that he can do. She, an idealist, has a vision of what she wants, but it is a vision that can change. This drives him wild. "Tell me what you want," he says, "and I'll tell you what is possible given my ability and our finances." Her reaction is to see this as unsupportive of her ideas, and she becomes upset. He's already upset, and worried that he'll be expected to create something beyond his abilities. What could have been a collaboration that brought pleasure to both has become an argument. Yet the real issue, here, is not that they don't like each other but that they see things very differently in this one instance. Home improvement can be a powerful symbol of investment in a relationship, and so would seem to be a statement of loving commitment. As each person sits, furious with the other, we have to ask, what went wrong?

When I worked with this couple I asked them what each admired about the other. Not surprisingly the man said he admired the woman's artistic and intuitive abilities. She said she envied his practical and cautious side. Yet these were the same attributes that were causing the dispute! So here is an exercise for you.

EXERCISE 1:

❖ List the things that you admire about your significant other.

Notice I used the word admire. On the occasions I've asked for what one loves I've received lists that include toe-nail varnish colors and choice of underwear. What one tends to admire is a quality that one wishes one had oneself - in short, a different way of encountering the world.

"I admire his calmness, rationality. That he's good at bargaining, when I always get too excited and pay too much."

"I admire her spirit, her boldness in life's decisions. Her pushing aside of details."

Each list is simultaneously a naming of what it is that each person admires and wants, and a naming of what the writer characteristically is. Someone who admires another's boldness is indicating a preferred level of caution in himself.

❖ Now: list the things in your significant other that are similar to your own qualities.
❖ When you've done that, list the things that are different.

The list of similarities can be extensive and reassuring. Knowing that you both like Korean cuisine and Expressionist painting can remind you of activities you can plan that will build on your commonalities. Noting that you both come from difficult families, for instance, can also be a useful indicator of exploratory work to do together and may signal a deeper similarity. Affirming one's shared beliefs and values first makes it easier to look at the things that are seen differently. By the time you'll have finished the list of differences you'll have a clearer sense of the otherness of the other person, and perhaps a new sense of wonder at whom this person is.

It is after all, the wonder that I want you to recapture. When one truly sees how different one's mate is and why those differences exist, one can often begin to change an annoying attribute into something far more valuable. As one man in his mid-forties put it, "She sees things differently. And I love that. And occasionally it drives me nuts."

This can be a particularly strong dynamic with people who are highly creative. A photographer I worked with had an undeniable, unusual vision that he brought to his art. It had made him successful and it had always been a source of satisfaction to him that he did 'see' things in a different way from others, literally and metaphorically. The challenge was that this uncompromising vision was not just something that stayed in his photography. He could be uncompromising in his every-day life, too. And that caused friction. The point is that if he had grown up being 'nice' and considerate of others all his life he probably would not have had the determination and the belief in himself necessary to allow him to become truly himself as an artist. D.W. Winnicott, the British psychiatrist, has commented on this type of artistic temperament in similar ways. Like him, I have to conclude that one cannot have the good aspects without paying for them. If one really values what is good, fully, one has to be prepared to pay the cost - and also to attempt to moderate the worse excesses of the other person though gentle persuasion. Picasso certainly was a great artist, but he was a difficult man to live with. Yet he was also immensely energizing to be around, as his wives and lovers attest.

EXERCISE 2:

❖ What are the areas of discomfort between you? Are there any repeated discussions? Write about one or more of them.

"She wants kids and I don't," wrote a man of twenty-eight and that was all he was able to write, which indicated to me how he felt the discussion had reached a stalemate. In such circumstances it's hard to predict a happy ending for the discussion. It would be necessary to ask why he didn't want children in terms of what that would mean for his view of the relationship. Was he afraid he'd be less important to her? Did he have a fear of diapers and interrupted sleep? What lies behind this?

In the end the solution to this problem, and others like it, may well be for the couple to part - it's as well to admit this possibility honestly and openly. Otherwise the tendency is for the information to be used as a weapon. How often I've come across the words, "if you persist in this view then I'm leaving!" The trouble with this is it implies that the other's choice is causing an undesirable outcome. It's a way of blaming the other. I'd prefer couples to try to see that if a solution cannot be reached within the relationship then it may be necessary to reach a solution beyond it, by parting and getting their needs met elsewhere.

To return to the man who didn't want children, when asked to look more closely at himself he admitted that he enjoyed the mother-like caring that his lover gave him. In fact he loved her for the very same qualities that she now wanted to explore further, in real motherhood. Although it took more work before a solution could be reached, I give this example because what had been a deadlock in fact contained vital information within it that allowed both partners to see the situation more clearly.

In the case of the couple who fought over home-improvement projects the same underlying currents seemed to apply. He loved her sense of vision, she loved his practicality. What disappointed each of them so much was when they weren't able to see things the same way anymore, when the qualities each loved became limitations. In Dickens' *David Copperfield* David loves Dora's perfect dainty prettiness and her genteel upbringing, but he becomes increasingly disappointed by her impracticality and inability to be a housekeeper. To put it in common terms, it's a little like buying a convertible Porsche and then complaining that it can't carry five kids and haul a boat-trailer.

The hardest issues and the most difficult arguments come from situations in which a person's good qualities work against him or her. The solution is to go back, recognize the good qualities, value them, and try and appreciate that other qualities may need to be coaxed to life, in a way that is non-judgmental, before progress can be made.

In each case, though, knowing who we are is the single most important first step. It's also a two edged sword. I know who I am, and I know what I'm good at. However I also need to know what I am less good at, which is usually the flip side of my strengths. So, the decisive person is good at decisions - but may come to them too quickly. The compassionate person may be kind - but may also be taken advantage of. The observer may be wise, yet not good at taking action. The key to good problem solving may be to see who one is rather than who one might wish oneself to be.

This next exercise may help.

EXERCISE 3:

- ❖ Think of a particular dispute you have had with your partner.
- ❖ What for you would be the ideal outcome to this dispute?
- ❖ What would be a reasonable outcome to expect?
- ❖ What is the absolute least expectation?
- ❖ What will you under no circumstances accept?

We always want it our way. We want to be right, and we want that recognized. Unfortunately I think we can all remember times when we did the right thing, and were still criticized for it. If we are truly looking for the best outcome it may be as well to consider that 'the best' outcome is not always that which we, personally, find most attractive. By phrasing the problem in the way I have here, in a sort of best, good, acceptable, and unacceptable hierarchy, we can begin to see what we may desire and what we consider to be non-negotiable points. If we find ourselves caving in on the non-negotiables we can expect only to feel badly about ourselves.

The point is not to think of winning or losing but to think of a productive solution that does not undermine our own sense of self. If you go into a discussion with this sort of thinking there is a far better chance that you'll protect your needs. We've all been in discussions, I'm sure, where one person becomes deeply upset. In such circumstances I've found myself giving in totally to others' demands, only to regret it later. Sometimes I've been the one who was too emotional to see clearly what I was doing; at other times I've been so moved by my partner's emotions that I've been tempted to give in to everything she wanted. Neither is any use if I've given away my non-negotiable points, the things that are vital to me. Eventually it will simply lead to yet another discussion, except that, as we all know, whenever anyone has the same discussion several times you can be pretty sure it'll get more tense with each repetition.

What is a 'non-negotiable' point? That depends on you, but most people I've worked with have been helped by spelling out such things. Responses have included needing the partner to be sober, drug-free, monogamous, financially solvent, non-violent, a non-smoker (the woman who demanded this had asthma, and so this was not just a preference), and so on. We can all think of people who have partners who have failed in one or more of these categories, and we have most likely seen the effects of that.

Another exercise is one already used in a different way in the section on *Stress*, in Chapter 9, but it serves just as well here.

EXERCISE 4:

- ❖ Make four columns. At the top of the first write: 'Things that are impossible to change.' Write down several things that are impossible to change in the relationship.
- ❖ When you have finished (and only then) write in the next column what it would take to change those items. You can be as extreme as you like. Include things like 'winning the lottery' and even 'leaving the relationship' if you wish.
- ❖ When that list is complete proceed to the next column. At the top of this write, 'If the items in column 1 really did change, what would it mean I'd have to do?' This list may well be more extensive. You may wish to write at length about what you feel here. For example, if your spouse were to stop insisting on buying a larger car, would that mean you would still feel as enthusiastic about the qualities of a smaller vehicle? Sometimes, when someone else stops ramming an idea down our throats it gives us a chance to warm to the merits of their suggestion.
- ❖ In the last column write, in response to each entry, what is to be gained by staying with the situation unaltered.

This last can be the most valuable column of all, and also the hardest to deal with. For instance, the man who did not want children reflected in this section that he had actually enjoyed the fact that someone had wanted to bear children he'd father. It had flattered him. He'd felt loved, needed and indispensable, and he'd like that. If the discussions were to stop, he'd miss that feeling. This underlying agenda had kept him in that mindset, which had nothing to do with the real discussion at hand. He had come to enjoy his role in a drama that was potentially destructive to the relationship. So, what is the pay-off for you in leaving this argument unresolved?

This is only the start of the work that can be done by couples. Use the exercises as a first step to loosen up deadlocks. You may find it necessary to call upon the skills of a couples counselor. If you feel it to be necessary, don't hesitate; your local phonebook or health clinic will be able to help.

And remember: some people like having running disputes that are unresolved. It reassures them that they are part of a relationship that is at least alive (if unhealthy). If they cannot get joy from the relationship then they'll settle for discomfort, because at least that's better than being alone. Being nagged, or even abused, is better than being ignored, to some people. If you are in that sort of relationship you may want to reflect upon why you consider happiness to be something you do not deserve, and why you have chosen this situation.

Given the chance, though, most people want to be happy with their partners and they accept that a certain amount of work may be necessary to achieve this. I have found that the majority of people prefer a compromise solution most of the time. It makes each person feel generous and understanding; it is in fact a way to show love, and to receive love, also. Every obstacle overcome also tends to bind couples closer as they see how they can come to amicable understandings and so value the levels of communication they share. Occasionally the compromises may be trade-offs. I'll agree to your golf games if you'll agree to my Tuesday nights at the bar with the boys. This is healthy. What is not healthy is one person seeking always to have it his or her way. That may be a short term solution to the difficulty, but it is likely to breed contempt on behalf of the dominator and resentment on the side of the one being dominated. This can only cause future strife.

In looking at problem-solving for couples in this way I am not trying to over-simplify the situations that may arise. If one partner has an addiction, for example, there really is no 'solving' that can be done, since the addiction is a situation in which the person puts his or her relationship with a substance (heroin, cocaine, alcohol) or with a behavior (such as gambling) before the relationship with the partner - or anyone else. In such instances professional help only works when the individual asks for it, and is ready to receive it. The exercises we do here will not be of direct help. All they can do is to remind the healthy partner of the attributes that first were attractive in the unhealthy partner. This may help in the process of assessing just how the situation has changed. It can certainly help in the process of letting go - which is what we have to do in relationships where one person is an addict. We cannot let go of someone fully until we have acknowledged all our love and all our hopes for that person, and faced the sad truth that for the present those hopes are empty. "This was not my son," said a woman of forty four. "This was an addict. Once I'd said that, I could save myself from the pain that was unbearable, and get to work on getting him the help he needed." The same thing applies for couples.

What these exercises can do, however, and do well, is to remind each of us of the core of the human being we love, who exists beyond an inability to wash dishes, for example. Inside the person who cannot remember where he left his car keys, or who forgets your birthday, is someone whom you have found to be worth loving. If we focus on the core and not the periphery, we can do ourselves an enormous favor.

This leads me on to the next exercise, which was suggested to me by Melissa Katz at Wellesley College. It can be a long exercise, but it can yield surprising rewards.

EXERCISE 5:

* ❖ Identify the ten or twelve major turning points in your life, occasions when something significant happened that changed the course of events for you. When you have done that, write a few lines about each event.
* ❖ When you have finished (and not until then) do the same thing again but this time take the point of view of the person you are having difficulty communicating with and write about the events in his or her life.

This is a way to see things from the other's point of view, and because it is such a detailed exercise, and one that demands that we engage imaginatively with how the other person thinks and feels, it can reveal some unexpected insights.

Since each individual is unique there's not much point in giving extended examples of responses to this exercise, but a few may help. Two friends who wanted to start a business were highly exasperated with each other. They literally could not understand each other's viewpoints until one of them, doing this exercise, was able to see that his friend and would-be business partner had come through a childhood which had included long periods when he did not expect to be happy. He compared this to his own happy childhood, and began to reflect upon what it meant to be in his friend's situation. Although the friend presented himself as a cheerful person in adult life there was within him a profound sense that the best one could hope for was stoic acceptance of less than perfect situations. When the writer saw this he stopped being annoyed at what he saw to be his friend's lack of vision. Instead he began to question his own eager optimism and to consider that he might have things to learn from this contrast - not the least of which was how to respond to his friend.

I've chosen this last example of a 'couple' that is not a sexual union but a working relationship because I wish to remind you that these exercises can be used in many ways, and indeed probably are best adapted to what you need. I've certainly used this exercise when I've had difficulty understanding family members, and several writers I've worked with have produced novels based on exactly this attempt to understand others in their own terms.

FURTHER PROBLEM-SOLVING EXERCISES

I'd like to take the time to explore further possibilities with you, specifically in the realm of understanding differences that can cause misunderstandings between couples.

One of the things that can happen when opposites attract is that we move beyond our usually self-imposed boundaries to meet that other person. This is normal. So your partner likes to travel to Mexico but you've always chosen to go to Colorado? Well, then, try a trip to Mexico anyway. You may love it. Difficulties can arise when we decide that, perhaps, we do after all prefer Colorado, or New Jersey, or staying home, and the partner is still keen on going to Mexico. Many couples I know have had to deal with this or a similar negotiation. What we can almost always see is that in the rush of enthusiasm in the early days of a relationship we may agree to things that later become onerous. We have extended our boundaries. Sometimes, having sampled the experiences, we find that we want to redefine things more to our usual comfort level. One woman wrote about how she agreed to accept her partner's pet into her life and her home, yet discovered after several months that she had developed an allergy to the beloved dog. Rather than cause trouble she chose to swallow anti-histamines each day in an attempt to block the symptoms. Finally, when she became ill with respiratory problems, she decided to speak out for her own needs, her real boundaries.

EXERCISE 6:

❖ Think for a moment of some of the boundaries you have had to redraw in your relationship. Can you list them? Write about one or more of them. Do you feel your concessions are appreciated?

The replies that this exercise has elicited have included everything from dealing with a partner's smelly feet to having to cope with a partner's children from a previous marriage. Many replies have been tearful. How does anyone cope with a partner who has affairs? Or with one who is more in love with her career than anything else? In each case it's worth recalling that in order for us to give up our precious boundaries we had, once, some very good reasons. We were, in fact, prepared to accept the lover's shortcomings because our love, or our needs, or our sexual desires, urged us to do so. The challenge here is to remember and to value the feeling that prompted you to break your own rules. The danger is that we'll simply be self-critical. "How could I fall for a person who has such boorish manners!" This statement criticizes the writer as being foolish, and the partner as being uncouth. Yet at some point the writer must have been blissfully accepting of those minor blemishes. If we can recall what principles we chose to compromise we can see again more clearly what our wishes and desires for the relationship were at that time. Perhaps you believed that love and gentle tutoring would improve your partner's table manners. If that didn't happen, why not? Did you insist, or did you give up trying? When we give up trying we give up expecting that the other person will extend his or her boundaries to accommodate what we want. The other person's foible thus becomes our failure.

I'm not suggesting we should insist on every little thing we may demand of our partners. That would be absurd. I'm suggesting we can turn a complaint ("he eats with his mouth open no matter how often I tell him") into something else, before it becomes destructive. It could be rephrased as, "I love him and I've been prepared to overlook him eating with his mouth open. Now I'd like to change that." Asking another person to change as an expression of regard for who you are enables you to ask for, and receive, a gift of caring, willingly given.

By making this process conscious we can avoid painful conflicts and move towards productive discussions. The aim is to avoid an unpleasant stale-mate. Here is an example to consider that can show how easy it is to become stuck. In the stereotypical situation it is usually the woman who criticizes the man for not dressing nicely, and the man might then respond by moving into defiant and defensive slovenliness. Angry at being nagged, he provokes more anger because the woman feels he's not listening. Often he's listened only too well. He just doesn't like what he's heard because he feels it as an attack. The challenge here would be how to effect a change in behavior without putting either partner on the defensive.

An extreme example may help illustrate this point further. When I was working with disturbed adolescents one young woman related to me how she never used to wash when she first came to the Home. After several weeks the other young women in her housing unit physically dragged her to the shower, pulled off her clothes, and began to soap her. At first she was terrified, and fought all the way. It wasn't until several months later that she was able to admit her gratitude. "That was the best thing anyone ever did for me, up 'til then, I mean. They showed me they cared." If we can express the caring first there's a far better chance that we can persuade the other to change without having to force a confrontation.

EXERCISE 7:

❖ This is a variation on the previous exercise. Write out your list of boundaries. What are the things you want done differently? Now write it as if from your partner's position. What are the things you imagine he or she wants you to do differently? If you wish you can do this exercise with your partner and compare the responses.

What emerges can often be startling. One man thought his wife wanted him to earn more money, when what she really wanted was for him to take time off, relax, exercise, and stay healthy for a long life ahead. He'd interpreted her requests to go on weekend getaways and vacations together as her wishing for a more glamorous life. He imagined she hankered after five star hotels and fine dining. What she wanted was walks in the country. The complication came when she saw him working harder and still not taking those country walks, and she deduced he was losing interest in being with her. Yet all the time he was working harder because he loved her and wanted to give her what he thought she wanted - at great personal cost.

We all have expectations, which I have here called boundaries, which represent the limits within which we want to live. Periodically we may want to check with our partners as to whether or not these boundaries are still acceptable and still useful.

Here is another example. A man in his forties related a tale that may seem familiar to many of us. He was a quiet man, and after receiving a promotion to a new job he would often come home from a hard day at work dealing with many people, feeling exhausted. What he most wanted at such times was just a few minutes of quiet, to collect his thoughts. His wife, however, was a more extroverting person. When he came home, wanting some quiet time, she was eager to talk about all the experiences of her day. He experienced her enthusiasm as overwhelming, and she saw his quietness as a lack of affection. You can imagine how unhappy they both were with this. Yet each was only being true to who they were. The solution was for the husband to ask for twenty minutes of quiet time when he got home. The wife was happy to do this, as it allowed her to give him a gift of what he needed so that he, in turn, could give her the gift of what she needed, later, in terms of conversation. The new job and its new demands had upset their previous pattern of existence and so their mutual understandings had to be reassessed. The overt acknowledgement of, and respect for, needs and boundaries paved the way to a more harmonious relationship.

Another way to think about it is that we each have our own particular sense of reality. It can be exciting to see someone else's reality - like visiting a foreign country - but it can be exhausting to live there. Each of us shapes that reality through our memories, which in turn define our expectations. Richard Carlson's book *You Can Be Happy No Matter What* has a similar idea. He calls it 'separate realities' and he encourages us not only to look beyond the behavior to see the person, but also to be aware of downward spirals of thinking. These spirals are habits we form that lead us to destructive thinking. If we think, "she always does that..." about someone, no matter who, we are fabricating our version of what we imagine someone else 'always' does. In truth, no one can be said to 'always' do anything, with the possible exception of breathing. Yet there it is, in our minds: this always happens; it's intolerable; why do I put up with it? The reality is far more likely to be that the person we are complaining about has a habit of doing certain things under certain circumstances, and in response we have developed the habit of watching for those things and then responding in a set way.

This is a behavior pattern that we have chosen, and it leads us only to a place where we are disappointed and angry with the other person, a place where we look for more confirmation of what the other 'always' does. Do you see how destructive this is? If I look at someone expecting to find faults, I'll surely find them. Then I can triumphantly claim that, yes, she really does do that, always. I'm right; I'm justified in my rightness - just look at the evidence! Yet I'm only seeing what I've programmed myself to see, and I've probably overlooked many good attributes in the process. This is the 'reality' that we are all capable of manufacturing for ourselves. Notice, we do this to ourselves, and we insist that it's real and that we are right. But it's only a habit of thinking.

Here is an exercise that may help.

EXERCISE 8:

❖ Think of things that your partner does that you like. Make a list. Write in detail about one or more of these. Can you apply the word 'always' to any of the actions?

"He always does the dishes." "He always looks after the cars." "She always deals with the bills." "She always has a little stash of candy that she pretends doesn't exist, and I help myself to it, or hide it from her, and we laugh about it." Each of these responses is a valuing of the other person. Can you replace negative thoughts with positive ones? Yes, you can, and you may want to do so. Look at some of your responses done for the exercises so far, especially exercises 2, 6, and 7. If you see the word 'always' or its equally negative counterpart 'never' linked to a critical comment, try saying instead that your partner tends to do this or that, or has a habit of doing something. Then look at the list of things that your partner does that you like. Preface each one with 'she/he chooses to do...' See how different that is?

These exercises may seem to have focused on trivial annoyances only. I do not think this is the case. I believe that it is the accumulation of trivial annoyances, unchecked, that leads to serious problems in relationships. If we can look beyond the surface, and see the core of the person we love, then the annoyances become less damaging. When we look at another's soul it may not even matter that much that he or she has different religious or political views than we do. It is eminently possible to love and respect another while holding different beliefs. In the contrast we can often find much mental and emotional stimulation, and both partners can grow as a result.

This is not to say that there aren't major and insoluble problems in some partnerships. If one's partner is a substance abuser, or promiscuous, that can be devastating to any relationship. In such cases I'd suggest that what has happened is that one partner has fallen in love with the surface attributes of the other, and has chosen to ignore the true core of the loved one. This is an exact reversal of what I've been talking about so far, in which I've stressed a valuing of the core *first*. If you are in such a relationship you may want to reflect on why you have chosen to overlook this central and most important aspect of your partner's existence in favor of the surface. You are doing the same thing as those couples I have already described, because you are choosing to see only the surface. The only difference may be that for you the surface remains the attraction.

And here is a word of warning: if you find you have a pattern of being drawn to addicted or self-destructive people you may want to note that and get professional help. These exercises will be of use to you, but the situation is too dangerous for you to rely on them alone.

FIGHTS

All couples have arguments. Ideally the arguments clear the air, and both will continue their lives with a renewed sense of what it means to be a couple. It's often been said that successful unions depend in great measure on the ability to have fights and still love each other. I believe this to be true, and the question is: how does one have a productive fight, one that ends up benefiting both?

Successful fighting is usually learned in the family. There siblings can learn all about clashes of interest and rivalries, and they also learn that they can survive them without destroying the love they have for each other. Often fighting can bring us closer. "Women call each other sister only after they've called each other a large number of other names first," so wrote Oscar Wilde, with a gentle mockery that contains a great deal of truth for both sexes.

The major consideration here is how can one learn to fight if it wasn't modeled successfully within the family? The center of this is that one needs to learn how to fight fairly. Here are some guidelines that may help.

1.   Allow enough time and space for the discussion. It's never fair to drop into an argument just two minutes before one of you has to leave, and it is never fair to stage an argument in front of others, such as at a party. The participation of others always muddies the waters. If this discussion is at all important, make the time, and keep it where it belongs. If that means biting your tongue until later, that's what you may have to do.

2.   Choose to fight only about the issue at hand, and don't get side-tracked. In the preceding paragraph the argument that takes place in front of others can become as much about how the disputants feel they are perceived by the crowd as about the topic itself. This is classic side-tracking. Another form this can take is allowing yourself to take a diversion. If you are annoyed about your partner's spending habits don't let yourself to get diverted into a discussion of your mother-in-law's foibles.

3.   When you fight, know that the aim of the fight is not to hurt, or to win, but to make the relationship work better. If you don't want that, don't fight at all.

4.   Only criticize what can be changed. Behaviors can be changed, but physical characteristics cannot. If you are annoyed with your partner, criticizing looks, age, history (for one's history cannot be changed), or even sexuality is not helpful. I have come across men who in argument have made unkind comments about their lover's genitals or breast size, and women who have accused men of being sexually inadequate. Such comments can only humiliate. It's a short term victory and a long term disaster. Focus, instead, on behaviors.

5.   Never walk out of an argument without saying when you'll be back. Everyone has a right to take a time-out, but make sure you announce it and make sure you are back at the stated time, preferably sober and reasonable. What is never acceptable is grabbing the car keys and announcing that you are going to drive off a bridge. That's not fighting clean. That's a combination of blackmail and terrorism. Anyone who uses that tactic loses all respect, and practically invites a callous comment like, "Go right ahead!"

6.   Don't lie. Like putting phony data into a computer, lying will not get you any useful return.

7.   Don't say sorry unless you mean to change the behavior that caused you to have to apologize. Hollow apologies, like blackmail, will kill a relationship in no time at all.

8.   Never use strength or force. I can't think of any situation where it's justified. Some men try to intimidate women by smashing random objects. I've also come across women who have destroyed things that the men in their lives have held dear. This is just another form of terrorism and it's never acceptable.

9.   Try not to let arguments simmer unresolved for a long time after they've happened. Make a time to re-establish peace, and assure your partner of your continuing regard.

10. Be careful how you say what you say. In particular, avoid absolute statements which may sound useful at the time but aren't true. "I never loved you," is not a line of discussion. It can only be a statement that precedes a permanent departure. Just similarly, "I only married you because..." is rarely true or accurate. People

marry for many reasons, and if someone only had one reason to marry then that person's a fool, or a liar. As we know, the concept of 'being in love' is not one reason but two, since the love had to be returned in some form.

With this in mind an important thing to be aware of is the 'you make me feel...' statements. They are simply a form of blaming: you do this to me. No one can make anyone else feel anything, however, so the words are actually not even true. They only have the effect of attempting to make one person into the villain. Try instead saying something like: "when you say/do that I feel..." This has the advantage of avoiding blame and being a more accurate assessment. What is at issue is the action and the reaction, and the aim is to change that pattern. Other words that should be treated with caution are 'always' and 'never' (Exercise 8 discussed some aspects of these) because they are rarely true and usually punishing. A simple 'you don't take out the trash' is less inflammatory than 'you never take out the trash' - and just as true.

All these thoughts may help you to learn how to fight more cleanly and more effectively than before. They may help you to re-negotiate boundaries and understandings so that you can both get what you need from each other. I hope so. So I'd like to add one more observation; most couples, in my experience, fight because one wants to be closer than the other. Think for a moment of how that could be articulated. "I want you take me dancing" might be one way of asking for more shared time. A request to go to Paris, or a desire for a diamond ring may be just different ways of expressing the wish to be regarded as special by the other. Hearing these requests, though, the partner may be taken aback by the expense involved and so miss the emotion that lies behind the wish. And that's how arguments can grow.

MONEY

I've included this after 'Fights' because many couples fight about money. In some ways it is a uniquely volatile area, since money can mean so many different things to people. How hard one has to work to get it, who earns more, who gets to control how much - all are important matters, and have to do with one's sense of independence, also. How much am I allowed to spend on myself? What am I entitled to? Is my partner being responsible with the money?

The following exercises are best done by each partner alone, first, and the results then shared.

EXERCISE 1:

❖   How was money treated in your birth-family?

Being born into a wealthy family does not necessarily mean that money was regarded as a plentiful commodity. Often I've come across poor families in which money was available in a far more open-handed way, although there was clearly less of it than in some richer families. What was your family like? What were the messages you received about saving, spending, and good value? Who controlled the finances? Sharing the results with your partner can be very profitable.

EXERCISE 2:

❖ Do you have any ambitions for your money?

Two people may earn the same amount, but one may be saving for a new kitchen while the other wants to dine out. Or perhaps one is saving for early retirement by investing, and the other anticipates working until seventy. Stating your ambitions for your money can be crucial, since if you are in a partnership it is, presumably, for some years to come and so you will need to clarify your aims to each other as early as possible. Investing all you have in a business venture may be your aim in five years time, but does your partner feel as enthusiastic? Perhaps not.

EXERCISE 3:

❖ What do think your personal style is with money? What do you think your partner's style is? Write down any doubts you have about your partner's ability with money, and anything you admire, as well.

This exercise can bring up some very real worries. The man who spent all his money on his collection of motorcycles but refused to heat the house had a very clear series of ideas about what money was for - it's just that they didn't include much bodily comfort and his wife objected heartily. She admired the fact that his collection was worth a fortune, but she resented being cold. He thought she didn't understand what he was doing. It turned out that she did, but she felt he was a little too extreme in his pursuit of his ambitions. When they shared their perceptions they were able to reach a more equitable understanding while not diminishing either person's sense of being appreciated for who they were.

Clearly there can be many different discussions that arise from this sort of exercise, and I'm not about to go into them all in detail. However, it's well worth remembering that in this, as in all discussions that may arise from this chapter, it's advisable to set aside some time to talk through the issues that arise. If money is a problem, set aside some time to talk freely and non-confrontationally, and do this on a regular basis if necessary. Major companies do it to ensure their survival, and you can, too, since your survival is every bit as important. If you need to hire a money adviser or a debt-restructuring person then do it, but you'll still have to have a very good idea of where your money goes and how it goes there before anyone can advise you. These exercises will help you get to the point where you know what's going on so that you can choose to change, rather than running to catch up to the most recent crisis.

Chapter Twelve

DIVORCE

It's common knowledge that half of all marriages in the U.S. end in divorce. This doesn't necessarily mean that half the people who marry get divorced, simply because quite a few people go through several marriages. An even larger number go through several domestic arrangements that are, to all intents and purposes, exactly like marriages except that they have not been formalized in the eyes of the law or by a religious group.

For some, at least, divorce is so traumatic that risking the same thing again is felt to be too risky. "I'll never marry again," said a university professor after his divorce, and fifteen years later, with three children by his new partner, he's stuck to that. This may seem to be entirely illogical - after all, he is to all intents and purposes married to his new partner - but there is, perhaps, something about the breaking of a formal, legal, socially-sanctioned promise that he sees as being exceptionally difficult, and he has decided not to risk taking it on again. In part this could be because lawyers and strangers become involved in what is essentially a personal and soul-searching decision, and so it is as well to see that there may be an added component to formal marriages that makes them more difficult to break away from.

Whether we define divorce as the end of a marriage or as the end of a long-standing relationship that involved partners living together is less important than an acknowledgment that it can be painful. It can also be a relief. Several people using these written exercises have explored feelings of relief, of freedom at being on their own again.

In this chapter divorce will mean the dissolution of a marriage with the understanding that the non-formalized domestic partnership may well share the same issues. You will be able to use the exercises in several ways. You may be contemplating divorce; you may be in the midst of it, looking for some clarity; or you may have already gone through it, and are seeking to make sense of what has happened. The exercises also work for those directly affected by the actions of others in a divorce. If you are contemplating divorce you might also want to look at the section on *Couples* in Chapter 11 for additional exercises and ideas.

Before we start, though, it may be worth thinking about the pervasiveness of divorce. Christopher Lasch in *The Culture of Narcissism* contends that the proportion of fragmented families is roughly the same in 1980 (when he was writing) as it was in 1900. The difference is that at the turn of the century families were much more likely to suffer the death of a parent, whereas today modern medicine has made this much more rare. Divorce has taken the place of death as a way of terminating marriages. Logically, that doesn't mean that people are just as 'happy' as before - death doesn't strike just the unhappy marriages - but it does give a different perspective. Today children are much more likely to have to deal with the 'absent' parent, usually the father.

In some ways this is much harder to deal with than a death. A father or mother who is lost to death can be seen as a loving presence who has been unfortunately removed. However great the perceived loss, no real blame can be attached to that parent no longer being around. By contrast, a divorced parent who disappears and becomes an absent parent will always be seen as someone who chose to leave, to withdraw affection, or who saw other affections as more important. Children are especially likely to take this personally, and to feel that the parent left because the child was in some way unlovable. This burden of guilt is a frequent phenomenon, and one that can severely damage the child's self-esteem and later relationships.

Having said that, divorce can often be positive. If two people are unhappy together it can be better for both, and certainly better for the children, that they divorce. Divorce at its most basic is an assertion of the desire to be happy, and that is a desire that should surely be honored. The problem seems to be that some people expect happiness to arrive without much effort on their behalf. These are the people who may have trouble staying in a relationship of any sort, and they may not know what happiness is for them, anyway. The restless search for happiness without any true idea of where it is to be found or how one will recognize it, is probably a search that is doomed. If you feel yourself to be like this you may want to pause and ask yourself why you think happiness depends on the other person, and not on yourself.

The ease with which divorce papers can be obtained sometimes works to prevent people from thinking seriously about their emotional commitments. If it doesn't work it's easy to get out, they may think. A string of unsuccessful attachments can become a substitute for the search for real happiness. If one is constantly on the look out for another partner then there's little impetus to think about whether or not one may want to reassess the way one runs one's life. The thrill of the chase may be so great that we forget what the whole point of the matter is.

In this chapter I'd like to suggest that no divorce is ever entirely easy. The disruption, the dislocation of life for all concerned, can never be taken casually. Whether you are a person who has divorced, is considering divorce, or if you are the child of divorced parents you will find this section useful.

EXERCISE 1:

- ❖ Think of the marriage. Recall one of the best moments.
- ❖ Pause.
- ❖ Now recall one of the worst moments.

Some people can only recall the bad moments, which is why I started with a suggestion to work first on the good aspects. Often, when prompted, people can think of several good things about even very poor alliances. Remember - it was the good stuff that made you link with this person to begin with.

It is important to recall this for several reasons. The first is that what attracted you once will probably attract you again, to someone else; and if it does you'll want to make sure that you know how to identify the good aspects and see any potential red flags, too. Sometimes the good and the bad are inextricably intertwined. A man recorded that he fell in love with the woman he married because she was 'strong' and didn't put up with any manipulation. He loved her independence. It was when he felt this strength of character was being used against him, when he felt criticized and belittled, that he sensed the relationship was beyond repair. In this example the best qualities of the partner, the reason he had admired her to begin with, were actually those which caused him the greatest pain. Best and worst are sometimes linked in this way.

Another reason to recall the best moments is that we need to value a relationship before we can understand it, and so let it go. If we continue to cast the rejected partner in the role of villain we can't understand that person or why we loved him or her. Instead all we can do is blame ourselves. "Why was I such a fool?" we may say to ourselves. We may have been foolish, certainly, but by criticizing ourselves all we do is make ourselves trust our own judgment less than before. Blaming doesn't allow us to learn so we can do better next time. An illustration may help. A teacher who wishes to be effective must do many things but two are especially important. One is to correct errors; the second is to praise what is done correctly. The teacher from hell is one who only points out faults, leaving the students crippled with the fear of making mistakes. In fact the students may not know what the correct way is. All they may learn is what the wrong way looks like. A better method is to praise what is done correctly, to build up strengths. By valuing the good aspects of the relationship you are building on your own strengths. So, ask yourself, what did you love to do together?

The exercise produces bittersweet replies. A typical one would be from the woman who said that she had such fun with her spouse, but he was so irresponsible she couldn't live with him, and he was constantly doing things that put them in debt. Again - the same aspect has two different sides to it; at least two.

EXERCISE 2:

❖ With Exercise 1 in mind write an apology. You can apologize to your spouse or to someone else. If you are looking at this from the point of view of the child in a divorce, write an apology you would like to have heard given to you, or that you would have liked one of your parents to have given the other. If you wish you can write an apology to a parent.

❖ If you prefer, you can write a sarcastic apology.

An apology, even a sarcastic one, is an admission that you had a part to play in the failed relationship. It can be very hard to admit this at the time, but it's never too late. In some cases, particularly the child's apology, it may show the perception the child had of being responsible. In reality the child is almost never responsible. It's important, though, to get the information, the feeling, to acknowledge the self-blaming and so move beyond it. We must admit the feelings before we can let them go.

Sometimes people write very moving apologies to their spouses - a recurrent theme seems to be that if they had both been a little wiser or calmer or a little better as people, then they might have been together still. Realizations such as that are probably not enough in themselves to allow two estranged people to link up again, so do not jump to any conclusions. The apology is the place in which one can see one's wisdom. The relationship may be over, or changed for all time, but that does not mean that the time spent together was wasted. Quite the contrary. It is the ore out of which one mines the gold of wisdom.

EXERCISE 3:

- ❖ This builds on Exercise 2.
- ❖ What would it have taken to put the relationship right? If the relationship is going on now, what would it take to save it?

Asking this question and answering it honestly is a way of accessing one's learning about the past, and one's wisdom. In response people have said many things such as, "If I'd been more patient..." or "If we could just have been better at communicating our needs..." In each case there is an admission that another tactic could have been applied, but it wasn't possible at the time. A middle-aged man made this very telling statement: "Given who I was then and who she was then, we did the best we were capable of doing. That was then. I could have done better now." Notice what he said: "Given who I was then..." We are, in effect only as capable as we can manage to be *at the time*. The great solution that comes to mind too late is not useful. Wisdom is not just knowing something, but it's being able to access it when needed. Possibly something in your relationship stopped you from gaining full access to your wisdom. If you are unhappy or anxious, it's hard to see things clearly, and so making good choices becomes impossible.

The purpose of this exercise is to re-value what you know. After a failed relationship we all tend to feel useless, that sense of "I'll never get it right" which lets us see only our errors and not our strengths. It's a frame of mind that prevents conscious learning about what happened. If we don't take the time to acknowledge what we've learned, how can we ever hope to do better?

The next exercise can be demanding, but also rewarding.

EXERCISE 4:

- ❖ Write about divorce from the other person's point of view.
- ❖ Write about it from the other person's parents' point of view.

This takes an imaginative effort, and every response requires us to consider that our actions, which made perfect sense to us at the time, may well have bewildered others. Thinking our way into the other person's place asks us to reassess ourselves, certainly, but it also asks us to reassess the partner. Was yours a very bitter divorce? Who was the most upset? It wasn't until he began to write about it that a forty two year old man was able to see his ex-wife's bitterness as the negative aspect of her original love of him. "It was as if I'd been a child, and she'd given me more and more toys to play with. When it all fell apart she wanted to take all the toys back."

Very often divorce includes arguing over who owns what and who is entitled to what. Seeing it from the other person's point of view can help to reduce the sense of personal injury we may initially feel. Stories abound of course: the man who wrecked the family's Mercedes rather than let his ex-wife get it. In a TV commercial, recently, a rich man is seen reading the divorce papers he's been served. Realizing his wife is asking for half of everything, he takes out a chainsaw and begins cutting everything in half. This is comic, but blind rage such as that is what often comes to light in the real world, too. What I want you to do in this exercise is to give some space to the rage you may have felt, and then move past that impulse of wanting to make the other person pay. That sense of injury can only keep us angry, and as such it stops us seeing what really happened. This is shown very movingly in these words written by a man in his late thirties. "When I saw it from her point of view, I stopped feeling she was out to get me, and I began to see how her anger was an aspect of her sorrow. Once I saw that I could feel my own sorrow. If we could have got there sooner perhaps we could have avoided hiring those lawyers. Those guys were the only people who got rich off this."

Often the other person's point of view is hard to achieve, but it can be a revelation once one gets there. One couple went to a mediator, who calculated the child support the husband had to pay. "I never realized how much kids cost until then," the man confessed. He'd never made much money and his wife had struggled to raise the family and hold on to her job. "When I saw that, I could see why she resented the way our marriage had gone." Obviously this example didn't come as a result of the exercise, but I offer it to you because it's such a clear example of how we can fail to see the other person's point of view. Until we do see it, we can't make the changes that will allow us to stop repeating the same disastrous errors. That's what this exercise is about.

Writing the exercise from the point of view of the spouse's parents can be a stretch as well, although one that can often be worth the effort. In-laws certainly do exert a pressure on a relationship, either good or bad, and sometimes they can sense things that the participants don't. The mother-in-law who claims they were never right for each other may, in fact, have some wisdom to share. This sort of insight, however, can be used in many ways. Did this person's feelings lead to actions that helped to undermine the relationship in some way? Parents know their children very well but they know them best as children, and the grown adult may be different. So what were the pressures that came from the parents? If you found yourself swayed by their point of view were you allowing yourself to fall into an old pattern of child-like deference? Or were you, perhaps, scornful of what they said because they represented many things that you had long ago rejected? And could they have been right, despite this?

If you are married, you can still do these exercises as imaginative experiments. Here is an exercise that you can do if you are contemplating divorce.

EXERCISE 5:

❖ Imagine the impact divorce would have on you. What would it do to others in the family circle? What about the children?

Again - it's difficult for some people to project into the realm of possibility, but it can be very useful. Many people don't look behind the event to see the reality of what it means. Divorce usually means at least one person has to find a new home, often both, and it can involve substantial financial re-arrangement. Imagine if both partners have to find new homes. The old home has to be sold (which can take a long time), the proceeds have to be divided equitably; cars may have to be sold, furniture sold, or stored, and then new furniture purchased for new homes. Children may have to leave neighborhoods where they had friends. They may even have to change schools. None of this is news, but all of it may surprise us with how demanding it can be to settle these aspects of life. And that is just the practical stuff - before one has faced the heartbreak. Who gets the kids? For how long each week? What are the visitation rights? What does that feel like? Some people's careers never fully recover from divorce - even though they themselves may insist that divorce is the best and only way. Relationships with children are almost always damaged, or at the very least, dislocated. The fact that one's father may be a lazy wastrel doesn't stop a child loving that father and needing that person, if only to see his short comings and ultimately to reassess the relationship at some point. The absence of either parent is a profound loss.

It may seem that this exercise is not very helpful. Consideration of all these changes would probably stop most people contemplating divorce from going any further. I am aware of this. But I am also aware of the reality of divorce. My point is that many of us, when we are unhappy in a relationship, decide that leaving our partners may be the only way to proceed. Since we are unhappy we may not be able to make the best decisions or see as clearly as we might wish. The important thing, here, is to ask you to look at the reality of what you may be proposing. Look at it soberly, then decide. Pretending that it's "no big deal", as one man put it, is stupid and dangerous.

"I never thought I'd miss the kids so much, even though I see them almost every day." So wrote a woman of 48 who had chosen to divorce her husband and move out. She could not have predicted how that would feel before the divorce, and yet, as she went on to write, even if she had been able to see into the future she would still have chosen to leave the husband. As she wrote the pain of regret became transformed into a clear-eyed acceptance of what she needed to do for herself, and the price that she realized she had to pay.

EXERCISE 6:

❖ Write about money in this relationship.

❖ When you've done that, reflect on how your partner may feel about the things you've written.

Responses to this exercise are often very long and detailed. Some people who have written about this question have produced page upon angry page about how much they gave to the union, and how it wasn't appreciated. Once one is past the initial anger, however, it is worth looking at the second part of the question.

Money is in itself just paper, but it is a symbolic exchange that can mean more to some people than to others, and so it is an area of emotional tension. A man who earns $8:50 an hour may resent his wife's desire to see movies at $9 a time and he may focus on the money. While he does so, he may fail to see how his wife is enlivened and energized by the outing, and so he fails to comprehend that this is a good way to spend money as far as the relationship is concerned. Similarly, he may regard the movies as 'a waste' as he saves for a down payment on a new car. The question has to be, does his wife feel the same pleasure in the new car that he does? She may not. In a worst case scenario, he'll accuse her of being wasteful and silly, and she'll see him as cheap, and having bizarre priorities. It's an argument 'about' money, but really it's a clash of values. The wife may need the movies as a way of mentally refreshing herself; the husband may need the car as a way of feeling important, that he has something to show for his work. Both may feel they need these things to be happy, but if the focus is just on the money the discussion might never get to this point of mutual comprehension.

Money can be a useful discussion point in other ways, too. Money means independence. Did each partner have his or her own money? Were earnings comparable? Who supported whom, and what did that feel like? Some men feel very insecure unless they earn most of the money - and if they do they may feel they have a right to dictate how it's used. Does any of this sound familiar?

Money, of course, is what comes into focus in divorce. Partners claim back what they feel to be theirs but they do it in terms of money. The irony is that marriage is not like a job in which every hour of overtime is paid at a certain rate. In any relationship there's a huge amount of unrecognized - one could say, unpaid - labor. This can never be truly factored into the dividing of possessions, although we may feel it should. "She'd never have had that job if I hadn't spoken to..." one man raged. Yes, he did a good thing for her. But to use it as a reason to cut back on child support is not a good idea. Again, a mechanic in his thirties was forced to sell off a car he'd restored. "It's worth $10,000, book value," he said, "but I put in all the work that made it worth that. Now she wants half!" One can almost imagine the wife's response, that he'd put their money into the restoration, and his work was part of the partnership, so why not half? After all, she brought him sandwiches, cleaned the house, did his laundry. Without that he wouldn't have worked so efficiently, so she was a partner, wasn't she?

My favorite example of money comes from a practice adopted at one time by British marriage guidance counselors. They gave both people in the troubled marriage some plastic coins with different values written on them. They asked the partners to give each other this money whenever the other did something that was particularly appreciated. So the wife might give her husband a twenty pence coin for bringing home the groceries, or fifty pence if he cooked a delicious meal, but only five pence for a cup of coffee. He might give her forty pence for fixing the car and so on. The plastic money helped couples show when and how they appreciated each other, something they might not have been able to express otherwise. The fact that the money was plastic also helped to show that in any domestic relationship there's a huge amount of unpaid labor for which thanks is the only reward. Still, because it's unpaid, thanks become doubly important. It's this unpaid work we tend to want to claim when divorce occurs, because that's where we felt least valued, and we claim it through the other material things that can be priced.

"She was lost when we met. I made her who she is. Now she wants half of what's mine." So wrote a man of fifty. I don't know that there's any right or just answer to his complaint. What was important to him was that he felt he should be paid, somehow, or allowed credit for what he contributed to his spouse's development. And didn't she contribute something to her own development, too? I'm sure she did. He did not 'make' her who she became. He may well have helped her see possibilities, but it was she who took that and did something with it. And that's what a partnership is, when it works well - an arrangement that allows each to help bring out the best in the other. Why should one of the successes of the partnership now be used as a source of contention? This is a classic example of someone who wants to be angry and who wants to hold on to that anger, even though the circumstance gives no reasonable justification for it. If we choose to do this - and there will be times when we will - nothing can change in our own lives.

This leads us to the next exercise, but I'll also refer you to the exercises on pages 158-159, which are specifically about couples and money.

EXERCISE 7:

❖ Draw up a list of all the things you feel you contributed to the relationship. What did your spouse contribute? Did either of you gain from what was provided by the other? How? If this seems too analytic, focus on one main thing you feel contributed to you or your spouse's future.

An older man from Europe wrote movingly about how he felt his wife had gained from his emotional support, without which she might have remained very confused. In return he had gained because she had been the reason he had come to the U.S. His life had changed materially for the better, even though he missed his friends and relations. When the couple divorced she tried to make him feel an obligation to her for bringing him to the States. She felt she'd done him a huge favor, and she therefore deserved thanks. He felt he'd been equally generous, as it were, by helping her through some difficult issues. When the man began to see that both of them had contributed in different ways, he was able to let go of his resentment and move on with his life.

The chances are that you may have forgotten to see how each of you gained in the relationship. "He was exactly what I needed at the time," one woman reported, "even though I knew there were things in the marriage that weren't properly balanced. And he needed me to be that way. Neither of us want to keep on being that way now." There's an implicit sense in this of two people who are beginning to see that they were right for each other at the time but that something had changed. They'd supported each other, and that in turn had allowed them both to grow to the point at which the relationship needed to be redefined.

Here's a different exercise:

EXERCISE 8:

❖ Suggest divorce to someone else. What would it involve? Would it be the only solution?

It's said misery loves company, and one could expect a large number of responses in which people claim that this major step is the only way forward. In fact, by the time people have finished writing this exercise one can often note that they've put in a lot of 'if' statements. "If he won't stop drinking…" "If she insists on treating you that way…" Statements that begin with if are usually hopeful, since they mark behaviors that have to be changed and expectations that have to be met, all of which could save the marriage if relayed to the spouse.

Sometimes this exercise has allowed people to write about the heart-ache of their own divorce, and occasionally they'll make statements that show just how hard the decision was, and how hard it has been to live with it. People who might never let on that they'd suffered will write with tremendous emotion when advising someone else. Again, what these people are doing is contacting their own hard-won wisdom about their experiences, and questioning the price they had to pay. Any teacher will tell you that the only way to learn something fully is to teach it. This is a chance to do just that. In the process we are more or less forced to come to some conclusions about our own past actions and what they meant. You may even find that you admit to making a number of mistakes in the relationship, and that there may have been other options open to you that you didn't explore. You may have been so eager to leave the situation that you just couldn't see it clearly, you jumped to conclusions, you missed opportunities. We all tend to do this. The point is that unless we notice these things, unless we take the time to reconsider relationships and why they failed, there's not much chance of getting it right in the future.

An example may help. A man of forty eight wrote about how he felt strongly attracted to a woman during the time that his marriage was in difficulties. "I kept torturing myself: should I leave and live with this woman, or should I stay with my wife? And then it got so I was seeing all the things I didn't like about my wife and comparing them to the fun I was having with this woman, and it was driving me nuts. It wasn't until I realized that this was not an either/or proposition that I began to make sense of it all. The fact that there was trouble in my marriage didn't mean that the other relationship was better." The tendency to jump from the frying pan into the fire could hardly be better illustrated.

Within this section on divorce I've encouraged you to raise some questions and I've tried to put the answers others have provided into a perspective that may be helpful. There will always be more questions, however, and some are too specific to be able to benefit from the sorts of general answers a book can give. One woman asked how she could deal with her ex-husband's new wife, whom she had to see whenever she dropped the children off. She felt nervous about this because the new wife was the 'other woman' in the divorce. There's no straightforward answer, here. This is made more complicated because the children may or may not like the new spouse. There may be a tendency for the children to be wooed by one side or the other as a consequence of the divorce struggle. It may turn into a case of: 'Come stay with Daddy. You'll have a much nicer time, and lots more toys.' This sort of crude bribery can only do damage and drive the antagonism into a different phase. I'd maintain that the exercises we've looked at here are a way to head off such tactics before they happen. The problem is that one can't make one's ex-spouse do the exercises! If you find yourself faced with a situation in which the children are at risk of being used as weapons, you can do several things. The first is not to play the game. Children are very sensitive to many things and they know when they're being bribed. What they appreciate is not gifts, treats, or whatever, but a parent who is open and honest about what's going on. Since approximately 80% of women find themselves financially worse off after divorce and only 45% of men are worse off (according to an *Utne Reader* survey) this means that many children will perceive that things are better at Dad's - and since most children are given to the custody of their mothers, Dad's will seem like a vacation in many cases. These seem to be the facts of present day America. The facts can help us put our feelings into perspective. There is going to be an imbalance. We have to see it and be aware of it.

EXERCISE 9:

❖ What do you feel you've been left to take care of as a result of the divorce? What do you think your former partner feels?

The answer here, most frequently, is "the children". Often one spouse feels he or she is left to raise the kids. The other feels he or she (usually he) has to pay for kids he hardly sees. Each side feels cheated. The reality? Children take a huge amount of time, energy, love, care, and money. In addition, children can also be a source of love, satisfaction, and delight greater than anything else on earth. You may feel you've been left with a burden. You may feel crushed by the demands of work, survival, and children. These are real demands and the source of great stress. Several women have written, movingly, of their desperation at being left to take care of the children with inadequate resources, and yet all of them have expressed a sense of pity at what their former husbands missed in the way of daily interaction with the children. No amount of money can compensate for relationships that did not grow.

Divorce is never easy, and poverty is a terrible strain that should never be underestimated. Under its pressure we may stop being able to think creatively so we can shape a better future. In this book I cannot tell you how to get a better job. I can only suggest that the exercises here may put you in a better place so that you can deal with your divorce and leave it behind you. Then you can use the energy liberated by that to find the job and the life you really want. Get those feelings out and then realize you've also been given a wonderful opportunity. It's your choice how you rise to the occasion.

ILLNESS

Illness comes to us in many ways. It slows us down, causes suffering, and changes the whole attitude of our lives. Even something as common as an allergy transforms a normal day into a miserable one.

Illness can be seen as existing in three forms. The first is acute illness, the type that hits hard but which we recover from, even if some of our capacities may not recover fully. Pneumonia may lay us low: we fight it off, but our lungs are perhaps weakened. This experience is qualitatively different from that of chronic illness, which may not be quite as dramatic but can continue for years or even decades. This sort of struggle is very different for the sufferer, and the issues it raises for family and friends may be different, also, as they watch the ebb and flow of the ailment. The third category is chronic and fatal illness. There is no known cure for AIDS, although there is often a time of remission, as there is with some fatal cancers. In the case of many of these illnesses the initial onset is almost unnoticed.

Accidents, on the other hand, are usually accompanied by shock and trauma, and we may take months to recover. We may not recover fully.

Whether you are ill, personally, or close to someone who is, these exercises can be useful. If you are in the company of a sick person just rephrase the question so it includes you. If you are particularly concerned with accidents you may want to jump ahead to the next section of this chapter which deals specifically with accidents. I'll point out, though, that there may be much to be gained from working through all the exercises as they are presented here, since many of the same issues will arise.

I take the trouble to spell out these obvious differences because the nature of your illness will, in one way and another, shape the way you respond to it. It may seem, however, that writing about one's feelings regarding illness can only serve to soothe or to vent emotions. It can certainly do both of these, but there is more. James Pennebaker's *Opening Up: the healing power of expressing emotions* (1990, 1997) makes it abundantly clear that disclosing emotions can not only help heal us when we are ill, but can keep us healthy throughout our lives. Professor Pennebaker's studies are based on over twenty years' worth of research and analysis of data, rigorously tested. His conclusions show again and again that writing out one's emotions can lead to an enhancement of physical health. What this means for this chapter is that writing has been shown to lead to better physical health, as well as mental health. It is able to do so because it can help us to gain a sense of understanding about what happening to us, and that allows us to feel less helpless. When we are ill we are likely to feel at our most vulnerable and at our least empowered. Paradoxically this is also the time when we may find that those around us don't want to hear what we have to say. They may see it as us complaining - or we may be afraid that they will. This sort of inhibition has, in itself, been shown to cause disease and worsen existing conditions. In fact not being able to communicate good news has also been demonstrated to lead to the same sorts of stresses that can cause illness. Pennebaker puts it like this:

> Wonderful and traumatic experiences are often intertwined.... The central physiological similarity, then, between the disclosure of positive and negative thoughts and feelings is in the reduction of inhibition. (p.122)

It is the inhibition - the failure to write, speak, or in other ways disclose the feelings that we may have - that is so damaging, even if original feelings are those of pleasure. With this in mind, this first exercise may help. It can be useful equally to those who are ill and those who are caring for them.

EXERCISE 1:

❖ If you had to see yourself as an animal, or could wish to be one, what would it be?

A man who was dealing with his wife's illness described himself as an Eagle. When asked to reflect on this image, what attracted him to it was that as an eagle he could soar above all the difficulties, alone and free. Seeing himself this way gave him the chance to reflect on what he was really feeling about the demands his wife's illness would make on him, and his desire to escape from it all. An answer from a young woman whose glandular imbalances had made her severely overweight was that she wished she could be an elephant, since elephants were large but they were fully protected by a thick hide. Her reply was 'thin-skinned' one might say. She was as much afraid of what others said about her as of the disease itself. A different reply came from a young woman who was watching her mother recover from alcohol-related illness. She said she wanted to be a little furry caterpillar, curled up asleep under some leaves. Her image of herself was of a helpless creature that just wanted to be left to sleep. It's not hard to see in this a desire to avoid pain and even to slip into depression - which is often characterized by the desire to sleep, to pull the blankets over one's head and not be present in the moment.

Reflect for a moment on your choice of animal. How vulnerable was the creature you chose? What qualities does it have? The woman who likened herself to a deer might have been expressing a timid and gentle nature. You may want to spend some time writing about your choice of animal. If you can, develop a narrative about the life of this animal.

EXERCISE 2:

❖ Can you recall when you first discovered what was wrong with you? What was your reaction? What's your reaction now?

The exercise works for accident victims as well since it sometimes takes a good amount of time before the doctors know the full extent of the damage and what may need to be done. Memories of the event vary hugely. For some people it's an instantaneous change: "I'll never walk again" for example, can only fill one with fear. For other people the event may be confusing - the reaction may be, "What does it mean, this disease I can't even pronounce? What will happen to me? How do I find out?" In all these cases keeping the feeling bottled up is about the worst thing one can do - yet that's usually what happens. We feel we have to be strong in front of our families; we can't weep in front of our doctor, we have to seem calm. In responding to this question some people write with relief, because they've never had any chance to unload those feelings until now.

It's important for you to see where you have gone, emotionally, since you were diagnosed. You may be more relaxed, calmer, more resigned, or more depressed than you were initially. Why? Because often when we are suffering we collapse into ourselves until it feels as if we've always been suffering. Faced with pain we sometimes don't know we have any choices for dealing with it. Sometimes we can't even remember what it felt like not to be in pain - that world is a dream to us. This type of thinking is dangerous since it leads to depression and depression has been shown to retard helpful healing processes and accelerate the effects of chronic disease. Use this exercise to look into your disease and see which reaction you have chosen, even if you didn't realize you'd chosen it. Could you choose a different reaction?

EXERCISE 3:

❖ How do you talk about your illness?

Some people talk and write about their illnesses with an air of defeat, and so convince themselves of the validity of their depression. "I can't seem to shake it," is different from: "I'm not going to let this thing beat me" - and not just in the sense of the attitudes they convey. One is an expression of not being able to do something: "I can't". The other is filled with determination to "beat this thing" - notice how the illness is referred to as an external item. Do you feel your illness is part of you or as if it's a strange and alien item that has temporarily got hold of you? The refusal to accept that the disease has any right to be in your body has been cited in many studies as a helpful attitude, one that promotes more successful outcomes. Surrender to the ailment is rarely productive of anything but more misery. In these circumstances anger at the disease may be beneficial as well as being a natural feeling. This mind-body connection is well worth emphasizing. Brian L. Weiss, M.D. puts it succinctly in his book *Through Time into Healing* (1993):

It is well known that the mind can strongly influence the body, causing symptoms, disease, and even death. All physicians know of hospital patients who gave up on life for one reason or another. Despite the best medical treatments and technology available, these patients wither away and die. (p.58)

How you talk about your illness reflects how you feel about it, and it can also shape how you feel about the possible outcome. If you see the illness as a judgement upon you, or as a curse - as people I have worked with have sometimes said - you may not be as able to raise the energy necessary to fight it off effectively. Try seeing it as something that will have to be dealt with and can be defeated, if it is an acute disease. If this is an incurable disease you may want to try thinking about it as something that, for all its pain and distress, still leaves you the chance to live your life and experience happiness.

Caroline Myss in her impressive volume *Why People Don't Heal And How They Can* (1997) puts this even more strongly: "As terrifying as disease is, it is also an invitation to enter into the nature of mystery." Seeing disease as opportunity is not a new idea, but it may feel impossible to those in pain. It's hard to respond to mystery when you're in agony. Nevertheless, to give in to the physical symptoms is the first step in giving in totally. Myss is very emphatic about this, which she calls "woundology".

When we define ourselves by our wounds we burden and lose our physical and spiritual energy, and open ourselves to the risk of illness.

Myss' main interest is in tracing a link between physical illness and unresolved mental distress, the 'wounds' in question, which I like to see as the tendency that many of us have to play the role of victim. In fact Myss describes as well a tendency that exists in physical illness: if we identify ourselves by our illness it can open us up to even more disease. Myss is very brusque about this, pushing aside wishful thinking and dreaminess. Determination is what gets us through disease. "You don't need a wishbone, you need a backbone," she writes.

I quote Myss here because she reminds us of something we very much need to recall. None of us would dream of allowing ourselves to be categorized as being merely black, white, or hispanic, for instance. It's not only degrading and racist, it's also illegal. Yet we routinely seem to do this to ourselves when we describe ourselves in terms of illness. You may have lung cancer, or a heart condition, or whatever it is that ails you, but you are not your illness. You are more.

The next exercise takes a different tack.

EXERCISE 4:

❖ Write a letter to a child under the age of five, whom you know and care about, explaining what is wrong with you. Alternatively, write a letter addressed to a pet you have or may once have had, to explain the situation. You may need to imagine the recipient, or think of someone as he or she once was at age five.

The disadvantage here is that you may not have a pet or a child to whom you can express your thoughts, but the chances are good that most of us have a young relative somewhere. Obviously, children under the age of five are unlikely to be able to read, and pets can't read either, but they can see and they can feel, and they want to understand what will happen. The exercise therefore demands a specific sort of writing in which details are kept to a minimum and concealment is useless.

This exercise came into being because a woman I worked with chose as an exercise to write a letter to her beloved dog, who could see she was ill but had no clear understanding of what that might mean, and so had become very protective of her. When she had finished the letter she then wrote one back, as if it had come from the dog.

What makes this exercise so powerful is that pets and small children know instinctively that something is not right and they need reassurance. In reassuring others we can often find our own way to calming ourselves. We are, in effect, writing to the frightened child within ourselves, and we know we can't fool ourselves. Furthermore, pets and small children are wonderful examples to us of unconditional love - which is something we may feel we need before we can speak openly about our fears.

This exercise can lead us to state our true feelings quite simply, also. So often that can seem impossible as our lives become tangled and our relationships become complex. Writing to those with whom we've had differences takes care and courage, and is beset with doubt. It might be the next step after this exercise, though.

And here it's worth making a few comments about what pets and children can tell us. A dog will always love its owner, totally; and a young child will, also, love those who care for her. This experience of unconditional love can teach us a huge amount. The dog doesn't care what you look like today, or what sort of day it's been: the dog is always pleased to see you. If dogs can teach us about giving love, then cats can teach us about accepting love and loving oneself no matter what. Every cat I've ever met, except those which have been mistreated, has lived in no doubt whatsoever that it is absolutely lovable. The ugliest, most scruffy cat in the world will come and sit on your lap and never consider that she is not acceptable company. We can learn about self acceptance from cats. If you are ill this can be a very important message to hear. Even though you are ill you still deserve love.

EXERCISE 5:

❖   What has your illness taken away? What has it given you?

A man who broke his legs in a car accident keenly regretted the loss of mobility, and the fact that he was dependent for so many things. He wrote with anger and annoyance in response to the first part of this exercise. Then, as he tackled the second part, he wrote about how he wished he could have learned how to slow down in some less dramatic way. He'd learned that he didn't need to rush about quite as much as he used to, and he'd learned to take time for his own needs, and for his family. He saw that his accident had given him something he didn't even realize he needed - a reason to stop doing so much busy work.

For some of us, being dependent goes against everything we feel we are. These are the people who will most often write about how the illness has allowed them to ask for, and accept, help from others. One man wrote about how at first he'd been embarrassed at his incapacity, but that he'd noticed how people liked to help him - how those he'd been kind to in the past had responded with something close to relief when they'd seen they could be of service to him. "I guess my pride had sort of kept them at a distance. When you don't let anyone help you, you don't let yourself need them. And no-one wants to be where they're not needed." Illness had hurt him, but it had given him the chance to deepen his friendships, and he was thankful for that gift, a gift of love.

This leads to the next exercise:

EXERCISE 6:

❖ Has your illness made you depend more on others? How do you feel about this? If you prefer, write about an instance of someone helping you. If you're already the helper, you may want to write about what it means to be in that role.

Inevitably any illness makes one depend more on others, but it makes us dependent in new ways. A woman who had always cared for her husband's needs found that he was now only too eager to care for her. She had depended on him for the family's income (she was a full-time home-maker), but now she was astonished at how he organized his life and the children's lives so they could attend to her. The whole question of who depended on whom was raised to a new level. It wasn't just physical help that was offered, because each person was helping out of love for the woman, and love for the family as a unit that needed all its members to cooperate.

A man whose wife had cancer, and who had been given less than a year to live, related a very touching tale. As soon as she knew how much time she had left, the wife took him aside and said she was going to teach him how to cook. He said that wasn't necessary. She insisted, saying that she knew he couldn't cook to save his life, and that he needed to feed himself properly. "Besides," she said, "if you can't cook you'll go marrying the first woman who fries you an egg, and then where'll you be?" Her gift was a realistic gift of love. She wanted him to be well fed after she died (and in the final stages of her cancer, too) and she wanted him to be in a strong situation so he wouldn't feel he had to find another wife to look after him. She wanted him to have time and space in which to run his life, and even to choose a new spouse if he wished. Her gift to him was an unsentimental and clear-eyed gift of love, and he recalled it with great emotion. He also took great pride in his cookery, making sure he did it properly, "for her sake" as he said. What happened, here, was that a potentially disastrous situation had given rise to extraordinary expressions of love.

AIDS patients have also spoken and written about similar levels of caring, often made poignant because one partner may have full-blown AIDS while the other knows that he or she may have contracted the virus from the dying partner. This would certainly be a situation that would need to be written and talked about. When one is on a journey through pain to certain death the thoughts and feelings have to come out, or the individual feels close to explosion point. Explosions of emotion usually occur because the feelings have been left too long and have become too big to be easily manageable. By considering the questions in the exercise the huge, overwhelming sense of one's situation can be broken down into sections that are easier to handle, without causing the issue to be trivialized. We all want a handle on our emotions, on our situation. These exercises can provide it.

EXERCISE 7:

❖ Describe any medications you may take, or any special procedures you may have to be part of. If you are the care-giver who has to ensure these medications are attended to, write about that.

Some student nurses I worked with decided as part of their senior year project to ask geriatric patients to write about their medications. They expected to get only a few replies. In fact every patient they asked replied and many wrote ten pages or more. It seems no one had ever asked them how they felt about the tablets and injections they were given, or the procedures they were asked to undergo. What came out was a flood of emotion, much of it angry. They were angry that doctors made decisions about them without letting them make up their own minds; they were angry that most doctors didn't listen, or talked down to them, or failed to register their comments; they were angry at the side-effects; at the complexity of it all, and at the way they felt they had been marginalized as 'sick' people.

What came through these peoples' words was a huge amount of anger at being ill, at being old, and at having to approach death without much chance of dignity. "I haven't time for all that stuff," one man wrote, by which he meant that he had to face his impending death (he was 90) and all this medical "stuff" just got in the way. "When it gets too complicated I'll just stop eating. That way I'll be dead in a couple of days," said one old woman, who wanted to die with the minimum of fuss. She, like many others, perceived some of the doctors as out of touch with the realities of being old. These patients didn't want more time, they wanted more dignity in the time they had left.

If it seems to you that all this talk about death is unusually unpleasant in a discussion of illness, I'd point out that every illness reminds us of our mortality. Anyone who fails to think of that is probably defending against one of life's great realities. It's easy to do this in the US, which is a youth-based culture. Young is good. Young is praised on all our TV channels, and to be old is to be out of it. Entirely. If one were to take the ages of all the stars one sees on TV and average them, I suspect that the preferred age for a media personality is about twenty-five. If we then ask what age characters most of these actors play on screen, we'd have to reduce that to twenty or less. Tina Turner still looks 'great' at fifty plus, where 'great' is an implicit comparison to twenty year-olds. In a room full of ordinary people of her age she just might look like a freak.

To return to the medications, many people feel anger at being tied to a regimen of pills. One young woman reported she preferred to ignore her diabetes because she didn't want to think of herself as physically limited in any way, and so she tended not to take her medications or obey the doctor's strictures against alcohol.

Even when talking about this she wasn't able to face what she was doing, which was actually dangerous. This is the exact opposite behavior compared to a woman who said that she felt much better now she was on the medication and that she had a real reason to leave cigarettes and alcohol out of her life. She looked at her medication as something that had given her back her energy and her joy.

EXERCISE 8:

❖ Is money an issue for you? How has your illness affected you financially?

Often this exercise grows spontaneously out of the preceding one. The old adage is that the poor get sick, and the sick get poor. Even if you have good insurance, the chances are that your absence from work is not compensated at the full rate. Medical bills can be enormous, and the unfortunate may find themselves ruined by a long illness. Although one cannot put a dollar value on someone's life, the sad fact seems to be that when the money runs out, so does the provision of care. Even in countries that have socialized medicine, in Europe for example, decisions are made based on budgetary concerns. If a hospital can only fund a certain number of expensive surgeries, then when the money's gone, the treatments cease. If you are a care-giver or a family member and a relative's illness threatens your finances, how do you feel about that? An aging parent in residential care can cost a fortune, while the grandchildren may need money for education, without which their lives may be forever diminished. How can we reconcile these claims? Possibly we cannot, but by writing about it we may feel less trapped, be less hard on ourselves, and even be able to explore creative options. We can't do that however until the feelings have been expressed and released. I can't tell you how to manage your finances. I can only direct you to procedures that will help to clear your mind so you can make better decisions for a better future.

EXERCISE 9:

❖ What do you know about your illness?

A straightforward question, perhaps, but I'm always amazed at how little people know or understand about their ailments, as well as about the treatments. Some people actually prefer to know less than they could, "I leave all that to the doctors," wrote a cancer patient of fifty-four, normally an inquisitive and inquiring mind. I'm not suggesting you should immediately cross-examine your doctor or buy a large medical dictionary. A forty two year old artist had to give up reading her medical textbooks because she reported that by the time she'd finished reading she was not only frightened but was also convinced she'd developed a dozen new ailments. Clearly this is not a helpful situation. Raising one's anxieties can do nothing to help healing. If this is your characteristic reaction, then you may not want to do this exercise, at all. I'd suggest, though, that in the case of the artist the problem was too much information and not enough real knowledge about the illness.

The whole situation is compounded by the way doctors rarely have time to discuss illnesses in any detail. The patient doesn't have the same amount of medical knowledge as the doctor, usually, and so doctors generally tend to speak in vague terms about what a diagnosis means and how it was reached, because no one wants to confuse patients with technical terms. From my own observations, also, I can give examples of patients and their relatives who simply did not know what questions to ask and so did not ask any when the doctor gave them specific opportunities to do so. The result in almost all the instances was that the sufferers did not know how badly or well off they were, and so into that knowledge gap flowed anxiety. When the doctor says the results are 'good' does she mean good for a person of my age, condition, and history, or good in an objective sense (where 'bad' means I'm going to die), or does she simply mean the results were clear and gave a good indication of what the problem may be? Doctors, of course, are usually guarded in their replies. For fear of lawsuits they are unlikely to say, "You'll be dead in three weeks," and they may often be exasperatingly vague. That is why this exercise can be so useful. If one takes responsibility for oneself, if one decides to find out as much as possible about what's going on, one can reduce the level of anxiety and make intelligent moves to cope with the situation. Reducing anxiety helps the physical healing process, and prolongs life.

In many instances access to information has made a huge difference in the way an illness has progressed. A woman of fifty who was told that her bladder condition was incurable refused to accept this diagnosis. When one doctor after another told her the same thing she decided that there had to be a better way than to face the rest of her life taking painkillers. She explored herbalists, hypnotists, acupuncture, homeopaths - in short she did not give up but she took it upon herself to find out as much as possible about her ailment. It was a long and difficult struggle, but she is now (at the time of writing) almost entirely cured, and without heavy doses of painkillers or surgery to remove her bladder. Did the alternative medicine cure her? I don't know. Perhaps it was her determination that mobilized her own immune system to fight back. Certainly she could not have got better if she'd just accepted the diagnosis that was given her.

A different example of knowing about one's disease might be AIDS. There are several different strains of the AIDS virus, and they work differently and at different speeds. Knowing which type of AIDS is involved can certainly help the victim to design a lifestyle that will cope most effectively with the virus. It also will help to indicate how much time is left, and what one can expect in the near future.

There's a large difference between planning for death six months ahead and planning for it six years ahead. The more one knows the better one can decide what to do. A landscape gardener of thirty two decided, when he discovered he had AIDS, that he wanted to lecture to schools, colleges and prisons about the dangers of unprotected sex. He knew he could expect, with luck, three to four years before he would be too weak to continue. He set his time lines, made the arrangements, and gave presentations twice or three times each week for three years. He felt exceptionally good about it since he reckoned he was helping to save lives. He knew also that the fact that he was under a death-sentence made him a compelling speaker and so in a strange way he was thankful for that, too. "It's a lousy situation," he said at one of his lectures, "but you know what? It's doing some good things for people." This was not just bravado. This man was determined to have a life, even while he waited for death.

Accurate information is basic to clarifying our states of mind. It can be astonishing how often information is misunderstood. An AIDS counselor at a Massachusetts prison reported that men were being tested for AIDS and when the results came back the word 'positive' appeared on some of the slips the men received. Several men actually took that to mean that a positive result was a good result, which meant they hadn't got AIDS. Whether this was a result of poor education, or of denial, or of both, the mere presence of information is never enough without an understanding of its import. So, what do you know about your illness?

One highly intelligent and articulate woman I worked with, who was facing extensive back surgery, told me that she always took her brother along when she discussed her options with the surgeons. She explained that she was quite capable of listening to all the doctors said, even writing notes on it, and yet when she left the room she was likely to be unable to understand the importance of what had just been said. She needed her brother there to repeat back to her what she'd heard so that she could be sure she'd heard it correctly. She knew why this was. Part of her did not want to accept the possibility of surgery, and so she knew she would conveniently 'forget' unless she took deliberate steps to make sure she didn't. Fear can undermine us in this way, and incapacitate even the normally rational processes. The same woman began to notice, in addition to this 'forgetting', that whenever the doctors asked her if she had any questions she immediately forgot what she wanted to ask. Realizing this, she took to preparing lists of questions in advance. On one occasion she appeared in the doctor's office with a typewritten sheet of eighty seven questions.

This may seem to you to be an extreme and neurotic response, but I would like to suggest that something else is worth considering. Here was a woman who was battling against her fear, and taking control of her situation. If, in order to do this, one runs the risk of seeming a little obsessive, all I can say is that ultimately it is your body, your pain, and your life. Perhaps it's worth being exacting about such vital things. There's an old truism that realtors sometimes will repeat, and that is: the bigger the purchase, the more offhand people seem to be about it. Realtors of my acquaintance have confirmed that people who would normally be avid bargain hunters will frequently buy the first house they see and not argue about the price. Could it be that when it comes to our bodies we fall into the same sort of trap? I've known people who have sought second opinions for car repairs who have never even thought about doing something similar before undergoing major operations themselves.

Healers tell us that all healing begins with acceptance. This does not mean a passive buckling under, but an acceptance of the disease and what may be required to deal with it. Being angry and upset gives power away. If we accept the situation in all its reality, we accept and cherish our capacity for facing the truth. When we do this we contact the power of our own sense of self-love. We can love ourselves only if we first accept the dire situation we're in, and that liberates energy we'll need to fight the disease. The tendency many of us have is to tough it out. We deny we're ill. We say we're fine when we're not. Because of this we may not take care of ourselves when we most need it, or we may insist on doing things we're no longer fit enough to undertake.

The opposite tendency is the slump, the sense of I'll-never-get-well. This is just as unhelpful and ultimately just as damaging. Harvard researcher Herb Benson in *The Relaxation Response* (1975) and *Beyond the Relaxation Response* (1987) writes about healing as essentially facilitated by the belief in healing itself. He called it the "faith factor" and his research suggests that belief can heal something like 75% of all illnesses. Belief, however, can only function when we have accepted that there's an illness that can be cured. The "slump" is a giving up that does not allow this.

A seventy-five year old man undergoing cancer treatment found that he was furious with the effect the radiology had on him. He felt tired and weak and, rather than accept this he fought against it, refusing to take rests when needed. At the same time he was convinced that he was going to die. When the doctor declared the treatment had been successful he was relieved and yet ... disappointed. Although the cancer had been contained, his overall recovery had been slowed because so much energy had been involved in the defenses against and negations of his real situation. Now he realized he'd have to take care of himself, nurture his depleted body, and keep doing so for the rest of his life. The prospect depressed him, since it seemed to suggest years of gradually declining physical ability and increased discomfort. The fact is that diseases don't go the way we want them to. Often it's hard to tread the line between resisting and maintaining one's resilience, and the acceptance that becomes a collapse.

In this next section, I want to take the way you think about illness into a different realm, to consider what your disease may be trying to convey to you, the sufferer.

Many diseases, of course, do not have much to convey. The flu, colds, infections - all are caused by outside agents, items over which we have very little control. We may want to consider why our resistance to these diseases has failed us (depression reduces immune activity, for instance) but that would be about the extent of the useful enquiry one could make, aside from asking if one has been behaving in a way that would lay one open to possible infections. Similarly, blood poisoning resulting from a cut, for example, doesn't have much in terms of a "message," unless it be to take better care when near sharp objects. These are ailments that came from outside. But what if you find yourself constantly succumbing to colds? What if, like the British actor John Cleese, you find yourself suffering from flu-like symptoms for two years?

Freud was one of the first who identified the possible psychological roots of some illnesses, which he claimed were "hysterical" when the affected organ was usually the one that had been involved in an earlier emotional trauma. Whatever we think of Freud's evaluation, it's clear that there is often a substantial emotional component to many illnesses. A 1996 report in Britain suggested that up to 80% of people who went to doctors were thought, by the doctors, to be suffering from psychosomatic symptoms. The report is interesting to me because in England doctor visits are free under the National

Health Service, no matter what one's income level, and so there is less chance of sufferers staying away for fear of the cost of a medical examination. It would seem that there is, therefore, a substantial case to be made for looking at the emotional causes of ailments, as well as the physical ones. Peter Levine, in *Waking the Tiger; Healing Trauma* (1997) suggests that there is a similar proportion of psychosomatic suffering in the United States, also.

This shouldn't surprise us. Everyone knows that high stress causes heart-attacks, to give just one example, but few of us stop to consider that stress is a mental affliction we subject ourselves to, often in the search for more wealth rather than just for survival. Mental strain kills us, just as panic may make us feel sick, and shock may cause us to lose our hair, or our appetites, or our will to live. If we really look at our illnesses there may be a 'poetic' interpretation of them that can help us.

The pioneering work by James Pennebaker and others, extensively documented in his important work *Opening Up*, attests to the health benefits of confessional writing done by those he named "high disclosers." His book is eloquent testimony to the advantages of writing down what is on one's mind, or speaking it to a tape recorder. High disclosers, according to Pennebaker, visited doctors less frequently than the population as a whole in the months following the disclosing. Extending his analysis to whole towns and cities, he found that cities that had experienced a traumatic event such as a flood, an earthquake, or an assassination had higher death rates, murder rates and suicide rates than in previous years, and these rates were higher than those recorded in the same year by neighboring towns.

THE IMPORTANCE OF DIARIES

Writing, talking, and disclosing can not only prevent illnesses that are brought about by unresolved mental anguish, but can help reveal patterns of thinking about such illnesses as we may have. The problem is two-fold: when we are suffering we tend to undergo a cognitive down-shifting of the mental gears. Our pain and fear disable our better judgements unless we are very careful. Under these circumstances we lose track of the reality of our suffering. One of the reasons doctors keep records (and every cartoon of a hospital has a temperature chart hung on the end of the bed) is because pain distorts perception and patients become less than reliable reporters of the situation. If you are ill, I'd urge you to keep a detailed diary of how you feel, what you ate, how much you slept, and so on. Two days of pain can feel like an eternity, and remove the memory of a week in which there was actual improvement. One woman who kept such a diary said that in her times of pain she would turn the pages and note that, contrary to her impressions, the condition was, in fact, more stable than she realized. Armed with a new sense of how well she was doing, her optimism helped her through the bad days, kept her on her diet and exercise routine, and undoubtedly sped up her recovery.

Another useful diary technique is to record your negative feelings. This has two benefits. The first is that venting feelings can relieve stress. The second is that it is often not until we have written something down that we can begin to see possible errors in the way we have chosen to think about the situation. One woman wrote her recurrent fear as follows: "I'm afraid I'll never get better." This is a very reasonable fear, and not uncommon. Only when she had written it down was she able to think about what she'd actually expressed. The first part was "I'm afraid..." suddenly she realized that, whether or not she was getting better, fear was a large part of her distress, and because of fear the pain was less manageable. Patients who are fearful habitually need higher doses of pain killers than those who are unafraid. As she looked at what she'd written she was able to ask what the fear was about, and it was evident to her that it was focused on the terror of being a burden to her family. Since she wasn't, as far as she could tell, a burden of any great magnitude, she deduced that her fear was of a future event that might never happen; but that didn't stop it from adding to the pain now.

What was happening was that she was preparing herself to be a sufferer, to be the shameful one, the burden. This, as much as anything, was holding her back. As I've mentioned earlier, many doctors will testify that a belief that one is going to get better can speed up the recovery of most patients. A belief that one cannot get better will just as surely worsen the disease.

I give this example because it is relatively simple, and because it demonstrates how we can, almost unconsciously, give ourselves damaging messages that we need to examine for truth, and redefine. Whenever a message like this comes into your mind, write it down, and then break it down into its components. For example, let's consider the following: "The pain is so bad I'm afraid I'm going to kill myself." This breaks down into three parts: The first is: "The pain is bad". Ask yourself how bad? Has it done this before? What did you do then? What options await you? There is, after all, always a better pain-killer, although some have unpleasant side effects.

The second part is: "I'm afraid." Fear is natural, and unavoidable, but it doesn't help the pain to go away, it in fact makes us more helpless before it. Fear is a highly evolved reaction that tells us to avoid, to run away, because our lives may be in danger. We cannot, alas, run away from pain, and the evolved response works against us in this case. Fear did not evolve to be of use in such circumstances - it was an emotion that was helpful only in response to immediate danger, but we're stuck with it, even so. Realizing that fear is an inevitable part of the mental landscape, that it always comes alongside pain, helps us to live with it. We are going to be afraid, so there is no need to be ashamed of this or see it as a failing. Courage doesn't erase fear, and it doesn't come miraculously from somewhere else. Courage is what happens when we see we are afraid, accept it, and agree not to let that emotion dominate us.

The third part is: "I will kill myself" and links to the second part - I'm afraid that I may be so distressed I'll do something desperate. But if one thinks about this rationally the desire to escape pain is natural. Why shouldn't one, from time to time, fantasize about taking steps to end the pain? Thinking is not the same as doing, yet in this instance the sufferer seems to be criticizing himself for suffering pain and then for entertaining thoughts of desperation that he sees as morally indefensible. This really is a case of verbally beating oneself up!

If you find yourself writing "I'm afraid..." write down as many as you can think of. Then counter each one with a statement that begins "I want." So, "I'm afraid I'll die" becomes: "I want to live." There's a whole world of difference in those sentiments, but they are the *same* response, phrased differently.

The important point, here, is that language can distort our reality, and negative language can undermine our will to get better. If we can reformulate our negative thoughts we can conquer this dangerous situation. I call it dangerous because that is exactly what it is. Any doctor will tell you of patients who have given up and just died. My own grandmother, the last time I saw her in the hospital, said, "I'll never get out of here." She gave up, and her prophecy came true. On her death certificate under 'cause of death' it said, simply 'senility'. She wasn't senile. But she was afraid and she did give up. I'm only sad that I didn't know then what might have helped her to revive the will to live.

I'm not trying to suggest that some sort of shallow, 'don't worry, be happy' frame of mind is all it takes. That would be insulting to both of us. What I suggest is to make a habit of writing down one's recurrent thoughts and seeing if they can be rephrased in positive and attractive ways, or at least in ways that may help us to reach more understanding. An AIDS patient who addressed prisoners at Old Colony Correctional Center in Massachusetts put it this way. "When I was told I had AIDS my first thought was that it was all over. Then I asked the doctor how long I had, and he said, perhaps a couple of years, and that's when I thought to myself, Jeez, if I'm going to get anything done I've got to get a move on! So I started lecturing about AIDS prevention, and here I am, four years later, still doing it." He'd turned despair into something far more vital, because he'd changed his perception.

To recap this section, there are two main exercises embedded in it. They are (1) the illness diary of symptoms to help us stay in touch with what's really happening, and (2) the "I'm afraid..." list, which can tell us how to rephrase our fears in a more helpful fashion. Rather than present them in the way I have with other exercises in the book I've left them to this point because it is essential that you see how they can work first, and then apply them later. The nature of illness is that it tends to rob us of confidence and energy, and I know that if I asked you to write responses to exercises the outcomes of which were not clear, many readers would give up, turn the page, and never be able to progress by using them.

Now that you can see that these exercises can be useful, you may want to do them for yourself. They have proven most beneficial to many people, some of whom have suffered from chronic ailments and found that the renewed sense of understanding and purpose available to them has been able to help accelerate the healing process.

ACCIDENTS

Accidents come in many forms and they are best characterized by the fact that for the person who suffers there is an initial period of shock, followed by a slow reconciliation to the event. There may even be long-term anxiety to do with the source of the shock. The person who is hurt in a car crash may perhaps remain nervous about all forms of travel for years to come. This could be seen as an extreme reaction, but I suspect it is more common than we may think, and when we add to it the statistical fact that all of us will at some time be involved in a car accident of some sort it can lead us to re-evaluate this instance.

In addition in every accident there may be an overlay of fear and anxiety to do with the treatments necessary to become fully well again. Surgeries and hospitalizations can be very difficult to deal with for young children, and older adults may find the whole experience demeaning or embarrassing. And no matter what one's age, pain is for a certain time at least, a constant companion.

In all these circumstances there is an emotional component that needs to be dealt with before healing can truly be said to be complete. There is also the consideration that one's friends and loved ones will be affected by the accident, too, since they will find themselves taking care of the hurt person. If you find that you have become a care-giver to an accident victim many of these exercises will be useful for you, too. So let's start straight away with an exercise.

EXERCISE 1:

❖ How do you feel people see you now, after the accident? You can write about individuals' responses to you, or even about memories of other accidents if you wish.

I'm always astonished at the way people have of blaming victims, especially accident victims, for their misfortunes. I've heard judgmental comments made where no judgement can realistically be made. For example, a colleague was once in a car smash and I was told of this by an office-mate who then added, "But she's such a terrible driver." Whether she was a terrible driver or not (and who's judging?) is hardly the point. My father thinks I'm a terrible driver, and I think the same of him, sometimes. This may have nothing to do with the accident. My colleague might have been parked in a legal spot when the other car hit her. My informant didn't know, but had jumped to conclusions - and to judgment. In another example a director of an educational program was involved in a legal dispute with a fired employee, and on his way back from the first day in court the director was in a minor car accident. Talking with others about this event I was interested to note how many said things like, "It serves him right" or "He had it coming". This was before anyone knew if the man (or anyone else) had been hurt. The rush to judgment is not logical, and seldom kind.

Neither is the tendency to blame one's own actions always logical. A man I worked with was sitting at a stoplight in his car when a vehicle from the other direction ran the light, crossed the dividing line, and hit his car head on. There was no way this man could have avoided the smash, and it could not be seen as his fault in any way. Yet, as he struggled to overcome leg and back injuries, he found himself asking over and over, "Why me? What did I do to deserve this?" In the weeks of convalescence that followed, the sense of self-judgment would at times leave him depressed, sure that fate was working against him.

That's why this exercise is a good one for each of us to consider. Do we feel that there is a judgment being passed on us? The reality is that even our friends may have joined in this criticism, even if they are not conscious of it and profess to feel only pure good will. Unless we are aware of this we will feel confused that people say one thing but seem to mean another.

This tendency to put evaluative judgments on people because of circumstances that are often beyond their control is deep rooted in many cultures. The poor are routinely looked down upon, even when their only offense has been to be born. Parents may find themselves judged because a child has a birth defect or some other abnormality. In fact people who would deny that they believe in God can often be heard making statements that would seem to suggest they believe in a higher power that is devoted to revenging itself upon the blameless. The fact is that no 'misfortune' can ever be judged in the short term. An example of this was in my local paper a month or two back. The parents that gave up a Downs syndrome child for adoption, because they felt they could not cope, could not have imagined the joy and love that child brought to the adoptive family.

There is a famous Chinese proverb that expands on this idea:

One day some wild horses strayed into the village and were captured. When the village elder was told about this event and asked to comment, he shook his head and said, 'It could be good, it could be bad.' The villagers laughed at him and went away to inspect their newly-captured horses.

The second day the villagers came to the elder and told him that his son had fallen off one of the horses trying to train it, and had broken his arm. The Elder shook his head again, and said, 'It could be good, it could be bad.' The villagers looked at him aghast at his attitude to his own son.

The third day soldiers came to the village. They took the horses and all the young men were forced into the ranks, all except the Elder's son, who had a broken arm...

I'll give another example, from life. A man who served in World War Two wrote about how his plane was shot down and he was put in a prisoner of war camp. He was depressed about his situation, about the deaths of his comrades, and about the fact that he was stuck behind the wire while his chums were fighting for a better world and were also being promoted. He didn't quite believe he deserved to survive and felt only that he had somehow failed. Years later, after he had been released, he realized that he'd never have survived the war if he hadn't been lucky enough to become a prisoner. 'Bad luck' can in fact be good fortune.

There are other things to consider, too, when thinking about how others see you now, or how you may see yourself. A man rendered quadriplegic by a crash reported that he found his disability made him cease to appear fully human to some people. In a hospital one day he found his sister and his doctor (who were standing on each side of his wheel chair) talking about him, literally over his head. After several minutes of this he spoke up and said, "Hey, I'm here you know." His sister and his doctor both registered surprise - and he was shocked also. They had temporarily ceased to see him as a person. He was 'a case,' 'a problem' but not a fully feeling emotional human being. It is only too easy for us, any of us, to stop seeing the situation at hand and to categorize it as 'a problem' or 'a disaster'. In doing that we slam the door shut on being able to see the possible good in what is before us.

Attitudes to the sick may well go through several phases - at first people may be eager to help; then after a while they stop being quite so open about it, the upbeat good humor subsides and something else takes its place. What that something is will depend upon the person concerned, but I find it interesting that we seem to have no adequate words available to describe the act of caring for a sick person. In fact many of the words we may encounter to describe the relationship between patient and caregiver are tainted and debased. Just look at the word 'patient.' It suggests a sort of suspended existence that I find quite unacceptable as a description. When one is sick many things are going on, from blind panic to total physical rehabilitation, and although they all demand patience, because they all have their own time span, the sick person is going through far more than just being patient. In fact the word 'sick' is also inadequate, since the person may be getting better or getting worse. Similarly, I used the word 'caregiver' - as if one has to give or give up something in order to care for another. It's an interesting idea that one can 'give' care. I'd maintain that one can give objects or money but that care, like love, is something that is internal that manifests itself in certain actions.

Other words that have lost their meaning include sympathy, pity, empathy, and duty. If I sympathize I, literally, 'feel with' the other - and that may be so overwhelming that it renders me useless as a helper. Empathy by contrast, means accepting the other and not judging (according to Carl Rogers). Yet we may need to judge others, to tell them they are not making an effort to get well, if they are sick, or, if we are sick ourselves we may need to tell them how better to help. Pity, also, is a word that has religious overtones that may suggest the saint or savior is high above and looking down upon the sufferer. That's not much of a model for human beings to emulate! Duty, likewise, is not a helpful word since it implies obligation that is enforced by social sanctions. Each of these words carries an implicit emotional value that may encourage us to adopt unhealthy responses to the situation, since we all shape our reality by the language we use to describe it.

Perhaps the simplest and best description comes from the Bible, where it was originally intended as a different sort of message. If we take the original written version of the familiar "love thy brother as thyself" we see that it is better rendered today as "love your brother for he is as you are." Perhaps this could be usefully used at the sick bed. Love the patient, for he or she is as you would be if you were sick; and likewise, the patient can see that if the situation were reversed, the caregiver would probably act the same way. This is a first step towards honesty and dignity.

Another helpful aspect may be seen in the Hindu greeting *Namaste* - roughly translated as 'the divine in me greets the divine in you.' It is a greeting that looks past imperfections and honors the potential for excellence in us all. And as it does so it reminds us to be aware of the divine in ourselves.

EXERCISE 2:

❖   Was there any blame attached to the accident? Did someone behave negligently?

The replies to this exercise have often been a great source of relief to many people, since a surprising number of accidents occur as the result of careless behavior by a family member. From the person damaged as a result of a mother's drug and alcohol use when the child was still in the womb, to the child brought up by a mother who continually drank whisky so that the alcohol entering her breast milk would cause the baby to go to sleep, to the teenager damaged by a parent's careless driving, to the adult hurt when an aging parent left a pot on the stove too long and caused a house fire - the examples are numerous. These are the accidents we may feel we cannot blame on others, but which we are left to suffer from. These are hard burdens to bear, since these are feelings that are not being allowed to be recognized as such.

Sometimes an accident is fatal, and the survivors punish themselves for the result. The loss of a child, even when linked to no imaginable negligence, can still affect parents so that they feel blamed, even cursed. If things are beyond our control, why should we blame ourselves? Yet we do. Sometimes, in our confusion over apparently random, meaningless events, we apportion blame as a way of trying to get free of the memory. After all, a meaningless universe is a terrifying possibility for many. A reason, any reason, can be more comforting than the blankness of unknowing. Often the easiest explanation is that one is oneself to blame. It's an explanation that gives temporary closure, but in the long term can be a crippling weight to bear.

EXERCISE 3:

❖   Have you lost friendships as a result of this accident?

Friendships can be lost because we are no longer physically able to see our friends as much as before, or because we can no longer be part of the same activities we once shared. On the other side of the coin, people may be afraid of our disabilities, or our disfigurements, and may not want to be around us any more. It's easy to write it off: to say that it can't have been a real friendship, after all. We may express a lot of anger towards such people, and this is an emotion that is best allowed out. What is less easy is to look behind the actions and see the frailties of others - the things that make them run from us.

It is not until we see these frailties and acknowledge that, yes, for some people another's physical change may be more than they can bear, that we can see the human fear that is all too natural. We will learn who our true friends are, but we'll also learn to mourn those who fled, and as we mourn we can appreciate the wonderful things about them that we once enjoyed, and so claim back the value of what has been lost. Friendships change. That's the nature of life. They may deepen or fade even without outside disturbances. Thinking in this way can help us value those friends who stand by us still.

And this leads us to the next exercise.

EXERCISE 4:

❖ Have you gained any friends as the result of the accident? Describe them, or one in particular.

People often find they gain real friends, and rediscover old ones. I don't mean just those people who seem to enjoy talking about medical complications and swapping yarns about disasters in hospitals. A man of seventy who was diagnosed as diabetic related a tale concerning an associate who was paralyzed, yet always cheerful. It wasn't until he was himself unable to walk (as a result of the diabetes affecting his legs) that he began to appreciate the resilience of his friend. As a result, he made an effort to see his friend and to develop a whole new type of friendship. "I'd always been somewhat of an outdoor man. Golf, tennis. Now I began to see a friendship that had an entirely different aspect to it." This new aspect was something he called "soul." "It wasn't about doing things, it was about just sitting and reflecting on what it means to be alive." Human resilience, the sharing of a sense of smallness before the ultimate mystery of death that was surely not far away (both men were over seventy) - all this had added a new depth to this man's life. "It's certainly brought me closer to my son. And to everyone else, really."

Other people have written about becoming friends with their doctors, with their nurses, and with other patients. Some take this to the logical next step. Nurses have often reported offers of marriage from seriously ill patients, and they have learned in many cases how to deal with such well-meant proposals. Of course it's hard to describe this as 'friendship.' I mention it here because it's an example of the sort of attachment that occurs between people when all pretenses are down. These, surely, are moments and days worth writing about.

The next exercise builds on this.

EXERCISE 5:

❖ How do you feel about your body, now?

Although this question seems to suggest an artificial division between the self and 'the body', I still think it's an exercise worth doing, since we are, all of us, aware of our bodies as aspects of ourselves that do not always live up to our expectations. It can be frustrating not to be able to do the things we have been used to doing. Perhaps that lets us appreciate our bodies more - or become disenchanted with them. The truth is, of course, that as we get older our bodies will tend to let us down, more and more often.

What emerges from this exercise is that even though we discover our bodies aren't, perhaps, in the first flush of youth or fitness, they have remarkable resilience. We're tougher than we thought, even though we may not be as agile, or as sharp–sighted. Writing about this we can begin to appreciate what our body was to us, and how its new condition may change our lives. We can write a dialogue with our bodies, if we want. Many examples of this dialogue-with-the-body have proven very rewarding, since through the pain, the reproaches, and the disappointment one sees, over and over again, a tenderness and love for the physical body. This is, I feel, a vital aspect of learning to love oneself with all one's shortcomings acknowledged, the losses mourned. If we cannot love ourselves in this basic way, it is very hard to accept our situation intelligently, and by doing so, take steps to maximize our potential. A seventy eight year old man, badly burned across the face in a wartime flying accident, described how he'd learned to love his scarred features, and how he regarded his deformity as a bonus. "People take one look at me and they see what happened. But they can also see I keep myself tidy, that I haven't given up. I think it lets them see the inner me, more."

EXERCISE 6:

❖ Do you feel as if you were singled out for this event?

The tendency, at first, is always to wonder, "Why me?" We may feel that a cruel destiny has laid its heavy hand on us, and this invites us to accept the status of helpless victim. The twenty five year old who was in a car crash the day before his wedding, and was paralyzed from the waist down certainly felt that way. Who could blame him? The problem is that whilst we are stuck looking at ourselves as victims, as the helpless object of some terrible other power, we lose the chance to see ourselves in a more productive light, one that could empower us to see our situation differently. The victim has already given in, preferring to reject helpful suggestions because they do not fit with his or her mind set. This is a form of learned helplessness, and as we all know, there is no one so helpless as the person who will not help him or her self.

This is not to deny the other possibility for this question. If you do, indeed, feel you were singled out for this event, then push that idea further. If Fate, or God, or Destiny really has singled you out, why would that be the case? In the Bible Job is quite definitely singled-out for some devastating disasters. In his case God was testing him, fathoming his faith and resolve, and Job emerged from it all with a purified soul. Likewise with the early patriarchs and the later Christian martyrs, extreme suffering was the way that they were brought close to God. In some ways Christ's suffering was the guarantee that he was closely linked to the Godhead, and in the Bible suffering is often a sign of God's special favor. Is that the way you feel about your situation? And is your suffering a route by which you approach holiness and eternity? If this seems to be true for you it would be well worth exploring this feeling as fully as possible, in which case writing would, for you, become almost a form of meditation or of prayer.

No matter which of these possible responses you have, it leads to the next exercise.

EXERCISE 7:

❖   What can you learn from your situation? What was it sent to teach you?

Whether or not you believe in God or Destiny will, obviously, slant the responses you write. An unemployed man of twenty eight who had damaged his knee and back severely wrote about how he imagined he had been set the task of learning patience. "That's what this was sent to teach me," he wrote, with some sorrow, and also with a sense of self recognition. "I needed to learn patience," he added.

"I guess this was a message to me to slow down," wrote a man whose car accident had temporarily immobilized him. Previously a frenetic over-achiever, he found himself re-thinking the way he organized his life (he joked about how he 'ran' his life, and how it kept him 'running' so much of the time) and as a result he made changes. He used his physiotherapy sessions as a way to introduce regular exercise into his life - something he had neglected before - and he began to rethink his diet, since he knew that relative immobility would cause him to put on weight unless he was careful. Although it may seem that these are only external changes, in fact they were manifestations of a deeper series of adjustments. Faced with the fragility of his body he began to care for it more, and to love it. Previously it had just been a shell that got him around, and he'd fed it junk food, snacks, and starch-heavy meals because his body was, to him, just like his car. Fill it with cheap fuel when it needs it. Now, as he considered his situation, he realized he'd have to treat his body well so it could last him into old age, so he could continue to be a good husband and father. In a very real sense his accident had taught him what his family needed from him.

On the whole, when accidents strike we search for meaning, because that is what we desire from life, some sort of explanation for what is a happening to us. In fact there is reason to believe that human beings are born with a sense of cause and effect, since this is a trait measurable in babies as young as six months old. They show surprise when confronted with events that have no definable cause for them. It could be the case, therefore, that when we are confronted with accidents that have no readily recognizable 'reason' that we find this disturbing because we are hardwired to expect reasons.

Of course, if only pleasant things happen to us then there's less of a pressing desire to know. We accept good things without too much thought. If I win $5000 on the lottery I'm likely to pocket the cash and feel I'm a good sort of person and that I deserve this luck. If, however, I have a burst pipe in my house that causes $5000 worth of damage, I'm likely to question the logic of the universe, since it does this to me. I certainly won't feel I 'deserve this luck' in the same way as I did with the lottery.

Whether or not there is meaning in the universe is up to you to decide. I can only state here that no matter what one believes, personal understanding is always an option. There is always a huge amount to be learned and understood from every event, because every thing that happens can be transformed into a more positive experience by asking: 'What can I learn from this?' It cannot take away pain or grief. Instead it can lead us to a place where the pain and grief can be transformed into wisdom and awareness. I realize this could be seen as just another version of the old idea 'that which does not kill us will make us stronger,' but I prefer to see it as more than that. If we fail to look for the human enrichment in every event, if we accept the role of helpless victim, then we are not looking to become stronger, and we are, in fact, killing our spirit. That's a self-inflicted wound, and far more serious than any accident.

Chapter Fourteen

Understanding Your Writing Better: What Kind of Writer are You?

I want to take the time, now, to reflect upon the writing you have done so far, and to suggest other ways of looking at it.

It may help you to consider that even if none of us write exactly the same way we can, in fact, reflect upon ourselves by looking at the way we choose to respond to these questions. I'd like to suggest to you that at any one time we are likely to engage in three different approaches to writing and that, no matter which approach we choose, we have four different types of response.

First of all, it's clear that there is a difference between a journal entry and a business report. In a journal we may well call our boss an opinionated incompetent, but in a business report we may have to word it differently: "Support was sometimes less than ideal from management, who were unwilling to accept the urgency of our findings." Something like that, perhaps.

This leads us to a consideration of the three levels of writing, any of which are available to us. The three levels are:

1. The personal (intra-personal): characterized by "I" statements;
2. The interpersonal (aimed at a confidante): "you" statements;
3. The expository (aimed at those may never have met): "we, us, it seems, it appears that..." statements.

Look at some of your responses. How did you write them? Did you write just for you? Or did you find yourself imagining these responses as being read by someone at some time in the future? Did this cause you to edit what you said? I know of at least one couple who used to write in their 'private' journals expecting the other would sneak a look at what they'd written. They carried this tactic on for over a year, at a time when other forms of communication seemed blocked to them. Another extreme was the diary of a New York surgeon, in which he recorded the weather, the temperature, and wind velocity, only. Nothing there to raise a blush to anyone's cheek, and done so intentionally. So, as yourself, who are you writing to? Are you writing to an imagined ideal reader? To a real person who may never see your words? I think that ideally, if you write, it should be to yourself, only. Otherwise there is always the chance you will be able to hide from yourself behind the mask of the person you wish you could be.

But there's another consideration, here.

Some of us tend to write with a feeling of dread, a sense of 'this is not good enough' whenever we think of our writing being read by someone else. This feeling is hard to combat, and many people have told me they have a sense of an internal voice that ridicules all they have to say, even as they try to write it. Variously called The Internal Critic and the introjected parent this is the voice that can cause writer's block.

I once worked with a woman who used to describe herself in the third person whenever she talked about conversations with her children. "You understand why Mummy had to do this," she'd say, reporting a conversation that had taken place earlier. "I said to him, 'Now, Mummy has no choice in this...' " This split into 'I' and 'Mummy' was a mirroring of her sense of her role as Mother, and how that role was more important than 'I'. One of this woman's challenges, it seemed to me, was to integrate these two voices. One of them, surely, was the Internal Parent who was supposed always to be the loving mother ("Mummy") and the other was herself.

One of the advantages of responding to the questions on these pages, or reacting to playful suggestions for writing topics, is that it can help by-pass that internal voice. It can suspend that sense of judgement that keeps us self-conscious. After all, when we're just jotting things down we can say to ourselves, 'This isn't really writing, is it? It's just playing with ideas, thoughts meant only for me, so there's no point in editing it just now... ' And yet, from the exercises we have done here, the questions we've asked and answered, can come the true stuff of self-discovery, without which no writing for the public domain can hope to come to completion. Or, put it another way - we can, in using these exercises, understand ourselves more fully and, at the same time, disable that internal critical voice that keeps us silent, that prevents us from speaking out and saying what we really mean.

There is also another way to look at one's writing, and what I'm going to suggest next is somewhat theoretical, but it has useful practical applications. Carl Jung (1875-1961), the great Swiss psychoanalyst, suggested that there are many ways of interacting with the world and that we are all likely to favor some rather than others. Jung is best known for his idea that people are either introverting or extraverting in their preferences, and perhaps this is most easily understood as the difference commonly to be seen between those who are quiet and private (introverts) and those who are social (extraverts). This work was expanded by Isabel Briggs Myers (1887-1980) of the United States. A self-administered series of questions was developed in order to test out the theories about personality preferences Jung had hypothesized, and this has now been tested extensively and supported by a vast array of statistical data. The instrument is now called the Myers Briggs Type Indicator (MBTI) and is widely used in businesses and colleges as a way of getting people to recognize how they work so they can work better and more harmoniously with others. You may already have some experience with the MBTI, in which case the following pages may be familiar to you. If you have not come across the MBTI before it is worth taking the time to think of your writing in these terms. Briefly stated, Jung's initial idea that people are either extraverting or introverting, (outgoing or private) can be extended to show other preferences.

A preference is exactly that, what we *prefer* to do.

I can be formal, wear a tuxedo, and attend dinner engagements, but I prefer not to. It doesn't mean I can't do these things. It simply means that I feel more comfortable in a different mode, and if I give a party it is likely to be far more casual. This is fine, since I'm a private citizen, but if I were an ambassador or a diplomat this might be a serious impediment to my career, since such people tend to do those things frequently, and if they don't feel comfortable doing them then their effectiveness is reduced as political forces. Our preferences, then, are where we feel most comfortable and function most effectively.

The Extraverting and Introverting preferences are described as "Life Attitudes" because they are descriptors of the ways we may choose to use our energies. The extraverting person likes to be social, finds social activity energizing and may have many friends. It is the outer world that appeals most to this person. Talking, group activities of any sort, and a pleasure in taking action seem to be characteristics of such a person. It does not mean that this person cannot be the opposite, of course. It simply indicates that this is the preferred sphere of action.

The introverting person, by comparison, is more engaged in the inner world of ideas and thoughts. Such a person may be a good listener, quiet, have a few close friends, and be deeply focused on whatever interests him or her. As you are reading this book it is likely that you are using your introverting preference in the act of reading. It doesn't necessarily follow that you are an introverting type. That is for you to decide for yourself. All I can say, here, is that the private act of reading utilizes the introverting preference. If you are reading this as part of a group discussion, then you may well have an extraverting preference. Reflection on the situation is important for an understanding of which preferences you have, and when you choose to use them.

We are all capable, Jung believed, of certain ways of receiving and processing information from the world about us, and these abilities exist along a continuum. For example, I am right handed. This does not mean I cannot use my left hand, but it does mean that if someone tosses me a tennis ball I'll prefer to catch it in my right hand. In fact, if I already have something in my right hand I'll transfer it to my left hand and then catch the ball. Logically it would be much simpler just to use my left hand. The point is that I choose not to. This is a preference. The preference even remains when I'd prefer it didn't. As I said, I'm right handed. At parties I hold my drink in my right hand. This means that when I greet someone and shake hands I have to fumble to get my right hand free, whereupon I offer to shake hands knowing full well my right hand is cold and clammy from holding an ice-cold soda. Oh, I've tried telling myself to use my left hand. But it never feels quite right, somehow, and after a short while I'm back to my old habit. Preferences can be very strong in this, and other ways.

Jung suggested that preferences exist in other realms, also. We can take in information about the world in a variety of ways, of course, but one choice seems to be whether we choose to rely on our five senses (what we can touch, see, taste, hear, and smell), or on our intuition (the so-called sixth sense). Ideally we use all these capabilities, and we find ourselves favoring one set as more suited to us than the others. The Sensing preference shows itself in a reliance on what exists here and now that can be proved, seen, and touched. For the Sensing person seeing is believing. In contrast, the Intuitive person may often not be able to explain why he or she feels something to be true, and yet intuitives have been some of the greatest inventors of our time, because they have dared to go beyond the accepted logic of the day. The computer, the telephone, electric lights, the airplane - all were created by people who were not being practical in the conventional sense. After all, who needed an airplane in 1903, when the Wright brothers made their powered flights at Kittyhawk? It was just a toy. There was no ready market for it. The Sensing person might well have been the one who said, "I'm sticking to the horse and cart!" And he'd have been right. The airplane didn't become efficient enough for general use for another dozen years. Now, this is not to say that the Wright brothers were not adept at using their senses. They were supremely practical engineers, very much hands-on people. Their genius was they put their sensing skills at the disposal of their intuitive abilities.

What this means is that we all have both sets of skills, sensing and intuiting, and we favor one over the other. The Sensing person trusts what he or she can see and touch. Such a person may well be practical, thrifty, and save regularly. There are considerable advantages to this way of being! The intuitive may seem to be dreamy, a visionary, impractical. And yet... the intuitive may be the one who gambles her money on a stock investment and makes a fortune. Or she may die impoverished. An intuitive friend of mine spent twenty years as a penniless author until she hit the big time with a novel. Her advance for the manuscript was $200,000. She was elated until her friend, who is sensing, pointed out that averaged out over twenty years that was a wage of merely $10,000 per year, and thus very close to the poverty level. "You could have taken any office job and made more money," she said. Who was right? The Sensing person or the Intuitive? Your answer may well indicate how you choose to respond to the world and what *your* preference is.

I'd venture, though, that if you're reading this book you're probably a little more of an intuitive than a sensing person. A purely sensing person might not believe that writing could have anything to do with mental health, and so would be more likely to resort to antidepressants, or other medications, to deal with the symptoms. I'd like to stress, here that we all have both abilities, and that they exist on a continuum. The following comparison may help: which of these options seems to fit you?

Sensing Preference (S)	*Intuiting Preference (N)*
factual approach	imaginative approach
detail matters	Big Picture possibilities
pragmatic, here and now	idealistic, future oriented
evidence, or proof valued highly	hunches valued highly
likely to ask 'what?'	likely to ask 'what if?"
sees objects clearly	sees patterns and correspondences

Possible Vocabulary Preferences

It is...	I've a hunch
Anyone can see...	I'd guess
common sense	Could it be..?
really, realistically	possibly...
practical	Imagine...
experience shows...	reading between the lines
here and now...	in the future...

As you can see from the chart, the more you trust your senses, the less you'll trust your intuition. Intuition is not 'provable' - which matters greatly to the sensing preference - although it may be right, even so.

The second axis that Jung spoke of is that of Thinking and Feeling. Feeling, in his analysis, means a concern with human values, the feelings of others, and the exercise of compassion. Its opposite is Thinking, where this is defined as the ability to use logic, assimilate and analyze data, and put it into a logical framework - sometimes at the expense of the feeling domain.

Imagine the scenario: a general comes in and announces to the troops that an attack is imminent. He says he expects a casualty rate of 20%, which is "very reasonable." And he's right, in a sense. Losses of 20% during an offensive may be 'reasonable' because 80% of the troops survive unharmed. Yet to the 20% who are dead or wounded that is hardly reasonable. The question has to be, how can we think about wars if we're going to respond to human cost? Well, we can't. Generals are necessary because they can use the Thinking preference over the Feeling preference. Doctors and nurses are valuable precisely because they don't.

Another example may help: the Feeling person may well be the sort of person who spoils children and animals by showing too much kindness and indulgence. An associate of mine who had a particularly beautiful two year old girl reported that she was constantly fending off well meaning strangers (often retired people) who bought candy for the child as they were standing at the check out line. She reported that she was afraid of offending people, but the sheer bulk of candy that was showered on the child each week was certainly not healthy. I think you can see the dilemma. The thinking dominant person, by contrast, may forget to show emotions, may consider what is logical rather than what is fun. Here is a chart that may help.

Thinking Preference (T)

Impersonal, objective data
Logic
Analysis
Cause and effect
Clarity, firmness, principles
Truth, Justice
How?

Feeling Preference (F)

Subjective realm of emotions
People-centered
Mutual valuing/ appreciation
Trust
Caring, compassion,
Harmony, making 'nice'
Who?

Possible Vocabulary Preferences

I think	I feel
It seems, it seems to me	From my point of view
Obviously	In my experience
Clearly	Emotions
Reason...logic	What's best for all...

This chart is only intended as a guide, but you may already have identified aspects of yourself in these paragraphs. We all choose one aspect of each pair as our preferred way of being, and each preference pair corresponds to a different type of mental function.

Sensing (S)   or   Intuiting (N) --   Perceiving Functions
(how we *take in* information)

Thinking (T)   or   Feeling (F)   --   Judging Functions
(how we *process* information)

This gives us four combinations of preferences:

- ST or TS
- SF or FS
- NF or FN
- NT or TN

Notice, one cannot be SN or TF because, just like left handed or right handed, we tend to choose one preference over the other in each function.

I've grouped them like this because in each pair it's likely you'll favor one preference more than another. An ST, therefore, can be seen in this notation to be someone who prefers Sensing first, and then uses Thinking next - and that's likely to be a different cognitive procedure than someone who approaches the world with a Thinking preference first and then confirms those thoughts by referring to Sensing experiences. The Sensing dominant ST will be the person who will look out of the window, see that it's a sunny day and 75 degrees and dress in summer clothes, trusting the five senses first and foremost. The Thinking dominant TS will also notice the fine weather but may also examine the situation, and so say that this is very unusual weather for early March in Boston. Notice how the logic (T) is valued more than the sensory input (S) of what the day actually is. Both people may end up dressing roughly the same, but the Thinking dominant person might well take a jacket or umbrella, just to be safe, and even check the weather forecast. The processes are different, and under other circumstances may lead to quite different actions.

When you've reflected on this for a while you may want to decide which of the four pairs you feel is a reasonable description of you. I've also added a chart for you to consider. It was developed by my friend and colleague Dr. Ronald Warners, and he and I have used it for some years, now, to excellent effect when we work with writers on understanding how they characteristically see the world. Take a moment, now, to read the chart and to fill in the blanks so that you can approximate your own Myers-Briggs Preferences. You'll notice that the chart asks you to consider eight possible letters as descriptors. This represents the full range of the Myers-Briggs Type Inventory. It is not my intention here to give a substitute for the full Myers-Briggs. If you are interested it is best to take the Type Inventory yourself and have a trained interpreter relay the results to you. What we have here is a guide, only.

In our work together in this book we will be most concerned with the balance of Perceiving Functions and Judging Functions, since they have the most direct bearing on the type of writer one may be. So, now please look at the chart on the next page. Fill in the blank spaces at the bottom. Don't agonize over your choice, but give it your best try. After all, there are no right of wrong answers.

Now you have your answers let's see what we can make of them. Look at the middle two letters of the sequence. Depending on your preferences it is likely that you will be one of four different kinds of writer. Please note that I'm not saying you can only be one kind of writer. The creative writer may well have to hold down a job that requires some very uncreative writing skills. The question is not what you can do, but how you prefer to be. Now look at the following descriptions.

THE ST WRITER: (THE REPORTER)

This writer will tend to process information in a factual way and write it logically. Strengths will include an eye for detail and fully supported statements. I like to think of this writer as 'the reporter' because events will be meticulously recorded. The disadvantages this writer faces are that it may be hard to link these specific events to a larger picture of what it all means, and it may be hard for this writer to include full expressions of emotions. Such a writer may often be very brief, believing that one sentence sums it all up and there's no more to say. The disadvantage is that often there is more to say. Simply recording that your mother abused you, for example, is not quite enough for full understanding of the events, let alone for letting go of the trauma. Such a writer will need to develop the Intuitive (N) and Feeling (F) domains in order to come back into balance.

Look at your writing. Did you tend to use personal anecdotes only? When you were asked to imagine a situation did you prefer to avoid that task? Did you prefer to stay with factual discussions? Do you see yourself using any of the preferred vocabulary listed? These can be the attributes of the ST.

The Feeling domain (F) can be accessed by asking questions about personal response to others and to events. So, for example, the victim of parental abuse might like to address questions like: what did it feel like to be the child who was abused? How did you relate to others as a child? Who were the people you liked and trusted?

Understanding Preference Patterns

*Personal Energy
Attitude*

Extraverting
Energy directed to the outer, immediate environment of action, objects, persons. Meaning through personal experience. Energized by being with others. Active, sociable, easy to know. Unloads emotions easily. Afterthinker.

E *or* **I**

Extraverting Introverting

Introverting
Energy directed inward towards ideas and understanding. Energized by being alone. Engrossed by inner events. Often shy. Cautious about surprises. Intense, reflective, reserved; bottles up emotions. Able to concentrate. Seeks to understand in depth. Moves from thinking to doing back to thinking. Forethinker.

Sensing
Focuses on sensory information. Practical, observant, detailed, here and now, concrete, sequential; craves enjoyment, comfort, luxury, beauty; relies on experience. "Give me the specifics" Asks: What?

Perceiving Functions

S *or* **N**

Sensing   Intuiting

Intuiting
Oriented towards possibilities and the future; imaginative; sees the big picture, full of expectations, enterprising and inspiring; thinks in abstract patterns; ingenious; motivated by inspiration, hunches, meaning. Asks: Where?

Thinking
Analytical, logical, objective, truthful; forms categories; works by principles and policy; naturally businesslike, executive; appreciates firmness, concern for justice. Contributes intellectual criticism. Asks: Why?

Thinking   Feeling

T *or* **F**

Judging Functions

Feeling
Values based, social, concerned for effects on people: tactful, naturally friendly, seeks harmony: appreciates compliments;loyal;loyal;persuades rather than debates: full of mercy. Asks: Who?

*Personal Life-style
Attitude*

Judging
Seeks closure, completion; decisive; plans ahead, is punctual, scheduled, purposeful, in control, rational, exacting. Dislikes the unexpected. gets the job done. Confident in their own opinions. More decisive than curious. Asks: When?

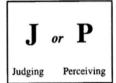

J *or* **P**

Judging   Perceiving

Perceiving
Keeps decisions open as long as possible, adaptable, curious, easily adjusts to the unexpected, tolerant, responsive to the moment; flexible, spontaneous, open-ended, leisurely, laid back, adapt as you go. Appreciates newness, aims to miss nothing. More curious than decisive. Asks: Where's the party?

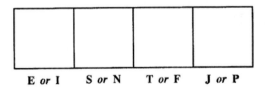

E *or* I   S *or* N   T *or* F   J *or* P

The Intuitive realm (N) can be made available by asking questions about the long-term impact of events, and whether or not they affect present relationships. Another good tactic for accessing the Intuitive realm is to ask 'what if...?' questions. What would have happened if, for example, your parents had divorced/stayed married/never met? Allow yourself to speculate. Sometimes for such writers the important word is 'because'. Try this as an exercise now. An example of this for the abused child might be as follows: She hit me *because*... she was abusive. She was abusive *because*... she was angry. She was angry *because*... she'd had a hard life. And so on.

One can see how this can go, and occasionally it can open up new awareness.

THE SF: (HUMAN INTEREST)

This type of writer will tend to be compassionate and practical. Nurses, doctors, social workers—anyone who enjoys caring for others in a practical way may be in this preference group. As a writer this person will have access to the emotions but may, on occasion, be swamped by feelings. Nurses, teachers and healthcare workers are always at risk of emotional burn-out from their work. As a writer this person will have no trouble illustrating events from the past and the emotions attached to them. The disadvantage may be that if you are an SF you may find yourself amassing examples of people's situations without taking the time to spell out what they may all add up to. You'll need to ask why the events happened, as well as recording them in detail. This involves developing the N and T functions. Remember, the N function is the 'big picture' awareness, and the T function is the ability to be coolly rational.

The SF writer can be usefully helped by asking such questions as: what does it all mean? or, what can be done about this? Sometimes it works even more effectively if one asks: what do you intend to do to make it better? SFs will always give great value to personal, lived experience, and sometimes it can valuable to step outside this personal world and see other viewpoints.

THE NF: (THE STORY TELLER)

The Intuitive and Feeling writer will be likely to have strong emotional responses to human situations and then link these feelings to a bigger picture. Such people can often "see it all in one little detail." They'll notice the way two people act and draw conclusions about how they live - even if they've never seen those two people before. Such a writer is a born storyteller, and has no trouble imagining others' lives, feeling others' situations. The disadvantage for such a writer is that when upset he or she may tend to blow small things out of proportion and base a big decision on too little evidence. This person may well find herself saying things like: "If that's the way I'm going to be treated, then I'll leave/change job/leave the country..." The feelings are honored, perhaps at the expense of practical considerations. The sense of what events may mean is valued - but the reactions may be overstated and the logic lacking. NF people may well read a sad story in the newspaper and conclude that the whole country is going to the dogs. Whether or not the country is in a mess may depend on more evidence than just one news story.

The NF writer may well be helped by asking for more evidence. Is this personal impression really the only one available? NF writers may find that to be a productive challenge. Evidence and data are aspects honored by the Sensing person (S) and the logical assembly of such details is what the Thinking preference (T) does best.

THE NT: (THE ANALYTIC WRITER)

The NT is the thinker who will most likely be rather cool, dispassionate, and controlled. Such a writer is often deeply analytic as he or she strives to understand what makes the larger events happen. Such a person will be very much at home with history or sociology - big topics that have to be understood by not getting bogged down in detail. Such people may well argue about how logical another's viewpoint is, and they tend to withdraw when confronted with emotional outbursts in others. As a writer, this preference type will be incisively analytic, but may find it hard to value those with emotional reactions. In fact, this writer may even be blind to another's "non-logical" preferences. If you find yourself, in response to the questions in earlier sections, analyzing a particular incident with great care, you may well be an NT, especially if you then used your analysis to demonstrate a larger truth about your life.

The NT writer will need to be reminded that what is logical is not always the best way forward. Asking this writer to consider human attachments (F) may be useful. NTs will be good problem solvers, but the question to ask might be: is this what will make people feel comfortable?

Reflect a while on this.

You may have noticed that all the preferences have good aspects, and yet all of them may need to be balanced out by introducing other preferences, also, if the whole topic is to be grasped fully. For instance, how does one react to world poverty? The feeling person may well want to get involved with helping, possibly at a local level. The sensing person will be more likely to contribute money and clothing. The thinking person will want to know how this happened and what can be done. The intuitive may well want to reform governments to put a stop to world poverty.

I do not intend, in this section, to try and diagnose you as a certain "type" of person. For one thing the Myers-Briggs is far more complicated than this, and it is not a diagnostic tool. It reflects back to you only what you have chosen as a description of yourself. Furthermore, I don't consider it likely that there are only four types of writers. We could reformulate this whole discussion and say that some writers will respond just to the letter of what is asked in the exercises, and no more (likely to be STs); some will record personally experienced incidents but with little analysis (SF); some will want to write stories, even fantasies (NF); and others will choose incidents to analyze, but may fail to mention much in the way of emotions (NT). Practical; emotional; storyteller; analyst. The chances are that you have aspects of all four.

What I'd like you to do is to consider what you seem to be good at in your writing, and then consider whether there are other ways of writing that may be worth exploring. Knowing how we write can reveal how we tend to take in the information the world throws at us. Sometimes it helps to know how we work so we can understand the particular tint of rose color we may have on our spectacles. Remember - no preference is better or worse than any other. The lady who once confided to me that she took in stray cats and dogs - eighteen at the last count - was exercising her Feeling domain in a way she found important. As such she was not likely to respond favorably to those neighbors who complained to her about the noise, the mess, and other details of the practical, thinking kind. The two sets of people speak, literally, different 'languages' when it comes to their preferences.

When considering the likely MBTI preferences that seem to describe you best it is not always necessary to be slavishly attendant to details. What's important is to get a general sense of how you prefer to work. I mention this because our preferences can change slightly depending on circumstances - and this can be very important for our work here. You can use your knowledge of the MBTI to predict how you are likely to behave when under pressure, and so you can be more aware of what is happening to you when it happens. Here's an example: We find out how well our cars cope with ice and snow by driving carefully under those conditions. We touch the brakes when we know there's no other vehicle near and we feel the skid, mentally noting that this is what we'll have to be prepared for on this trip. And just as brakes that work well in dry conditions can be the very worst thing to apply suddenly in icy conditions, so we can appreciate that our strengths of character do not always work if our personal conditions change. The hard-nosed lawyer cannot cross-examine her own child, for example, in the same way she may grill a witness in court - at least not if she wishes to retain the child's love and confidence.

I give these instances because the MBTI can be a useful indicator of what we will do well, and when we are in adverse circumstances it can tell us how we will not manage to do well. In short, it can tell us what sort of a sufferer we may be, or what sort of caregiver when around our loved ones (which is always harder than caring for strangers. That's why professional nurses are so good).

When faced with a crisis - be it illness, or work-related - what tends to happen to us is that we dig in firmly to our dominant traits. Unless we are very aware and flexible we may tend to get stuck into 'more of the same.' We couldn't move the widget by using a small hammer? So let's use a bigger hammer... Actually, the widget may move if we oil it, or heat it with a blowtorch, or freeze it so the metal contracts, but the chances are good that we'll look for a heavier hammer, and risk damaging the whole assembly. So the rational, thinking person will respond by becoming more rational, even if the situation is highly charged emotionally. In such a circumstance the rational person may seem to be cold and uncaring - which adds to the confusion of the emotional people present.

If we take this into the realm of illness, let's just imagine a Thinking-dominant man who gets the flu. At first he'll tend, perhaps, to shrug it off, deny his physical misery, and keep going to work because he doesn't see a valid reason not to. Appealing to him to take care of himself just will not work for someone like this. So, our poor flu sufferer will search out the best flu medicines but will not go to bed and stay there, because there's no 'reason' to do so. However, if one suggests that he has to stay home because he'll give the flu to the whole office, and the project will be put in jeopardy, then that's a rational argument that makes perfect sense to him. When people who are Thinking dominant are ill or stressed, all they can see is the Thinking viewpoint. This is true of every preference.

If the illness persists eventually the Thinking dominant person will be overwhelmed. The usual way of coping with the outside world is no longer working. That is the point when the negative aspects of the dominant can become troublesome. A Thinking-dominant person will be an inspired and annoying complainer about every detail. Notice, the Thinking faculty is still present, but it's being used even though it cannot bring about any constructive outcome.

As the discomfort and pain increase the Thinker may tend to slip into the inferior - the opposite of the thinking domain - which in this case is the Feeling domain (that's the opposite of the Thinking preference on the charts, above). The Thinking dominant person is not as well acquainted with the Feeling domain, of course, so entering this domain is confusing to this person. Such a change may be manifested in despair, depression and collapse, all negative aspects of the emotions. Like the car on ice, the individual has discovered that nothing works quite as expected, and so may be overwhelmed with panic.

As suffering becomes deeper and more protracted we are all capable of falling into our inferior functions. Fear will do this to us - and which of us has not been frightened by illness at some stage? It will keep us paralyzed in an unsuccessful mindset, if we are not aware of it. Fear and illness will take our strengths and use them against us, unless we are aware of this and take steps to be prepared.

To recap, then: when stressed our dominant rigidifies. If the illness lasts longer than usual eventually the dominant is overwhelmed and the sufferer (or the panicked care-giver) collapses into the opposite of the dominant mode - the inferior. People going through this will often need help re-establishing their dominant in a more flexible way before they can get fully well.

An example may help. A woman of great creative talent (an NF) became ill at the age of fifty. Because of her circumstance as a mother of two, and the number of people she saw as relying on her (Feeling domain considerations) she delayed in getting medical help. When she became worse the intuitive (N) function became over-wrought and she found herself imagining terrible diseases at work in her body, and that she was near death. Her imagination, which she normally used to earn her living, was now working against her. She collapsed into despair. Then something very interesting began to happen. She began to work from her tertiary (Thinking) and inferior (Sensing) functions because she refused to accept the fate she had imagined she was destined to suffer. She began to devour medical books, made hundreds of pages of notes and explored every medical route she could find, searching for information. She stuck punctiliously to directions about treatments, exercising the Sensing domain (her inferior) in a way she never had before: "I've never studied so hard in all my life," she declared.

The results of her researches were mixed in terms of clinical improvement. In fact, once she began to shed her fear and could re-engage with her dominant (N) she became less devoted to medical textbooks and was able to listen to her body a little more. I give this example because it can show us how any of us are likely to behave when under strain, or when ill, or when we are caring for someone whom we love who is ill. We'll dig in to our dominant preference - whatever that may be. We'll stay there until it is overwhelmed by the situation. Then we'll be propelled into the unfamiliar world of the inferior. We'll tend to do this unconsciously. My point is that if we know what is likely to happen we can give ourselves more choices.

It's as well to remember, also, that individuals are not dissimilar from governments in this respect. Governments are notorious for acting from their dominant paradigms, as is the military. "Sending the troops in" may work very often as an idea for achieving short term peace, but as the British discovered in Northern Ireland, it was never a successful long-term strategy. More troops did not necessarily mean less violence, yet in response to each violent act more troops were deployed. It wasn't until troops were withdrawn that peace negotiations could begin.

At risk of oversimplifying, we can chart in general terms what is likely to happen to us when our dominant function seems to be overwhelmed:

- The Intuitive (N) will be at risk of feeling snowed under by details (the Sensing realm), and will obsess about them;
- The Thinker (T) will find the emotions (the Feeling realm) to be flowing more freely than is comfortable;
- The Feeling person (F) may well become overly concerned with the difficulties of what is logical and sensible:
- The Sensing person (S) may well be overcome with shapeless fears.

As I said at the start, it's important for all of us to know who we are and how we work best, so we can be aware of what our strengths and weaknesses may be. Words like 'equality' tend to assume that we are all somehow, fundamentally the same, and that one treatment suits us all. Yet we know that we are not all the same, just as a racehorse is not the same as a plough-horse. We know that we don't all think the same way, or have the same abilities, whether these be the sixteen different combinations of the preference types of the MBTI or Howard Gardner's eight different intelligences.

This section may well have seemed very theoretical and abstract to some of you (particularly those who are Sensing dominant, I'd expect) and to others, especially the NTs, it may be more engaging. My intent is to ask you to consider your particular gifts and how they may differ from others' preferred ways of seeing. Your 'take' on the world is likely to be original and wonderful, and I wish you to honor that. What I'm suggesting here is that your viewpoint is unique, and it is also understandable by others. I'll give you an example. A man I used to work with in England was hired to teach English in Mongolia, of all places. He spoke to various people who knew the Far East, all of whom gave him useful information. When I met him again years later I asked him about his experiences, and he said that before he'd left he'd been told he'd never understand Mongolians because they were so different. After he'd been there a while he found he did understand them, quite well, much to his relief, and he began to enjoy their company. The trick was in not expecting them to be explainable in western terms, but only in their own terms. "Once you see that, they're just folk like anyone else," he said. His understanding of them did not make them any less wonderful. It was the relinquishing of his own point of view that allowed him to see that wonder and warm to it. If he'd simply stayed in his British point of view he would only have found his time in Mongolia frustrating.

My hope is that using this chapter you will be able to reflect on how you prefer to see the world, to make that process fully conscious. Once you have done that you can reflect on how others see life, and decide whether or not there's anything to be learned from a different perspective. Most of this book is predicated on you seeing yourself, your responses, and then considering whether these are the only responses available to you. The chances are that you have more choices and possibilities than you think.

Chapter Fifteen

THE MATERIAL WORLD

William Manchester, the historian, said that during the renaissance the average Italian merchant lived better than the King of Scotland. I'd go further and say that today pretty much everyone in the U.S. lives above the level of that middle-class mercantile trader. Even those on welfare can buy out of season fruits that even a few decades ago would have been unbelievable luxuries. Marshall McLuhan put it succinctly when he said that soon the only difference between rich and poor would be the brand of automobile each drove. As of 1996 for the first time the U.S. had more automobiles registered for road use than the total population- babies and octogenarians included. That means the driving population has, on average, far more than just one vehicle per person.

The objective of this chapter is to get you to examine the way you interact with the material world and to encourage you to ask whether there may be a more productive way to treat its daily assault on our senses.

Naturally there are all sorts of things in the material world that we could use, and so for this first exercise let's look directly at that.

EXERCISE 1:

❖ Imagine you have just had a 50% pay raise. Write "I want..." and fill in the blanks. Do about twelve of these. When you have your list, then write beside each one "but I really want..." and fill in those blanks. After you've done this, repeat the process and, after each one, complete the sentence, "I need..." When you've done that, beside each one write, "but I really need..."

By limiting the amount of money to a 50% pay raise we can keep the desires within reasonable bounds. A million dollars would lift this exercise into fantasy. What I want to do is focus on those things that you've been hankering after that are just beyond your immediate means. These are so often the things that we think would make us happy.

What I find whenever I do this exercise is that respondents quickly make the distinction between what they think they'd like in material terms, and the things they'd really like in less tangible terms.

"I want a bigger refrigerator so I don't have to go shopping so much. But I really want more time, because I hate shopping for groceries, and waiting in line, and feeling tired, so by the time I've cooked dinner I can hardly talk with the family ... and that's what I really want to do."

The refrigerator may help ease this situation, but as the answer indicates, buying a new appliance will not necessarily improve the family relationships. Here's another example:

"I'd love a new vacuum cleaner," wrote one woman, "but I really want it to be a present from my husband. What do I need? I need him to notice what I do, how much I do. I need him to notice me."

The reply says it all - clearly the woman would like to have her work appreciated by her husband. Here the new vacuum cleaner would make a tangible difference, but it is the donor who would make it truly a gift the woman wants. An object is never just itself, but a focus for other deeper wants, and here this woman was able to peel back the layers.

What I'm at pains to point out, here, is that very often we find the world of material goods and advertising can direct us so that we imagine we need certain things. Luxuries are wonderful, of course, and can bring great pleasure. My concern is that sometimes those easy, immediate pleasures can direct us away from the real issues. The old clichés of love-songs are "Money can't buy me love" (the Beatles) and other expressions of happiness despite poverty - if the personal relationships are adequate. This exercise is a way to approach a relational problem that may be masked by an emphasis on purchasing power.

EXERCISE 2:

❖ Recall a bargain that gave you pleasure, or, if you prefer, a purchase that was less than satisfactory.

This exercise, I find, quickly separates the optimists from the pragmatists. Optimists nearly always can recall bargains that were great pleasures for years to come. Pragmatists, and those of us who are jaded by the material world, can always recall the pair of shoes that looked so good in the store but which proved murderous to the toes, or the handy item that looked so useful but has lain unused in the cupboard, untouched, from the day it arrived home. And yet... weren't we all optimists when we made the purchase? The point here is that the material world consistently plays with our hopes and our optimism. If it leads us on and then lets us down repeatedly, what we can learn is pessimism. This can, on occasion, take us to a realm of self-fulfilling disappointments. "Just my luck" we say, and we're blaming ourselves for being optimistic! Suddenly we're in a vortex that can undermine self-esteem, and actually hurt our outlook on life. Our response, all too often, goes beyond the purchase itself. I'd suggest there is a confusion here. Self-esteem should not, necessarily, be confused with one's ability to identify a bargain. If it is we can see the familiar signs - the person who has to get a bargain at all costs, whether or not the object will ever be used. One can see mild examples of this at any Saturday yard sale. There are always a few people who can be seen muttering to each other: "You know how much these cost new? We can't pass this up!" Pleasure, for such people, often comes from the bargain rather than from any practical purpose it may serve, later. Please don't think I'm criticizing a harmless activity. I love yard sales. But I notice elements of compulsive behavior in them at times as people strive to fulfill their lives in unproductive ways.

EXERCISE 3:

❖ Describe a "pack rat" you may have known. What sort of things were saved? If you prefer, write a fantasy about an 'Aladdin's cave' of stored objects.

This exercise usually gets a welter of replies, from the man who described cleaning out his grandparents' home (the grandfather had saved all his old newspapers, amongst other things) to the confusion of the woman whose mother had taken to hiding her jewelry around the house, to deter thieves, and had forgotten where she'd put things. What always strikes me is that one person's treasure is another person's trash - that the objects we value and cherish are not always recognized by others. What are the things you save? Why? What are the things you saved as a child?

Compulsive hoarding (and homeless people can often astonish us by the sheer amount of stuff they carry, drag, or wear) can be a sign of compensation for needs that have gone unmet at other stages. The trouble is that once one has accumulated all the items and all are similarly shabby, how does one sort out what's salvageable from what isn't? In Charles Dickens' *Bleak House* the despised and illiterate rag picker, Krook, consoles himself by keeping large heaps of legal documents, even though he has no idea what they mean. The secrets they hold, unintelligible to him, comfort him with a sense of power.

All material objects are consolations. Even clothes are just another way of protecting ourselves from the elements to which we surely will return. Of course we need clothes, but we may not need some of the expensive items we have. The situation is compounded because of the relatively high quality of modern clothes. Nowadays it is not enough to look good, we have, also, to advertise the expense of looking good by having the maker's name on prominent display. If it's Nike sneakers or Gucci handbags or Hilfiger shirts, it makes no difference; the claim is both an assertion of power and a capitulation to an illogical system of self-valuation. In short, labeling clothes is a sign we are afraid that others will not notice who we are. Since when did the material world have such powers to explain us? In the controversial movie *Affluenza* about the material items we seem ready to die for, there are astounding interviews with teens who refuse to wear anything that is not designer-labeled. To the unformed ego external validation is very important and paradoxically this clamor for validation further reduces the individual's ability to feel adequate in and of himself. It would be going too far to suggest that the material world has helped to erode the ego development of western civilization, but it hasn't helped it much, either.

EXERCISE 4:

❖ 'Keep off my blue suede shoes!' Do you have a prized possession? What is it?

Responses to this question have varied from "my diary" to "my father's watch" to "my dog" and even "my stereo." Several times guns have been prized items. This exercise works well as a contrast to Exercise 3, since you are asked to limit yourself to just one item. In each case the item says a great deal about the individual - that is obvious. Prized possessions are those that we feel to be possibly monetarily valuable, or an essential part of ourselves. If the object were merely valuable but not attractive, we would probably sell it to enjoy the proceeds. Let's ask this question another way.

EXERCISE 5:

❖ In an emergency, what single item (other than a wallet) would you take with you?

Contrary to what advertisements suggest it's not the American Express Traveler's check ("Don't leave home without them") nor is it Cutex ("A girl without Cutex isn't dressed"). Nor is it, usually, any type of hair-care product. More often than not it's an object of sentimental value, such as a ring, a brooch, even a teddy bear. Often it is a medication. When the responses are gathered I'm always surprised at how many people cannot answer. When the decisions have to be made, it's astounding how little we need.

EXERCISE 6:

❖ What item do you feel you cannot do without?

Many people respond that their computers or their cars are impossible to do without, and usually that indicates a strong connection to work. If pressed, though, these people will tend to admit that they could do without these items on a beach at Aruba, for example. Once again, if you drew a blank here, you can sigh with relief. Objects do not matter as much as relationships, health, happiness, or a good night's sleep. Yet we regularly trade in all these aspects of well-being for everyday objects.

Now that I've been rude about the material world for so many pages, I feel I should at least clarify my stance. Material well-being is important to all of us. The only thing I wish to remind you of is that there is more to life than the accretion of toys. The seduction of material goods is the promise that if we just had … whatever … then we'd have perfect skin, perfect clothes, perfect poise, in short we'd be perfect. But being complete in that way also means we don't have to rely on anyone else, or care about anyone else's viewpoint, either. The illusion that we are offered is that with this car, or that lifestyle we wouldn't need anything anymore. Clearly, that's absurd. The promise is that we'll be cut free even of the desire to desire. This is the language of the compulsive gambler, the one who's waiting for that one big win that'll make everything turn out right. It's also the language of loneliness. If we desire to be elevated to this mythical plane of material well-being we cut all our ties to everyday humanity. That 1960s and 70s icon of material savoir-vivre James Bond had everything, and needed nothing. Certainly he never had a deep or meaningful relationship with others, and although he had plenty of sexual activity, he appears again and again in each new movie as unattached as before. I choose Bond as a figure because his appeal has remained steady for more than 40 years, from book to movie - and he's still with us.

My point is that the dream of material wealth is ultimately for many, a dream that involves increasing isolation. In slang terms, many people used to use the term 'outta sight' to express approval, or 'Can't touch this' is another version. The problem is that if one is truly out of sight and out of touch, then how does one have any meaningful personal life? If one is 'way cool' one is disconnected and ultimately alone. This is the paradox of the hunger for material things. An example may help here: a man has a car so he doesn't have to use public transportation. His wife has a car so she doesn't have to negotiate with him about sharing the car. In addition they can call up the local supermarket and get someone else to select and deliver their groceries. They have cable and satellite TV so they don't need to go to the movies; they have so much in-home entertainment they hardly need to go out ... and so on. If I compare this to the village I grew up in, in England, there was far more borrowing of this and that, car pooling, interactions with the local shopkeepers, lending back and forth of lawn-mowers. Less money meant more people interactions. As Sandro Chierichetti (1940) puts in, describing the vows of St. Francis of Assisi, being less than wealthy has some human advantages.

> Poverty - not laziness, not escape from action, but voluntary and heroic renouncement of possession, the tyrant of man - poverty is a source of charity and love.

St. Francis took poverty to an extreme, but that doesn't mean we can't learn from his example. We cannot complete ourselves as human beings by piling material goods into the void of our hearts. We can only become whole if we reorganize our needs and the human needs of others, and strive to do something about that. As Oscar-winning film director Roberto Benigni said, "I want to thank my parents for their great gift to me, their poverty."

EXERCISE 7:

❖ Write about what you would do if you won the lottery. Jot down your ideas. When you've done that try dividing your answers into several categories: Things to Buy, People, and Things to Do (travel, adventure). Which list was longest? What does that tell you?

If your list is full of things to purchase but short on human contact items, you may want to re-think the balance in your life. Similarly, if you have a long list of objects but very few entries under 'Things I'd do' you might want to think about what you really want to do. Wealth brings opportunity. It brings freedom from the necessity to work for money. How do you want to use your newfound leisure and resources?

There is, of course, no final word one can say about the material world. We all enjoy our luxuries, and they bring us pleasure and solace. They remind us of how well we're doing (and in America almost everyone is doing well compared to, say, Somalia). They reassure us that our lives have some rewards, even if temporary. They may even console us for the people we've lost, for we all have lost people and we all need consoling.

Perhaps the lure of physical objects is so strong because it is a compensation for lost youth. We stop being able to measure our progress in the world after a certain point in our lives. As children we can see how much taller we have become, how much more proficient we are at what we do, and there is a recognizable reward structure. We can check how we're doing. Once we're older we feel our bodies slowing up; we lose some pleasures such as the ability to party all night and still feel good the next day. We gather gray hair, and wonder what we have to show for our years on earth. This is the point at which the amassing of physical objects can be a comforting diversion. Possibly we would do well to recall the words of Henry David Thoreau in *Walden*.

> Men labor under a mistake. The better part of man is soon plowed into the soil for compost. By a seeming fate, commonly called necessity, they are employed, as it says in an old book, laying up treasures which moth and rust will corrupt and thieves break through and steal... The mass of men lead lives of quiet desperation. What is called resignation is confirmed desperation.

I'd like, now, to propose two exercises that may suggest a different way of dealing with the problem of the material world.

EXERCISE 8:

❖ If you could found a club or a society, what would it be? What rules might it have?

I like this exercise because it almost always brings light-hearted and humorous replies, behind which can be found important feelings. A woman who was about to turn fifty and who was childless decided to found a society to help women past fifty have babies. She was tired, she said, of the fact that men could father children into their seventies while a woman of fifty who wanted a baby was looked on as abnormal. She was able to speak out about how much she loved small children, about how she could only imagine what it would be like to be pregnant and give birth, and about how her two sisters had had to undergo fertility treatments before they could conceive. Her plan for the society was extensive, and included medical research grant writers, adoption specialists, and even sex education classes to be taken into schools. It was more of a foundation than a society, and this exercise allowed her to express her wishes for herself without any sense of self-pity. By creating a society, something that of necessity reached towards the outside world, she was relieved from the pressure of her personal wishes, and so was able to leave self-pity behind. Whether or not she ever managed to do anything to make this society a reality, she had been able to express a yearning about a subject that was potentially heart-breaking, yet she was able to do it in such a way as to reclaim her status as a self-directed person, not as a victim.

In contrast, a man of thirty six decided to create not one but three societies. The first was to value moments of silence; the second was to banish the use of pronouns; and the third was to establish moments of eye-contact. The common thread that linked them, as he observed, was that he felt his life was lived in a constant rush, and that people did not make the time for a few quiet moments, nor did they make real human contact - let alone eye-contact. He envisioned a society headquarters that had no written signs so people would be forced to ask the way and so talk to each other. At the root of his sense of estrangement was his belief that the use of pronouns - as in 'he said... they said... he replied' - kept people distant from who was actually saying what to whom. The pronoun 'they' was particularly insidious, he felt - and who could disagree? His three societies, just like the society for women over fifty who wanted babies, had taken ideas he held close to his heart and given them coherent expression. In the process the writers had turned areas of sorrow into personal affirmations of what they wanted to do, and how they wanted to run their lives.

In a different vein, a woman whose beloved cat was dying went one step further. She not only thought of a society for the appreciation of her cat, but she went so far as to call people she knew and ask, good-humoredly, if they would join. As she did so she was able to express, indirectly, what she had known for years, which was that she had tended to focus her attention and love on the cat, at times at the expense of developing human friendships. By reaching out to those that knew her, she not only acknowledged how she had been living, but she also invited them to see that she knew this, and gave them a way to respond to her. It was far more elegant than if she had tried to explain her whole life to everyone. The practical return was also magnificent. Her friends were able to show their love for her, which was something she had found difficult to ask for. And that fear of asking, after all, was why she'd poured her love upon her cat.... Her private grief at losing a much-loved pet had motivated her. She'd not only thought of a society but had chosen to live her choice - and she'd done so with a full awareness of the somewhat unusual and eccentric nature of her request.

I've described this at length because the idea of forming a society is a way of asking what is important in a person's life which may not be getting full recognition. Often those important aspects are slightly embarrassing, or things we wouldn't freely admit to just everyone. It also asks us to consider what sorts of people we want in our lives, and how we might begin to locate those people. At a basic level it is also a move from solitary pain to community empowerment, a point where the question, 'Does anybody care about me and my concerns?' becomes an affirmation that these feelings are important, and deserve a supportive network. So, one man who wanted to form a Charlie Chaplin society did so because, as he said, Chaplin brought magic into his life. He identified with the comic-romantic aspects of the character, and wanted to contact others who felt the same way. What could have been a depressive stance, an identification with a comic but pathetic figure, had become the start of an exploration of his own psyche.

Many times I've noticed how productive this exercise can be, and I relate to it very directly. I have always been interested in vintage motorcycles (the older the better) but as a college teacher it's not always easy to find colleagues who share this slightly offbeat hobby, so I've joined local clubs where I can be with those who share my interests. Why? Because my hobby has 'magic' for me, just as Charlie Chaplin had for the man I mentioned earlier, and I want to be able to contact that magic, even if many of my good friends shake their heads and wonder what the attraction of restoring old machinery could be. I need my hobby, but I don't need anyone to disapprove and spoil my fun. I've a sense that this is true for everyone. We all need a place, mental or physical, where we can contact our 'magic'.

This leads to the next exercise.

EXERCISE 9:

❖ Create a place of bliss, a safe place you would want to be. You can treat this as a fantasy, if you wish.

Versions of Virginia Woolf's *A Room of One's Own* have appeared in response to this exercise - comfortable rooms with privacy, quiet, and great armchairs. One woman produced a picture of her place of bliss which was a series of clouds, floating, weightless. Castles and estates in rural Maine have also figured, and everything else in between.

If the preceding exercise about a society was a way of asking how you might include people in your vital inner life, this exercise is likely to reflect how close we want them to be to us, and under what circumstances. The man who wanted the estate in rural Maine, complete with airstrip, was clear that he wanted lots of room for visitors, but that they would all meet for communal meals. Otherwise they had their own separate buildings to stay in. By contrast, a woman who wanted roses outside her open bedroom window only required that room to herself in a shared house. Community was just outside the door, just as the roses were just outside the window.

What I always find so remarkable about the responses to this exercise is that there is so rarely any insistence upon physical luxuries. It is unusual for someone to insist on, say, a new Mercedes, and on the occasion that this happened the man who had specified it was able to see that this was another way of talking about the sense of freedom and pleasure that could lead to peace of mind.

These two exercises can, in this way, reflect each other. We all want some degree of company, and we all want our own private space. By writing and reflecting in this playful way we can help to define to ourselves what we feel we need. For it is not until we do this that we can make the first steps towards bringing these needs into the realm of fulfillment. Writing, on its own, cannot make the dreams come true. By spelling out our wishes we can acknowledge that we'll need help to get what we want - and the only way to get help is to go out and organize it.

And that's true, broadly speaking, for all of us.

The danger that both these exercises confronts is the do-nothing daydream of 'if only...' We can spend decades hoping that someone else somewhere will make it all happen for us. We can spend lifetimes not expressing our wants because we feel that they may be selfish. A society, by definition, identifies that there are others out there who feel the same way - and so one's needs are no longer selfish.

Similarly a place of bliss assumes that we're all entitled to such a place, and to such bliss. The exercise is deliberately designed to ask the question, 'how are you going to get it?' This is a much more empowering question than, 'why do you want it?' Why always pushes a question into explanation format. We have to justify ourselves in the face of why. How demands no such reflection. If you find yourself asking frequent why questions of yourself you might want to rephrase them as how questions. A simple example may help. Try asking a twelve year old why he did something, and the chances are you'll get a very defensive answer.

"Why did you break the window?"

This is very different from:

"How did you break the window?"

To return to the woman of fifty who wanted a baby, the question why can only seem antagonistic, demanding justifications. How will you do this? On the other hand, is a question that will reflect just as much reality, and it has the advantage that it suggests the woman is fully aware of the difficulties and prejudices. It asks her to consider the situation, not to explain herself to a cosmos full of skeptics. For the sense of those skeptics waiting, out there, to criticize and question us, will silence us like nothing else can, and freeze us into immobility.

If we accept that we are all entitled to a place of bliss, then we give ourselves permission to shift our focus from the material world to the spiritual.

Chapter Sixteen

CARE-TAKING

This section can usefully be linked to some of the issues raised in Chapter 10 *Parenting* since many of us will find ourselves caring for sick or aging relatives at about the same time we're also raising children. Possibly your situation is that you have ailing parents and a pair of teenagers in the house, or your children are all close to being finished with college and you find yourself looking for long-term care for a parent. Whatever your situation, the most obvious stresses on you are likely to be claims on your time and claims on your wallet.

The standard expected response when caring for parents is that one should be motivated by love, by a sense of gratitude for all that the parent or relative did for you when you were younger. This is very persuasive. Most of us do feel gratitude for all that our parents did for us. But what does that mean in terms of obligation? Elder care can cost the equivalent of a year's salary if the person is actually infirm. One man, a professor in his late 50s, related that an aging aunt needed managed care, and that all the places he looked at were priced around $50,000 a year - roughly equivalent to his salary. Eventually he moved her to Tennessee, as it was the only place he could find good, managed care at a reasonable price. Since he lived in Boston that made visiting very difficult. He had done all he could for her. He couldn't give up his job and nurse her 24 hours a day, since he needed the salary. He couldn't find anything closer. His aunt, however, felt abandoned.

This is a no-win situation, and it's not atypical.

EXERCISE 1:

❖ What have you had to give up as a result of helping and being a caretaker?

If this situation hasn't happened to you yet, take a moment to think about what you might have to give up. Consider everything - from your Sunday morning game of golf to working late at the office when there's a deadline. Write about this, or create a list. You may even want to spend a day or so thinking in this vein, jotting things down that you feel you may have to forgo.

This may sound like a negative way to start, but in reality we will have to give up something. What have you had to forgo already? As you read your responses, look for words like 'I was forced...' and 'I had to...' Weigh those words carefully, because ultimately the chances are you were not coerced; you forced yourself. Why? A sense of duty, perhaps? A sense of guilt for having been a less-than-perfect child in the past? A sense of pride? When we look at words like 'I was forced' or 'I felt compelled' we notice that grammatically these are passive sentences - you are having something done to you, rather than being the active person. In reality you could choose to walk away from a situation. You might feel terrible about it, but you could do it. So what keeps you from doing that?

My aim, here, is to establish that you have made a choice. A choice, any choice, becomes much easier to deal with when you, the chooser, acknowledge that you took it on. 'Look what they made me do!' is the cry of the helpless victim. 'I chose to take up the challenge' is the statement of the self-directed, vital human being. Which way do you see yourself?

Look, also, for responses in which words like 'gave up' or 'sacrificed' appear. These are, for the most part, negative statements - even though to sacrifice originally meant to give something willingly and reverently to a deity. Isn't it interesting how words change their value? Even the most famously repeated statement of them all: 'I gave up smoking' sounds like a loss. Imagine if we reformulated that. It could be something like: 'I chose to take up healthy living'. The sentiment is the same, but this time it is a positive sentiment. This is not a quibble. We define our world through words. If we use negative wording to describe our actions we take part in diminishing who we are. Naturally this is open to abuse - an army rarely suffers a defeat, it instead undertakes 'a tactical withdrawal'; an air force doesn't have 'a lot of crashes' it has a '40% failure rate' (meaning four out of ten planes crashed), and so on. I'm not suggesting we fool ourselves with language. I'm urging you to look at your responses for those subtle negative messages that act as a form of self-criticism. For we are always our harshest critics.

EXERCISE 2:

❖   What do you feel you have gained from the experience of care-taking?

This can be a wonderful exercise, and it may take several repeats to understand, fully, what can be gained from this most intimate of encounters. Some people have reported that care-taking finally broke down barriers between parents and children, allowing them to see each other as loving, frail, and thoroughly human, perhaps for the first time ever. Nurses working with the terminally ill or with hospice patients have reported that although the work is hard and often emotionally wrenching, it can be uplifting. Working with people who know they are dying has a way of concentrating the mind upon what is genuinely important. In facing death we are forced to ask what life is about, and with some urgency, as our loved one grows weaker. There is much we can learn, if we are prepared to accept it.

"I think I learned most about patience. Mine grew as I watched my Dad struggle." So reported a man of fifty-three.

"She died at home. I'm so glad I was able to give her that," said a fifty five year old woman of her mother.

Analyzing statements like these is never very helpful, since they express emotions that lie deeper and extend further than the words can really convey. They speak of lessons learned on the pulse of life, felt in the blood, and they are not easily translated.

If we look for what is to be gained from the experience of caring for another we may find deeper wisdom than we expected. If you want, you could return now to Exercise 1 and reconsider it. Surely, you gave up things - income, freedom, leisure - but you may well have been put in touch with the greatest challenge of them all, what it means to face death.

EXERCISE 3:

❖ Do you feel you are doing more than your share? Not enough?

A couple in their fifties found they were the only people who were prepared to take care of the wife's aging mother – the other four children made no contribution. This led to strained relationships with the other siblings and a general sense of being used. Yet from this difficult set of circumstances the couple were able to emerge with an enhanced sense of themselves as people who cared and were prepared to act on their feelings.

A bachelor in his forties, who did not drive, talked about how he took a five hour train ride every weekend to see his mother during her final illness. "She was horrible to me," he related. "She'd criticize everything I did. My sister, who never went to see her, was idolized." What this man realized was the shocking truth of the old saying, 'you always hurt the ones you love.' Many years later he began to realize that his mother only felt safe enough with him, of all the family, to express herself. Unfortunately the expressions were all negative, sometimes even hurtful. The man began to realize that her negativity had more to do with her own sense of the unfairness of life than anything else. She wanted to say she loved her son, but all she could say were things that were less than pleasant. Behind this, he saw, lay her unfulfilled hopes. She had wanted so many good and loving things for both her children, and many of them had not happened. The man began to see that behind the disappointment lurked a huge, under-utilized capacity for love. The son was doing more than his fair share of helping, but he was receiving something, indirectly, that was golden.

Nurses have often reported to me similar circumstances. A ward sister was telling me about a particularly cantankerous old man in her ward, and I said that I thought it would be hard for me to care for someone who was as unpleasant as that. "Oh, we don't pay any attention to that. He's just angry he's dying. He loves us, really. You can see it in his eyes." The wisdom and the caring in this statement impressed themselves on me deeply. If one is dying then it must be hugely poignant to leave not only this life, but those people that one has come to rely on, to love, during the final illness. The point was that these nurses saw right through the old man's ill humor. They knew, intuitively, exactly what was going on, and accepted it. They even liked his testiness. How consoling, how sad, how absolutely important - to be understood and accepted finally, even at such a late moment!

EXERCISE 4:

❖ How has your life changed as a result of being a caretaker?

It is important, for some people, to list all the ways their daily routines have changed. Doing this can help us get a firmer grip on what life demands of us now. A list can also help us prioritize more efficiently. We see ourselves removing the superfluous items, making alternative arrangements. For example, one's children may have to learn to take more charge of some aspects of their lives since there is not enough time to do all the things for them that one used to. This is often a good thing in the maturation process. The family may begin to function more cohesively as a cooperative unit as a result - rather than the familiar 'leave everything to mother' routine that dominates some households. Siblings may find themselves helping each other, taking on tasks they might otherwise abandon in favor of TV. "It's amazing what kids can do if they see a solid reason for it," wrote a mother of two who had always done all the household chores.

Sometimes the extra burden of a sick relative has other healthy repercussions. A man of forty-one related how when he was a boy his sick grandmother would ask him to read out loud to her. He loved to do this, and it also gave his mother some time to herself. It wasn't until years later that he realized that his grandmother asked him to do this because he had a mild speech impediment, and the reading practice was good for his mind (he still loves to read) and his speech. He thought he was entertaining her. She knew she was giving him a gift that would build his confidence and self-esteem, while assuring him of her love. She helped significantly to develop a new direction in his life.

Look at your own experience. Are there any such hidden gifts? I'm convinced there are more of these than we may be aware of. Some of the gifts are seen immediately, others take time to emerge.

EXERCISE 5:

❖ Is there a better way to arrange the care-taking?

This builds on Exercise 4. Often it is not until we think about this, brainstorm about it, that new solutions can emerge. If we respond to the challenge of care-taking by seeing it as an inevitable imposition we will not be able to think creatively about it. A man of thirty eight, who ran his own business, began to think about how he could contact others who had parents to care for. A few weeks later he had organized a co-operative neighborhood arrangement in which people looked after their own parents and organized a roster to care for other's relatives, too. By means of a delicate juggling of schedules it was possible for blocks of time to be traded so no one's relative was left unattended. It took a lot of organization, but it saved a fortune in professional fees for nursing staff. The added result was that the caretakers were able to see that other people had similar concerns to their own, which broke the focus of seeing the needy parent as the only problem in their lives. The cooperative group in fact became mutually supportive for the emotional needs of the caretakers, as well as for the aging parents

A different example is provided by a man in his fifties who developed a brain tumor. Before he became too ill, he consulted with his wife and family and they arranged to reach out to all their neighbors. At first they asked that people come and visit for a half hour 'positive thoughts' gathering. This proved to be successful, and the caring that all experienced led them to repeat the meetings. As they reached out - and as neighbors responded - they discovered a whole new way of responding to the disease. More than this, his family was not left alone with its difficulties as the husband became steadily weaker. Strengthened by this support they were in turn able to help and support others. Meanwhile, others who were in similar situations have learned from this example, shaping their lives accordingly. No one could say it was easy, but it would have been far harder without the mutual support that was allowed to flourish. I like to think of this example because out of a simple request for help came a gift for the entire community: cooperation. Other caretakers have learned from this man's situation. The solution is far from perfect – no one would claim that it is. Those most closely involved have shared care-taking duties, cooking, childcare, and general chores. The community as a whole has been strengthened, and individuals have certainly been helped physically and emotionally. Potential disaster has been changed in large part to loving kindness.

EXERCISE 6:

❖   Who takes care of you, when you take care of others?

It's vital that we take care of ourselves, pay attention to our own needs, or we'll have only a constantly depleting stock of energy from which we have to supply others. As you go about your tasks, ask yourself if you are getting what you need to sustain you? "I hadn't realized I was running on empty," a man of thirty two confided. When he made time to eat, sleep and exercise properly he found he had much more energy to give to his nursing. He even found he was able to receive support from his patients as a result. The difference was that he was open to what they had to offer back to him. Looking after himself was not selfish, in this case, so much as life-enhancing for all concerned. If you aren't taking the time to replenish yourself, think about that. How could you make that possible? What would it take? What do you miss? "I'm really looking forward to having two days all alone all to myself," wrote a thirty eight year old mother of three. "No phone. No TV. Just me." A woman who headed several committees and organized everyone's life, she desperately needed this brief vacation so she could continue to be the person her family needed her to be. The hint here is that if you don't take the time to tend to your own needs, no one else will.

Obviously there is much more to the task of care-taking than can be dealt with in these pages, since every situation is different. As you read this you may be thinking, 'what good is this to me? I'm still stuck with the task.' This is where I have to relay to you that the solutions are in your hands. I cannot take the task from you. But I think that by doing these exercises you may be able to see your situation with a little more insight, and you may begin to realize you have more options that you had at first thought.

It is an interesting thing about people that when we are faced with a demand or a crisis that we tend to act cautiously rather than anything else. We tend to want to think 'within the box'. We may even find ourselves saying such things as, 'what does everyone else do in these circumstances?' The examples I have given of caretakers setting up cooperative care are, to me, creative responses that have very little to do with staying within the unwritten social norms of don't-bother-your-neighbor-with-your-troubles. These people dared to think outside the normally accepted limits. Perhaps that is the real lesson here. Creative solutions can only come about when we stop being fearful and see beyond what we expect to see. And this leads us to the next exercise.

EXERCISE 7:

❖   What are your fears about being a caretaker?

I don't think it's morbid to face one's fears about this. If we choose to state what we most fear we can begin to take steps to deal with it, to tame the fears, to manage them. Some people have chosen to respond to this by writing about how they're afraid that being a caretaker will tie them down for years, will blight their lives, wear them out, and so on. This is a very real fear. All situations are different, but I can imagine how frightening it must be to have to think about having an infirm parent on one's hands for five years or more. Since few of us have uncomplicated relationships with our parents, this may be something that seems like a major obstacle.

When you have made a list of your fears, you may want to make a second list of what you need in order to cope with the situation. Since you've written about your fears it may now be much easier to focus on what you need. Suggest resources you can draw on to deal with each fear you have listed. Now you've written them down you may find that some of the fears are not as bad as you thought they would be. Some may be worse.

It may even be a good idea to do this exercise with the person you have to look after. Share these thoughts and fears and discuss them, if you can. The best way to deal with those one has to care for is to be open and honest about what is happening and enlist them as part of the solution whenever possible.

Again, there are no easy answers or quick fixes here. What I offer are some ways to begin to see the situation differently so that it can be less overwhelming. Whatever you choose to do it will be hard work, I'm sure. But unless we take stock and decide what is possible, and what constitutes a task well done, we may tend to work exceptionally hard and still feel we haven't done enough. That can only lead to heartbreak.

The next sections will continue this discussion into the realm of death and dying, and mourning.

Chapter Seventeen

LOSS

Often we lose people. They drift away from us and we hear one day that they've died. Sometimes they leave us - parents, lovers, friends - and we never know what happened. Accidents may take our loved ones at times we least expect, and sudden health problems can deprive us of those we assumed would be around always. Wars can claim those we love and leave us without even a grave to visit. Our children can die, or be killed, or disappear - which is probably the most shocking loss of all.

This is a topic that cannot be dealt with very effectively by any book, since those who feel the loss may feel it at a profoundly visceral level. Often there is nothing one can do to soothe a father's pain or a mother's loss except to hold that person, and be witness to the grief.

Grief like this takes time, often several years. In some cultures there is a socially prescribed period of mourning. These days we may tend to look at that as just a way of honoring the dead person, but I'd suggest that the custom arose originally because the mourning person was likely to be, literally, changed forever by the experience, and so needed some time to adjust. In the west, widows and widowers used to have to wear black for a set period of time. This would seem to be counter-productive. After all, widows were often relatively wealthy as the inheritors of the husband's estate and so they would make attractive spouses in many societies. The period of mourning seems, therefore, to have evolved not in response to the male dominated laws of property, which would want to have as short a period of sequestration as possible, but as a real acknowledgement that unless people are allowed the time and mental space to mourn their dead they will not be fit to make further alliances.

If you have suffered a recent loss you'll need to have some good friends or some good counselors, or even both. If your loss has been less recent I can suggest an exercise.

EXERCISE 1:

❖ Complete the following. Write as much as you wish. "The last time I saw my (father/mother/child)....."

This can be an occasion to vent, or it can allow us to try to make sense of what we know. The last time we saw someone is always the most poignant in retrospect. We may recall the mundane things that we wished we'd got past. The fact that we were in a rush and so didn't say goodbye properly; the last silly joke; the fact that we were preoccupied and didn't even really look at the person; the argument; the words we wish we could unsay. All these thoughts can haunt us unless we take the time to release them through writing.

It's worth recalling that in many ways the last contact with any person can seem symbolic of aspects of the relationship. The last phone call, down a crackly line, may seem to be an image of distance and misunderstandings. Or you may recall the person being typically themselves, and that too can be heart-rending.

When you have written, review your work. Are you blaming yourself for the way the last conversations went? How responsible do you feel for the way the relationship was at that point? Could you have done anything differently? Of course you could, now, in retrospect. At the time you probably couldn't have done it otherwise. And it wasn't all up to you, was it? The other person made up half that conversation.

EXERCISE 2:

❖ What words would you like to have said that you didn't? Spend some time on this: you may want to respond now, and then again later.

Most frequently people want to express their love and affection. Sometimes they want to express anger and rage. I'd like to remind you here that the object is not to wallow in the past, nor to dredge up misery. The loss cannot be undone. All we can do in our lives is to try to learn from the loss. Ask yourself what you can learn from this, and what you can take into the future. That is why I ask you to respond twice to this question - now and later, when you may feel differently.

EXERCISE 3:

❖ If you had to talk about what happened between you and the missing person, perhaps explain it to a child, how would you do that?

If we attempt to explain things to an imagined child, someone who is sensitive and inexperienced, we may well allow ourselves to make a more careful and fair assessment of what happened, and we are more likely to be able to see the aspects we can learn from. When we explain things to ourselves we may well want to heap self-blame and criticism on our heads, and we may only manage to confuse the issues that most need clarification. So, please, imagine that child who needs to know, who deserves honesty, and who needs to face the world with knowledge that is genuine, knowledge to live by. In taking care of that child you take care of the hurting and helpless aspect of yourself, too.

If we follow Eric Berne's ideas of transactional psychology we can take this several steps further. Once we have explained to a child (really the child within us) we may want to try explaining to an imagined adult. In doing this we can develop a non-judgmental adult to adult assessment of what the loss means to us, one that is sensible in our own terms. It can be very hard to find an actual adult to do this with, since some will tend to be less than patient and others may want to tell you what to think, and that is why I suggest an imagined person, someone who will understand if only we spell out what we mean.

I do not intend to give more exercises here. More material appears in the next chapter, on death, although that chapter has to do specifically with the process of dying rather than the shock of loss itself.

Chapter Eighteen

DEATH: FACING OUR OWN ENDS

We will all die, yet we seem to behave as if we'll never have to face that challenge. Our own death may seem remote; we assume our friends and loved ones will always be there, and so we may not think about this until it's too late. In a culture such as ours, where youth and beauty are revered above all else, where our efforts are often directed to eradicating the signs of aging, it's probably not surprising that we seem to have difficulty facing death. The stores are full of products that are designed to make us look younger, combat wrinkles, gray hair, baldness, and the changing body shape that comes with advancing years.

Is it any wonder we're confused about death? Dr. Kevorkian's assisted suicide program kept lawyers busy for years arguing about whether he should be prosecuted or not before he was finally convicted. In contrast are those hospitals that regularly exert heroic efforts to 'save' the lives of the terminally sick. In fact it is thought by some organizations for elder rights that the last week in hospital for a dying person makes up, on average, over 50% of the total medical expense incurred during the rest of the person's life. This is hard to verify since there are so many variables, but we all know of families that have been financially depleted by the final hospital stay of a relative. This can be avoided, of course, by the use of such things as a living will and powers of attorney that spell out exactly how much care the person wants in those last days. The astounding thing is that so few people ever make those preparations. I can only presume that they think it'll never happen to them.

The desperate scramble to save lives that may not want to be saved is caused by many things. Hospitals make money; doctors want to try out treatments - this is commonplace. In addition, patients and their relatives alike seem to allow this to happen because they are confused as to what to do. They're confused, I'd suggest, as to how to value life, and what is appropriate in death. Letting go is hard when you've had no chance to understand what it means.

Our cultural confusion about death is probably nowhere more evident than in the New Age ideas of channeling and past lives. I am not criticizing these belief. I would merely like to suggest that any belief can be distorted, and that this is no exception. Whether or not reincarnation is real seems to matter less than the fact that many people believe it to be true, and the knock-on effect is that even those who are not particularly spiritual seem to regard reincarnation as likely. The result is that some believers may take their own lives less than seriously. There'll always be another life, right? My advice is to quote Gandhi back to such people, and Gandhi as a devout Hindu really did believe in reincarnation. He said that even though it may seem improbable that what we do in our lives can have much effect, "it is vitally important that you do it!" We could interpret that as meaning that even if you believe in reincarnation it is a much better plan to behave in this life as if there were no second chance to get things right. Interestingly, Hinduism does stress exactly that in the idea of karma. Every decision is eternally significant, since what is done well will produce good.

Another perspective on death is seen in the furious calls we see so often on our TV screens uttered by the relatives of murder victims. At the time of writing this, Massachusetts once again came within a single Senate vote of passing a death penalty. I'm not about to discuss the pros and cons of capital punishment. Every person has his or her deeply held views, and as the vote suggests, opinion is split pretty evenly. What interests me more is the idea that seems to motivate some of those in favor of the death penalty, namely that death is the ultimate punishment, that it is, somehow, a combination of pain and terror that the convicted murderer deserves. While it's true that the death penalty is frightening, is it really as fearsomely cruel as forty years of incarceration? Some might argue, as we do with our beloved pets, that a quick, painless death is merciful indeed.

As you read this you are probably saying: "But... But..." I don't wish to argue with your views. What I'm saying is that our society is filled with contrasting ideas of what death is about, and this confusion keeps the individual under-prepared. We see more death on TV, actual and staged, than any previous generation, anywhere. You'd think we'd have a better handle on things by now.

The objective of this chapter is to get us to ask ourselves basic questions about the end of our lives. If we don't plan ahead we may find ourselves in a situation where others are planning our lives for us. An acquaintance of mine, in her eighties, declared that if she ever were hospitalized she would simply stop eating and so die rapidly. She preferred this to "ruining her family" with medical bills, to use her words. This sounds good in theory, but the actuality is that once in the hospital, medicated, sedated, and fed through a tube perhaps, even this act of refusing food is not possible. We think we're prepared for departure, but often we're not.

EXERCISE 1:

❖   What do I need to do to approach death without fear? Make a list, if you wish.

This question can seem alarming, and yet it's only describing what we optimally all desire - to face the great unknown without panic. For many people religion and faith are great guides as to what we have to do to face our demise. Indeed, in other eras, when religion was more widely accepted, it provided set expectations of what one had to do. Undoubtedly this helped to calm the sufferer. Today religious practices are much less widely endorsed, and some of us may have to make up our own scripts. It might be as well to plan it out in advance, since we never know when death will claim us.

Many people respond to this question by listing those things they have to do to protect their property for their loved ones. Others have written about people they needed to see in order to forgive them or beg forgiveness - or simply in order to tell them they love them. I would take an even larger perspective. If one is at peace with one's world one can not only die with a clear conscience, but live with one, also. Approaching death without fear means living without fear; it means recognizing what living means.

We all have a tendency to feel that we can't die yet because there's so much we still have to do. That, logically, makes no sense at all - yet that's the way so many of us live. Material concerns tie us to the mundane. Such thinking doesn't even hold true for most jobs, let alone for life. It's like saying, "You can't fire me half way through this project!" But projects get cancelled all the time.

If your list includes seeing a lawyer, rewriting your will, and so on, by all means do that; and then begin to address your spiritual needs as well.

EXERCISE 2:

❖ What do I need to do to allow a loved one to come to terms with death? You can write about this if you are the person who is dying. You can also write about it if you are attending someone you love who is dying, and who may need some help with this.

If you are dying you may find that a considerable amount of pain can come from seeing the difficulties your loved ones experience in facing the approaching separation. This exercise can prepare you for their confusions and needs. Remember, they will be looking to you, in all likelihood, to see how you are dealing with this. They will want to take their lead from you, and may be confused as to what their roles may be. Sometimes Exercise 1 can be a great help with this. When loved ones are able to see that you have made practical arrangements for the disposal of property and so on it can reassure them that you are ready to face your death. Knowing this can often help them overcome the paralysis of not knowing how to be or what to say in the face of something they may see as frightening, as overwhelming. It has been said that whenever a parent dies the children, no matter what age they may be, adult or young, feel the death like children. The lead up to death may be the time when we want others to do the work for us, but the fact of the matter seems to be that others will be waiting to see how we manage the situation so they can see how to react. We have, very often, to take the lead in these things just when we least feel like doing it. Asking a loved one to help with these arrangements can break this sense of emotional paralysis.

The same is true for those who are attending a dying relative. Perhaps your spouse is dying, or your parent, and is having a hard time facing up to it. If you can encourage the dying person to make the necessary decisions about the practicalities this can relieve the emotional burden on the survivors and give relief to the dying person. So many times I have come across people who will not admit they are dying, not because they are in denial, but because they don't want to be morbid, or because they think it may be in poor taste to mention it. This seems especially true for the generation that grew up in World War Two, who may have seen death more often than other generations. It is not until the practicalities have been settled, and the dying person has openly admitted his or her awareness of the situation, that everyone else can allow honesty to return to the situation. The saddest responses I have read have come from those who were unable to reach this point. Here is one: "I just kept telling her she'd be fine, even though I knew she wouldn't be," wrote one man, " because I could see her fear. I wish we could've gotten to some honesty. Instead it all felt like pantomime. I was supposed to say these words, and she was supposed to be encouraged by them, and she tried to be. But it didn't work. We both knew it." Since the fear of death can confuse us in this way, taking care of the practical details can be a way of reasserting a measure of control and dignity, and of allowing a genuine, open, and loving dialogue to emerge.

EXERCISE 3:

❖   What were the important deaths in your family? What did you value about those
    people?

It's only by looking back, by observing the deaths and lives of those whom we have known, that we can begin to think of what we must do and how we must do it. The examples other people show us can have more impact than we know. I recall watching a family friend die of cancer and, at age fourteen, I was frightened to even be around this kindly gentleman in his late fifties. I realize now that he saw how frightened I was. Even in his pain he let me witness how he was just living, peacefully, one day at a time, and he enlisted my help in that. We had a long chat about what to have for lunch, and I recall thinking that it didn't matter much because he'd soon be dead, yet he calmed me, choosing fish (which was within his diet) and behaving for all the world like a man waiting for a train to come. Death would come when it came, and until then he'd look after his diet and make sure we had an acceptable lunch. At a time when he had every right to ask the world to be good to him, he was able to give me the gift of his calmness. From him I learned that a painful death can be faced with dignity and good humor, and that those who are left behind need guidance as much as anyone.

Another instance was related to me by a woman of fifty who had undergone a series of surgeries as a result of breast cancer. In responding to this question she described how her friends and colleagues at work, and the children she was mentor to, were all terrified to speak with her after they had learned of her need to return to the hospital. "They couldn't meet my eye," she said. That was when she realized how afraid they were of her possible death, and this made life harder for her, too. Her solution was to write an open letter to the whole institution, stating exactly what would happen, when, and what the situation seemed to be. She asked for their patience. The effect was to lessen the tension for everyone. Yet she was the one facing death, and she had to reassure the others.

A contrary example may serve to explain this further. A relative of mine was dying of cancer but forbade anyone in his family to mention this. As far as he was concerned they were to say he was "unwell," but "improving." My relative went to his grave with his so-called secret. He wanted to avoid the pity of others, he wanted to bear his illness bravely. It was a noble aspiration, but all he managed to do was prevent us saying goodbye, and he cut off any chance we might have had to tell him how much we loved him. As one woman in her sixties wrote about her father's death, being able to be with him, to see him through to the end, despite the pain and frailty, was "the greatest gift he could have given me." My relative unfortunately didn't allow that gift to be given.

This leads to the next exercise.

EXERCISE 4:

❖ Write a letter of condolence to someone who has just lost a loved one, or who may lose that person soon. What do you love and value about those people?

It may seem unnecessarily morbid to write a letter of this sort about someone who hasn't yet died, but I will remind you that we are engaged, here, on a task that will help to value the good things about life. The old cliche "you don't know what you've got until it's gone" is, to me, one of the saddest statements of the unconsciously lived life. We do ourselves an enormous service by regularly checking in with ourselves to value our experiences, consider our friends, and be aware of where we are. This is the whole miracle of diary and journal-writing. If done conscientiously it keeps us in touch with what we feel. As PBS sports commentator Bill Littlefield said to me, "Having to write every day is a great way to find out what you really feel."

When people respond to this exercise they often become emotional, realizing their own sense of loneliness in the face of death and loss, as well as gaining an awareness of how much their friendships have meant. The next stage is that some people take the next step, which requires a huge amount of courage. They go and see the people concerned, and tell them about their feelings. This can be a risky endeavor, of course, since others may not be prepared for such outpourings. If you decide to do this then I'd advise choosing your moment carefully. I'd also advise that in such circumstances less is often more, because sometimes we don't need to say very much for others to understand that we love and value them. A few words, said with the depth of feeling that one can reach as a result of doing these exercises, are all that are really needed.

EXERCISE 5:

❖ What do you fear about death? What might you welcome? Again, this question works whether one is dying or thinking about someone who is.

Some people answer this in essay format. Others produce lists, which may include the fear of pain, being poor, being alone, and losing sanity. The reason I have these two questions as a pair is that for the chronically ill death may offer a welcome release from suffering, from the perception of living in a degrading condition, and from the pain inflicted on others who may be observing the death. Those who are religious may be frightened at the thought of facing God, or eager to enter heaven. For many people, however, the greatest fear is that they face the unknown, and they wrestle with the possibility that their lives may mean nothing. It's a terrifying thought to some.

I can't give any answers. I can only suggest to you that whatever exploration you need to do in order to face death is best done before the final moments. Elisabeth Kubler-Ross' landmark study *On Death and Dying* spells out the phases we can expect to go through as people losing loved ones and as we ourselves go towards death. She points out exactly what the steps are that lead to the final stage of giving up false hope and allowing ourselves to let go. Kubler-Ross doesn't tell us how to get to the last stage, she simply describes the phases she has observed others going through. In addition, she doesn't emphasize that the progression is not straight forward, and that the dying person can choose to loop back to an earlier stage. What needs to said is that there are many ways to face death. The question is - how can we come to make peace with ourselves and the world? This next exercise may help to clarify that.

EXERCISE 6:

❖ Imagine how other people will look on your death. Is there anything you need to do? What do you need to tell the people in your life?

Sometimes by considering how others may react we can gain insights into what we may have to do in order to make peace. A good example of this can be seen in the strange poetry of the suicide note. These are sometimes reported in newspapers, and one of the things such notes frequently contain are apologies to those left alive. The apology, the confession of being too scared, too confused, too enmeshed in problems to carry on - these are things that often come as a shock to the survivors. My point here is that these notes often show a high level of awareness of the problems, even honesty. This is very hopeful - if the note is delivered as a request for help rather than as an apology after the event. By seeing how one's death may affect others we can begin to assess who may be able to help us, and how. The farewell note is a potentially useful communication, one that deserves to be shared sooner rather than later, and it can help those we care for see how we really feel before it is too late to do anything about it.

The irony, of course, is that many people who have had relatives kill themselves are angry for just that reason. "Why didn't he let us know!" shouted a man of 40 when his brother killed himself, "How could he do this to us?" This man took it as a personal affront, a rejection, that his brother hadn't come to him for help. He was raging angry. I'm sure the brother couldn't have foreseen that reaction - if he had, he'd have certainly thought twice about taking his own life.

All I'm trying to point out, here, is that if we can consider the way others might respond to our deaths we can begin to comprehend that there may be a contrasting view to our own. We'd all like to imagine being mourned, being wept over, a stream of loved ones following the casket mumbling things about how we'll be missed. Indeed, I sincerely hope that for everyone. It may not turn out that way, in reality. People may well be upset that we didn't reach out to them in the time we had left. It's a prompting we might wish to follow up.

Responding to this exercise, one woman of fifty began to write in scathing terms about her father's will. As executrix she had been left with the responsibility of hosting a party each year, to be funded out of the estate, for dozens of relatives and friends - the party to be held annually until the money ran out, which was estimated to be many years ahead. The daughter didn't care about the money, she was enraged by the rampant egotism that had made her father do this, especially as she hadn't got along with him since she was twelve. She couldn't believe that he could do this, as he'd never really cared for any of his other relatives, either. Did the father want to burden her? Did he really not understand how much resentment this will would cause? We'll never know for sure, now. Certainly the lawyers had advised him against it on many occasions. The question has to be: what on earth was he thinking? Whatever he was thinking, it seemed not to have been very clearly formulated, and led only to resentment.

Further discussions with the woman about her father revealed that not only had she not got along with him, but he had physically mistreated her, which had caused her to run away from home. When she was finally returned home after living a precarious life on the run, he had insisted she be referred for psychiatric assessment, as if the problem lay all with her. She found it very hard to forgive her father for this. One could guess that the father's will, in which he specified that the child he had mistreated was to be the hostess at a sort of annual appreciation party, was perhaps trying to signal to the world that he believed he was blameless and here was his daughter, running the party (and therefore forgiving him) to prove it. Here was a man who seemed to think much more about what would be presented to the outside world rather than about what was real in the relationship. It is a sad example of how muddled we can be sometimes, as we approach death.

Another example was related to me by a woman from Germany about a neighbor in her village some years before. The neighbor, an accountant, had cancer and decided to kill himself to avoid further suffering. He had no family, but he made the arrangements for his death with meticulous care, specifying the exact suit he was to wear in the coffin, even down to the particular tie and tie-pin. He left all his papers in perfect order and prepared the obituary he wanted published - a long document that owed more to vanity than to anything else, as the woman related. Then he fixed a hose-pipe to his car exhaust, turned on the engine, placed the end of the hose in the car, and asphyxiated himself. What he didn't realize was that the carbon monoxide that killed him would also turn his flesh a strange blue color within a few hours, destroying the tissues. It proved impossible to have an open casket funeral, as he'd hoped, and all his efforts to appear as an impressive corpse were thwarted. I give this gruesome example because I want to differentiate between those people who think about dying, eternity, and their souls, and those whose plans for death are so fixed in the mundane world of what people will gossip about that they never really manage to leave the workaday considerations of petty vanities. There is a double irony to this tale. The man who so wanted to be remembered was, indeed, remembered; it just wasn't quite what he'd intended.

In spite of all this I can't help thinking that this was, in fact, the action of a brave man. He wanted to avoid the long degradation of an incurable illness when there was no family member to care for him. That is a very reasonable thought. The thing that pulled him down was his pride. He wanted to let everyone know how brave and in control he was. In the attempt I suspect he never allowed himself to recognize the range of feelings were that were open to him.

This discussion leads us into the next exercise.

EXERCISE 7:

❖ Describe a memorial you'd like to leave for (a) yourself; (b) your best friend; (c) someone else you value. You can respond factually or you can imagine you have the resources necessary for a project of this sort.

One young man of twenty-six said he wanted to have a bridge as a memorial, "Because I like to think my job as a teacher has helped people make transitions." An older man wanted to preserve his colonial home and garden and donate it to the Parks Commission as a museum. An environmental engineer suggested that for his monument he'd like to gather the world's supply of Styrofoam, make a big pyramid of it, and then ban all future production. It would last forever, he explained, be easy to construct because of its light weight, and act as a warning to us all. "And at least we'd know where all the filthy stuff is for once", he added. This is, perhaps, a quirky response, but it's very much in tune with the central thrust of this exercise, which is to ask what "message" we'd like to leave behind us. If we adorn a friend's grave we value that person in a specific way, and the message we send to the world is that love can outlast death. This is the first, strongest message. The second, which is what we hear in funeral addresses, and see on gravestones, is the valuing of specific attributes: "loving father", "Beloved Mother", "gallant brother-in-arms."

By looking at what we have valued in others we can see more clearly what our own value systems may be. Usually that's hard to do. Ask the average individual what he or she believes in and values and, in my experience, one gets self-conscious one-word answers, for the most part. These exercises are a way of causing our values to surface so that we can see exactly what it is we do regard most highly. In the leaving of life, if one does not know what has been cherished, if one has never stopped to take stock of such things, it becomes all but impossible to relinquish one's grasp on the living. Those who beg for life even when there is no life left are those who have not been able to value others, to mourn the loss of those others, and to let go. Those are the most agonizing deaths to witness.

EXERCISE 8:

❖ If you had a lot of money, who would you leave it to?

This is a continuation of Exercise 7. George Burns, surely one of the most loved comedians of all time, put it this way when asked who he'd leave his millions to: "If I can't take it with me, I'm not going." Others see things differently and choose to leave their money to causes, to Universities, to educational foundations. This is a statement, of course, of what one believes in, and the beliefs are very varied, from AIDS research to zoos for children. Interestingly, most people writing this exercise do not choose to leave millions to their relatives. Instead they tend to leave enough money to make a material improvement for their loved ones, but not so that they are awash in money. As one older woman wrote, "Too much money can bring worse trouble than too little." Even those who have experienced poverty seem to agree that wealth can only soften the edges in life rather than solve problems.

Sometimes in response to this exercise people have written several pages about wealth, poverty, the impact money has had on them, and related issues. This shouldn't surprise us - we spend so much of our lives working for and thinking about money, and about what money can buy, that it has become a significant part of our identities. Even the ability to purchase without concerning oneself about cost (which is true for very few of us) is a defining feature. F. Scott Fitzgerald said it succinctly when he said the very rich "are not like us."

Since money is such a large part of who we are, giving it away, even in fantasy, can be a strange experience, one that releases us from any of the normal strictures we may feel. We can value something or someone by donating wealth, and we don't have to feel embarrassed, for once, at what we can "afford." And since we'll be dead when it happens, we won't have to feel embarrassed at gratitude or anxious about those who may criticize our choices.

What all these exercises are intended to do is to cause you to think about mortality, and how you will face your own death. I hope that in thinking this way you will have had the chance to revalue your own life, and the joys of living, for it is only by appreciating what we have, who we are, who our loved ones are, in life, that we can hope to understand what the experience of leaving may mean. This may seem more painful than the alternative. Many people may feel that if they don't think about it then they won't have the chance to feel the pain of separation. There is much to recommend this point of view, and the logical continuation of it is to subject ourselves to huge quantities of sedatives so we won't know our own names, even, and therefore are hardly likely to regret our own dissolution. I don't encourage this. Narcosis is not an option unless someone is in extreme pain.

All that has been written here is applicable to the loss of a loved one. In order to recover from such a loss it is vitally important to record and explore all this person meant to you; the good, the less good and the puzzling. Sudden death is the most difficult of all. We tend to believe our friendships and relationships are not threatened by time and change, so we put off our assessments, our re-valuations; we suspend our understandings. Sudden death gives us no chance to sort out these things.

I think that this is what is conveyed by the teachings of Buddha, and of Christ. Both men were tempted by the world's allure, and both men lived in the world, yet they turned aside to something larger. In fact Buddha's final temptation was on the threshold of attaining nirvana. The temptation was to give up the world and glide into the joys of heaven. He resisted, choosing instead to use his knowledge to guide others to the same point. He recognized that his personal achievement of nirvana was in fact a selfish desire, and that humankind would be better served by a deferral of his own wishes. We can interpret this as implying that leaving the world is not just a case of letting go, but a situation in which we have to ask whether or not we have done what we are supposed to do before we leave.

Christ, in his brutal sufferings on the cross, is a different emblem of what it can mean to die. Whether or not we are religious we can learn many things from Jesus' death, and one of these is perhaps that it is very hard even for the Son of God (who knew what was ahead) to tear himself away from the attachments of life.

If one looks past religious orthodoxy and sees these two deaths as symbols of what it means to die we can recognize that even those in direct contact with the eternal have had trouble just leaving. Christ's pain is a direct indication of the love he had for humanity, and Buddha's selflessness also indicates a deep sense of duty to his world and love for others.

Death is a topic that is certainly too big to cover fully here, so I'll refer you to some other works that may be helpful. Ira Byock's *Dying Well* offers a huge amount of information. Byock is the president of the American Academy of Hospice and Palliative Medicine, and he presents several categories of tasks that can help the dying person, and which he sees as the milestones on the pathway to personal growth at the end of life. I have listed them here in some detail because I feel there is much to be learned from his observations. He identifies eight tasks that need to be completed in order to achieve a peaceful death, and I take the liberty here of explaining them. I do this in part because they are interesting in themselves, and also because they reflect in a slightly different format many of the things the exercises have covered and so may serve as promptings for further writing. The eight tasks are as follows, with my connecting commentary attached:

1. Completing of worldly affairs.
    This is in tune with our first exercise. We are unlikely to be able to die easily if we feel we haven't sorted our worldly affairs adequately.
2. Coming to closure in personal and professional relationships.
    For both the dying person and those left behind it is important to allow time for those things that need to be said to be communicated.
3. Learning the meaning of one's life.

We all want to know that our existence was not useless, that we did more than take up space. Every life has meaning, if we can find and value it. I'm reminded here of Hermann Hesse's *Knulp*. The tramp and scrounger Knulp is dying in a snowstorm, agonizing that he never did anything worthwhile, until he hears the voice of God telling him that his role in life was to be a free spirit that others could feel had brightened their day. For us, too, our roles may be similarly humble and still be useful. The issue may seem also to be more complex. What did we learn as a result of being alive, and what are our realizations as we approach death? Learning from one's life means suspending judgement upon one's actions and experience, letting go of blaming, recriminations, and victim-hood. It means we try to see a pattern and pull out value, no matter what the experience may have been.

4.   Loving one's self and others.

This stage cannot be fully achieved until one has been through stage 3. It is the letting go of judgements that allows us to love even those who have been troublesome in our lives. As we love them, we open ourselves to self-love.

5.   Accepting the finality of life.
     Once we accept that our life will end, no matter what we may want it to do, it can liberate us to see what we have already lived, and value what is left. This leads directly to the next item:
6.   Sensing a new self beyond personal loss.
     When we realize that there is still something left, even when we've lost everyone and everybody - call it soul, if you will - then this knowledge can prepare us to see beyond the diurnal self and find something more enduring.
7.   Recognizing a transcendent realm.

One can choose to phrase this in many different ways: as heaven, as God, as nirvana, or as a sense that the world will continue its existence eternally even when we are dead. Whatever we decide is less important than the recognition itself, which is a powerful calmative for dealing with the fear of death and the great unknown beyond it. That prepares the patient directly for stage 8.

8.   Surrendering to the unknown.

Even though Dylan Thomas could write, "Do not go gentle into that good night... rage, rage against the dying of the light" it's pretty clear that his dying father, to whom he addressed the poem, was about to do no such thing. Fear is a construct of this world. The next world may not require it.

Byock sees these markers or stages as essential for a peaceful death, but he is also pragmatic about what patients need. "I help them with their bowels. They won't be thinking about the meaning their life had if they're worried about their bowels. Only when dying people are comfortable enough can attention be drawn to end-of-life issues." (*Utne* interview, March 1998)

He sees pain management as a major concern for dying peacefully, since drugs can dull pain but also can impair awareness. Byock is also very aware of the embarrassment of dying, as the patient becomes less and less capable, and feels him or herself to be more of a burden. Byock's view is that we are socially acclimatized to caring for incontinent and helpless babies, and it really is only social conditioning that makes adults ashamed of their neediness.

Elizabeth Smith, Associate Professor of Social Work at the Catholic University of America, Washington D.C., agrees in general terms with Byock, but she prefers to describe the successful approach to death as one that endorses a "trans-egoic" model of life. Based on work by Carl Jung, and elaborated by Roger Walsh and Frances Vaughan, the idea is that one carries one's conventional "identity" a little more lightly, and recognizes that as the body breaks down there is another identity available. This is difficult because the realization is the exact opposite of what we have spent our lives building up in terms of who we think we are. This is a version of Byock's stages six, seven and eight, perhaps, and I mention it here because I hope to show that even though there is no total agreement as to what constitutes a good death, there is substantial overlap.

For example, Christine Longaker, in *Facing Death and Finding Hope* also offers much useful advice, and notes that many terminally ill patients want to be able to do one good deed before they die. She suggests several things that can be done.

1. Donate or arrange to donate an organ, if feasible;
2. Change one negative pattern;
3. Ask forgiveness;
4. Make offerings to charity or to religions;
5. Offer up one's pain and suffering for others, through prayer.

Fear of death, she points out, is alleviated when the patient feels that his or her death has some meaning, and is not merely the same thing as a clock running down. These suggestions have all been found to give meaning and comfort to dying patients.

Obviously we can begin to see certain repeated elements in these observations. Perhaps it matters less which precise model we follow than that there is a model. Every civilization has had its models of dying and maps of the afterlife. From the medieval *Ars Moriendi* to the Egyptian *Pert em Hru* to the Tibetan *Book of the Dead*, *Bordo Thodol* we have many guides to help us through this central transition.

One book that may be useful is Marilyn Webb's *The Good Death* which gives ten aspects that help to facilitate the good death, as she has observed. Again, I've listed the main points here for ease of reference.

1. Emotional support:
   The dying person may well be depressed, and find it hard to finish old business, particularly family matters. No one can be expected to do it all unaided.
2. Open communication:
   This is necessary even at the early stages of illness. Openness with doctors and about treatment plans is vital or the patient will begin to feel that he or she is not being told the truth, or is being shielded.
3. Spiritual support:
   The patient may well want spiritual guidance, and this should be available, no matter what the caregivers feel about the way the patient defines his or her needs.
4. Preservation of the Patient's decision making power:

This relates to item 2. Medical staff have to be sensitive to this to avoid the patient feeling like an object at the mercy of experts. The patient needs, often, to feel confident that her wishes will be carried out, even if she can no longer speak or express those wishes.

5. Knowledgeable symptom control:
    In this case pain management is crucial, so that the patient is comfortable but not drugged to insensibility, for example.

6. Limits on excessive treatment:
    Knowing that limits have been agreed is often hugely relieving to the patient who may not want her life prolonged beyond a certain point. This is another version of item 4, and leads to the next item.

7. The preservation of the quality of the patient's life:
    At what point should one let the patient die? Often this has directly to do with the quality of life one can expect, depending upon treatment. Two days of lucidity followed by a swift decline may be preferable to six months of pain and hallucination. Open communication (item 2) is vital for these decisions.

8. Financial support:
    The dying should not have to worry about money. Since few of us are limitlessly wealthy this may mean that a certain amount of planning is done, in which a strategy is agreed upon, before the dying person becomes too ill. Often dying people imagine that the financial situation is worse than it is, and this can cause considerable anxiety at the very point at which they most need to be free from such concerns.

9. Family support:
    A hard death can scar and damage even the best of families. Families need to make decisions that include their own needs so their support can be willingly given, not wrung from them. This is an aspect that is very frequently not dealt with, in my experience. I have seen too many people wear themselves out doing what they think is 'the right thing' for the dying relative, and as a result inflicting huge amounts of damage on themselves and their own families.

10. Continuing support of the patient:
    The patient needs to know that she will not die alone and isolated. This sense can only be achieved when items 1-9 have been addressed.

EXERCISE 9:

❖ At this point it might well be worth surveying these lists and writing a brief response to each of the items that seems to apply to your situation.

In many ways these lists duplicate some of the items that may have already been raised for you by other exercises, and which you may have raised in narrative form already. The advantage of responding to an item on a list is that it allows you to approach the topics from an analytic point of view, whereas a narrative can become a more emotional expression. In all the other exercises we have done so far there has been an open ended quality. You could raise the issues and the feelings and then deal with them at leisure. Death is possibly the only occasion when there is likely to be a time constraint. The work has to be done before the person dies, and so I feel in this instance that it is desirable to have a second chance at some of these issues and review your ideas now.

If it seems as if I'm pushing a lot of lists at you I'll only defend my action by saying that death has become fraught with so many variables in our time, that there are no longer any generally agreed guidelines. One hundred years ago most societies had strict ideas about what was acceptable practice for caregivers and dying alike. Medicine was less advanced, and death was frequently close upon the heels of disease. The options were limited and one had the priest, rabbi, or mullah at hand for the final stages. We can no longer lay claim to such a simple life. We ignore the complications at our peril.

This inevitably leads to more difficult situations for the caregivers, as well as for the dying. Dale Borglum, director of the Living/Dying Project in Fairfax, CA, has written revealingly in *Tricycle* (Fall 97) about what he calls the shadow side of care-giving. He Identifies several psychologically unhealthy tendencies he has noted in care-givers. They are as follows:

1. Spiritual inflation: The caregiver develops an aggrandized sense of his "mission," or becomes an "expert" in helping the dying.
2. Laying a spiritual trip on someone else: Sometimes the caregiver wants the patient to be a certain type of person during suffering, and this may conflict with who the patient actually is.
3. Set expectations of "the good death": This is akin to item 2. Caregivers sometimes imagine the final scene and how it "should" be, rather than responding to what is true.
4. Fear of drowning: Caregivers can fall prey to a fear that the experience they will go through may suck them into some abyss from which they may not be able to return.
5. Unresolved grief: This will only distance the caregiver from the dying person, and force the patient into isolation.
6. Voyeurism: This is a version of item 1, where the caregiver wants good spiritual feelings for him or herself - more than he or she wants the death to be a good one.
7. Idiot compassion: The caregiver who always tries to be nice and gracious, who wants to protect the patient, does so at the cost of not expressing the truth. True compassion cannot emerge in this condition.
8. Sentimentality: A version of item 7, sentimentality occurs when the caregiver becomes "lost in our sweet, romanticized, emotional response to the dying process rather than maintaining a clear awareness of what we are feeling."

Borglum also identifies other sub-sets of behaviors, such as wanting the patient to live; wanting the patient to die; hogging the patient at the moment of death; the loss of healthy boundaries; burn-out; the seductiveness of the caregiver; and issues of transference and counter-transference. This last is where the caregiver wants the patient to be a certain sort of person, and in response the patient becomes that person. This can also work the other way round, of course. The patient may want the caregiver to be like an absent child for example, and the caregiver may well respond by obligingly becoming that role. In each instance it is a move away from what is authentic to a convenient mask, and the risk is of the patient feeling left profoundly alone in the final hours. Death, says Borglum, will "Shove into our face our need to know, to be in control, to cling to any identity" and prevent us from feeling real compassion for the sufferer. "When compassion deepens, it naturally leads us to a second approach for working with the shadow: the view that we can rest in the true nature of mind itself without the need to suppress, cultivate, or improve anything."

At this point I can only urge you to write about any thoughts these words may have sparked in you. The general consensus for all these writers is that a good, peaceful death is one that is approached with honesty and without any illusions. Some people may disagree with that. I've come across several instances of people who have said, "I never dared to tell so-and-so what really happened, and it is better that way." It's a philosophical position I'd find hard not to have some sympathy for, and there have been many people who have surely taken secrets to the grave with them - for whatever reasons. Yet, for all that, I have an instinctual sense that honesty confers respect and love on caregiver and dying personal alike, and so that would be my choice.

Here are some organizations that you may want to contact for further information, and some books that may help.

Upaya: The Project on Being with the Dying
1404 Cerro Gordo Road
Santa Fe, NM 87501
(505) 986-8518
www.rt.66.com/~upaya

Living/Dying Project
Box 357
Fairfax, CA
(415) 456-3915

The Natural Death Center
20 Heber Road
London NW2 6AA England
www.newciv.org/G1B/death
email: rhino@dial.pipex.com

BOOKS:

The Good Death: The New American Search to Reshape the End of Life. Marilyn Webb
   (Bantam) 1997 $24.95

A Year to Live: How to Live This Year As If It Were Your Last. Stephen Levine (Crown Books) $20

Dying Well: The Prospect for Growth at the End of Life. Ira Byock (Riverhead) $24.95

Signs of Life: A Memoir of Dying and Discovery. Tim Brooks (Times Books) $23.

Stay Close and Do Nothing: A Spiritual and Practical Guide to Caring for the Dying at Home. Merrill Collett (Andrews McMeel) $22.95

The Art of Dying; How to Leave this world with Dignity and Grace, at Peace with Yourself and Your Loved Ones. Patricia Weenolsen (St. Martin's) $22.95

Chapter Nineteen

ADVANCED EXERCISES

In the sections that have made up this book I've given you a number of exercises to do and think about. I hope you've done some of them, and I hope you've chosen to write about some of the things that came up in response to the questions.

In all the exercises I've had some particular goals in mind. One of these has been simply to give you the chance to write and get your feelings out. Sometimes just realizing that you have emotions about an event or an issue can be an excellent starting point.

The second goal is to help you to think and feel in relation to your particular situation. Often the problem that faces us is not that we don't or can't think and feel, it's that how we think and feel falls into somewhat predictable patterns. Each of us, as we have grown up, has developed our own preferred patterns of response, and so when a situation arises we tend to respond in certain ways - the ways we find most familiar. The image that comes to my mind is of a machine that sorts loose change. You've seen them, I'm sure. The money goes into a container that shakes the different sized coins into the appropriate slots that match their dimensions; dimes first, pennies next, then nickels, and so on. The system works well until we insert a foreign coin that looks like one of ours but isn't quite the same - a Canadian quarter, perhaps, or a British five pence piece. Then the machine places those coins in the division that is a close fit. Or it jams.

Emotions can be like that. We try to categorize them as a way of controlling them. Sometimes they can't be categorized. "This must be love!" we say, because that's the closest fit we can manage. And if the machine jams we don't know what we feel any more.

My aim in these pages has been to ask you to re-examine your various life-situations and to ask yourself whether they really are what you think they are. Do you really have to act that way? Is this a disaster or could it be something else? In fact I've tried to challenge you into asking whether things are as you have presupposed them to be. A careful assessment of what's really happening, as opposed to what we're afraid might be happening, can be the most useful thing we can do for ourselves.

And this leads us to the next level of discussion, which is to acknowledge that we all have certain roles we tend to adopt when faced with difficulties. With each role comes a story, and one that we accept. I'd like you to think, for a moment, of some of the roles you see around you. It may even help to think in terms of TV sitcoms, which are very adept at making fun of the various identities that people tend to take on.

To illustrate what I mean, here are some of the ones I've noticed.

1) The Soccer Mom. This can be a man or a woman, but I've seen more women in this role, since this person tends to be the wife who spends huge amounts of time driving kids (her own and other people's) to sports fixtures. She is usually pictured driving a minivan or SUV, marshalling kids and equipment, or even worrying about mud and grass stains on uniforms. That's a favorite role for her in the detergent commercials, of course, and part of her competence is that she always knows the best stain remover.

The Soccer Mom may well love her involvement in the children's lives and I certainly don't want to belittle her important contribution to the family. I'd only like to suggest that the soccer Mom shows her love for her children by becoming their servant. Her actions are a coded way of saying 'Look how much I'm doing for you kids. I must love you a lot to do this, mustn't I?' At the same time she signals to the community that she is a 'good mother'. And she is. Yet her kids may only see her as a taxi driver, a convenience. She may be very good at supporting them physically, but less good at dealing with them emotionally. In fact there may not be time or energy for her to engage with them emotionally, yet all the world can see she's a 'good mother'. Her children may be so scheduled and organized that they may gain no experience of organizing themselves, and she may actually be robbing them of initiative – with the best intentions in the world – by making them passive.

The male counterpart of this stereotype is even more familiar.

2) The Workaholic Dad. We all know this one. The Dad who's so busy earning money to keep his wife and kids fed and housed appropriately that he stops noticing he never gets a chance to see them. His actions signal 'Look what a loving person I am: I'm a good provider.' Yet his absence from the home may lead to anger, estrangements, divorce and despair. Perhaps this man doesn't know how to be comfortable around his children, so he flees to the office while consoling himself it's for a good reason.

Do you begin to see a pattern here? In each case the role that has been adopted has advantages. Social approval is more or less assured, as each is a version of the good parent. This is what psychologist Eric Berne has termed the 'payoff' for the behavior, even though the behavior itself stops the individual from being truly present. Whilst we're acting a part we can never be truly ourselves.

A third version of this would be The Good Kid.

3) The Good Kid is the child who tries hard, is honest, dutiful, and who is loved by teachers and parents alike. What could be better? Yet the good kid could have become like that simply as a way of securing love and acceptance. She may well have suppressed the rebellious or unacceptable parts of her character in order to get the assurance of being loved. But there's a price to be paid. In fact the conforming child may at heart have an impoverished sense of who he or she is when there's not someone else there expecting something.

I've listed here the positive benefits of these three roles, as well as the negative. Everything we do, every choice we make, means leaving aside a choice we didn't make. The good kid may be such a conformist that he or she fails to stand up for what he or she believes in if it goes against the norm. Choosing one route always means repressing another possibility until we literally cannot see any other choices. And so we fall into set patterns of being.

Here are some more examples.

4) The Long-Suffering Saint. This role can be adopted by either men or women. The basic form is that the individual has to be seen as extremely patient, endlessly kind and generous, and has to be seen to be carrying the heavy weight that entails. At various times the Saint is more heavily burdened than at others, and never does he or she ask for help. That's just not the Saint's way. Silence and endurance are the rules. The image here is that the Saint is somehow finer, better, than those people who make the Saint's life so hard. So the pay-off for this figure is to receive social approval for trying hard, and yet also to receive pity at the same time. These are substantial rewards.

Within a family, though, it can be infuriating to live with someone who may not state his or her needs, and who is always slightly removed from the real interactions of life (remember, a real saint puts the relationship with the divine ideal before any relationship with others). This can even prompt other family members to be cruel to the Saint since that seems to be what he or she expects, because it re-enforces the role of suffering-for-others. In fact the Saint does want this - for without a burden how can sainthood show itself?

And that is the very real danger for this role. When the Saint is so invested in being the one who is nobly suffering, he or she requires some disaster to labor for. Since the Saint is far more interested in the role than in what the family or the community needs, the reactions of the family are varied. Mostly they fall into two responses. The family members can leave, and disengage from the game. The risk is that they'll be seen as ungrateful for the Saint's sacrifices. The second option is more dangerous. Since the Saint is accustomed to reacting to events in the family with pain, that tends to send a message that the rest of the family can do nothing right. The effect of this information upon a child in this family can be shattering, leading to despair or even mental collapse - which incidentally gives the Saint even more to rise above. Alternatively, if the child gets the message that she is not acceptable then she may begin to welcome that role herself, and become delinquent.

I think you can see from this how the roles that one plays can be damaging to oneself and to others.

I could go on to give other examples of this persona-creating, but I think it's more important to understand how such roles appear rather than to see how many there are. I suspect there may be hundreds of versions. It cannot be very useful, therefore, to try to identify them all. The important thing is for you to try and recognize some of your own behaviors as scripted parts in life's dramas, so you can change the script.

Here's a comparison that may help. Imagine being an actor. You train for years then one day you get your big chance. A movie company wants you to play the villain. You do it well, and everyone loves your performance as the over-the-top evil character. More offers of parts arrive. The trouble is that they all want you to play the villain. You are type-cast for life. You can accept these parts, become rich and famous, and yet never feel you've used your full acting potential. But the money is a great compensation.

Children grow up like that. They are born into situations that make certain demands on them. They are offered roles that to some degree may coincide with who they are and what they can do. But as they accept or reject those roles they also have to suppress parts of themselves that don't fit - just like the actor.

We learn at an early age that certain emotions are not acceptable. Perhaps rage is punished; perhaps it's hilarity, or fear. And so we submerge those aspects.

These repressions can take the form of mental images that we tuck into our unconscious. The rage we feel is too risky for us to express, so we create a mental image of the raging person, and we say to ourselves that this person is not who we are. Or perhaps we see others being happy, and we observe our situation and see that this doesn't seem to fit with our home atmosphere. If the home is not welcoming of this ebullient emotion we may decide that energetic and open happiness is not who we are expected to be. So we bury the happy person, remove it as a possibility for ourselves, like a musical instrument we could learn to play if only the family wouldn't object so much to the noise It makes In unpracticed hands.

Our lives fill up, therefore, with roles we have seen in others, ones that our situation seems to welcome, and that seem to offer possibilities for development. It also fills with those possible roles that we have experienced but which don't seem to be welcomed or nurtured, and as a result these are consigned to the Unconscious, the Not-Me, sometimes called the Shadow Self. So we may find ourselves developing the roles of 'helpful person', 'listener', 'the reader', 'the scholastic achiever', and so on, much to the delight of our elders. The unacceptable roles remain undeveloped, primitive, and vaguely frightening.

Just as summer means nothing without knowledge of winter, so we cannot be fully ourselves until we accept the full range of our emotions, positive and negative. Choosing a role and electing to stay there is a very fine way of not having to look any further at ourselves, so we cannot access the considerable energy that exists in the roles we have rejected. Indeed, we expend a huge amount of energy trying to keep those roles under control. Observe anyone who is trying to be more patient that he or she can easily manage. After a while the stress is easy to spot. The mother who loses her temper with a demanding two year old may well release a torrent of anger - no shortage of energy, there - and immediately afterwards may be stricken by immense remorse, which takes an abundance of psychic energy. What's in short supply is the ability to use this energy productively. Like trying to keep a secret, it often takes more care and effort than the secret is worth.

An example may be useful. In the late seventies at the Massachusetts Maximum Security Prison in Walpole, the guards went on strike. They stated that the prison was so violent that they needed more pay. Negotiations broke down and the guards walked out, refusing to do anything more than man the outer walls and deliver food.

Everyone expected a bloodbath.

How could it be otherwise? The forces of restraint had left, and the powers of violence were in charge.

I interviewed many people involved in this event. What happened was that the prisoners took over and began to monitor themselves. They set up their own security committees, and other inmates were asked to be responsible for making sure the men were locked in their cells at the correct time, that food was distributed properly, and so on. The prison which had been a place of inmates killing each other and of daily acts of violence now ran far more smoothly than before. The murder rate plummeted. The situation remained peaceful and stable for many weeks. Eventually the guards saw their pay bargaining gambit had backfired. In response to an alleged disturbance they stormed the prison. In fact the general opinion amongst those I interviewed was that the guards had staged the whole thing in order to reassert their roles as bringers of order.

Since then the prison has once again regained its reputation as one of the most violent prisons in the nation. Now renamed Cedar Junction in an effort to escape its past, the actuality is even more brutal than before. What I want to focus on, here, is the fact that violent inmates, when given the chance to adopt a different role, were in fact ready to be part of the solution.

Our minds seem to work the same way. If we stop acting like our own jailers we may find we can help ourselves. I'm not suggesting we should release all prisoners, neither do I recommend that we all start acting on our aggressive impulses. Instead we might want to acknowledge that they are part of who we are. I may feel murderous, or angry, but rather than pretend I'm not feeling it I'd be better served listening to that impulse so I can try and understand it. What is that feeling trying to communicate to me? It might be fear, or it might be tapping into a sense of disappointment so deep that it existed long before I ever saw the person who brings up these feelings in me. If that is the case, then the person in front of me is not the cause of my anger or distress, so I do not have to behave aggressively towards him or her.

From my experience working with murderers, and the things they've said about themselves, I'd venture that most people kill because they haven't had time or the opportunity to face the feelings that well up before them, and so they haven't been able to see that there may be a way other than killing. Repressing our murderous thoughts - or any destructive thoughts - may just move us to severing contact with those feelings, and so make the conflict more likely to happen.

We can, if we wish, envision our minds to be like a large party, perhaps a family party. When we give this party we can choose to invite only the good members of our family and the acceptable acquaintances, of course, but that tends to make for a fairly dull gathering. Who will be there? The Soccer Mom, the Good Kid, The Long-suffering Saint, the Workaholic Husband..... Meanwhile those who haven't been invited feel themselves to have been wronged, and so they gather outside to throw rocks through the windows, while the 'good' members have to pretend it isn't happening. You can imagine how strained and uncomfortable such a party would be, and how afraid the guests would be to leave, since that would mean encountering the rough elements outside. It takes a vast amount of energy on behalf of these guests to block out their knowledge of what's outside, and to pretend not to be afraid.

So how can one avoid such an anxious situation? A better course of action might be to invite some of those troublemakers in. There are enough good influences to stop them from doing any mischief, and after all, they want to be there, so they'll be relatively eager to conform. And when you feel that you're ready you can invite a few more in. And so on. It's a version of the old saying, 'treat a man like a slave and he'll act towards you like a slave.' If we treat all people with respect we allow them to become the full human beings they are capable of becoming. They can't be that if we treat them like dirt. And this is true of the split off and submerged aspects of our psyches as well.

You may remember that when I wrote about facing the Internal Critic I suggested something similar. This figure, sometimes called The Self-Hater, can be very troublesome until we ask it to be present in our lives in its positive form, the Caretaker. We can allow it into the party in this form. Just similarly the Soccer Mom can be a wonderful example of loving others if only we can get away from the compulsive need to serve that seems to come with that role.

It's only when we allow ourselves to dialogue with those parts of ourselves that we can tame them. To do that we have to give up those pre-scripted roles. The exercises in this book have been designed with this in mind. What were your preferred roles? Did you notice any? And what's your pay-off for remaining in a role? Here's a way of finding out.

EXERCISE 1:

❖ How do you think people describe you in terms of character? Write a list of words they might use about you. They may use words like 'unlucky', or 'caring', or 'wild', perhaps. Include any nicknames, too.

❖ How did your parents and relatives describe you? Were you 'the friendly one', or 'the cute one', or 'the bookworm'?

❖ When you've done that, take a pause and review your list. How would you describe yourself? How would you describe yourself for a personal ad or a dating service? Write the ad in seven lines or less.

When you have your lists of words compare them. Do you accept what your parents and acquaintances say? Do you feel their nicknames and descriptors are accurate? As you review your lists I'd like you to be aware of their descriptions of you as messages you could choose to accept or reject. In adolescence you may have chosen to reject many of them.

One man reported that he was always being told as a child to put his books down and go and do something useful for a change. Clearly it was not acceptable to be a quiet bookish sort. Some families would have welcomed that, of course. As he thought about this he began to see that his love of reading had always been tinged with a sense that he was different, doing something anti-social. Far from being able to accept his reading-self and find others who were like-minded he had chosen to accept the role of the solitary, and he had lived it in his life. Since he'd internalized the message that reading would never do anything good he'd come to a strange compromise. He'd gone to college almost in rebellion against his parents, and once he'd graduated (with a degree in English) he'd continued to read but with a growing sense of hopelessness as to its usefulness. He'd become more and more alone and never dared to use his love of words to do what he most longed to do, which was write. Notice, I'm not suggesting that his dilemma was caused by one parental sentence. I'm suggesting that that sentence contained a clue to the role he felt he had had to accept and then shake off.

A woman in her early forties referred to the fact that she'd always been called 'the friendly one' by her mother, while her sister had been 'the pretty one'. She'd lived this out in her life: she was friendly. The disadvantage was that as she grew she turned out to be far more attractive even than her sister, but she had never fully accepted that.

As you scan your word lists do you see any discrepancies between what was said to you and what you feel yourself to be? This would be worth exploring. It would also be worth referring again to the birth order exercise in chapter 4. It can help to identify other messages that were relayed to you about who you were expected to be, and who others imagined you to be. You may want to revisit the section on the Myers-Briggs Type Inventory, too, to see how you may prefer to interact with your world.

Obviously no book can attempt a full decoding of all the personae we adopt in our lives, if only because we are all so very different. If you are reading this book it's likely that you are a seeker after knowledge, at least in part. You may also be a joyous person, or a person who feels victimized by the world. You may actually have been victimized. The question is, to what extent to you accept that role? That part lies within your choice only when once you've identified the role. Many people who have been victims have refused to stay in that mind set, and have changed their lives.

It's worth remembering that these roles are adopted whenever we are faced with emotions that we find difficult to handle directly. We love our children fiercely, and so we may become the Soccer Mom as a way of normalizing the emotion to socially recognized levels. We may feel confused by our children, but responsible, and so the Workaholic Husband steps up. And so on. A colleague wrote about a figure that always seemed to take over her life when she had to deal with her emotions, and whom she christened The Drama Queen. This histrionic and energetic figure allowed her to remain defensive and to drive off inquiries as to how she was actually feeling because the overblown reactions that were likely to result would silence all questions. The Drama Queen literally knew the words to use, she had her script, and this was an excellent way of not admitting the fear that the woman really felt about owning her own feelings.

A man in his thirties wrote about a role he found himself slipping into which he called 'the self-loather'. Examining this response, which he certainly didn't enjoy, he was able to articulate very clearly that he adopted this mind-set when he felt he needed change but couldn't seem to achieve it. So, as he worked with it, he decided to re-name the role, and called it 'the desire for change'. In doing so he freed himself from the negative judgmentalism he'd become accustomed to, and paved the way for real change. If we grasp a knife by the handle we have an excellent instrument for cutting through impediments. If we grip it by the blade all we can ever do is hurt ourselves. His recognition and renaming allowed him to seize the handle, the positive aspect, of this role.

These roles are chosen by us for one reason only: when we are playing a role we don't have to be fully present in the moment. All we have to do is follow a script we have in our heads. Uncertainty is therefore translated into certainty, at the cost of losing sight of reality.

The whole thrust of this book has been to urge you to let go of your preconceptions and be as fully present in the here and now as possible. There isn't anything else. We can choose to be dictated to by our memories, or we can choose to lose ourselves in fantasies about the future. In neither case are we present here and now.

Our work together is nearing its end. I'd like to leave you with a few brief reminders about how to look over your responses and so I wish to return to the question of the language we use when we write. I've already spent some time on 'ought' and 'should' as well as other ways we mislead ourselves verbally. Here are a few more to watch out for, since words, if used carelessly, can actually create roles we may not wish to be part of.

To begin with, there are many locutions that function the same way as roles do, to disguise our motives from ourselves. When we say "I've got to..." it may be worth asking who is compelling us, for if we are compelling ourselves then we have more choices than we may think. "I've got to..." is a version of the passive voice, and the passive voice always accords power to others. Look at the following:

"They made me..." "they expect me..."

"I ended up being made...." "So now I have to..."

If others really have made us do things then we may want to ask why we agreed to be in that situation, and if we want to do those things. Of course, we may want to do them because we'll lose our jobs if we don't, but then we are choosing to take responsibility for those actions. If we can't own our own actions we cannot hope to understand them fully, nor change how we operate. It's like saying "I'm sorry" if we don't mean it. As one woman wrote: "Don't ever say you're sorry unless you mean to change your behavior! Otherwise you're not sorry at all."

Words can, in this way, mislead us because we choose to see them as meaningful when they are not. If I say "I can't..." is it really true that I cannot do the thing? Or is it perhaps more true to say that I will not, I don't want to? When I worked with disturbed adolescents we used to take them once a year on a hiking trip. On one occasion, in the wilds of Snowdonia in North Wales, a girl of fifteen kept saying, "I can't walk any further." It was a reasonable thing to say, but it wasn't true. She didn't want to walk any further. Since we were in the middle of nowhere she was faced with a difficult choice, and she discovered that she could, in fact, walk further. What we think we can't do may be no more than a self-deception. Unmasking it can turn out to be immensely liberating. That same girl who absolutely, positively, could not walk any further reached the end of the week-long expedition with a revitalized sense of her own capabilities, and a greater sense of control over her life.

Another word I want to take issue with is 'know'. So often people have written things like, "I just know he's going to leave me," or variants of that. If we take the word 'know' and put in its place words like think, or fear, or imagine, we have a different proposition. "I imagine he's going to leave me," gives you the chance to check perceptions, moderate behavior, and consider that just because the individual thinks something is true does not automatically prove that it is true. Knowing this can allow you to avoid falling into a preset role you have prepared for yourself.

A similar slip of the tongue can be to ask a question as an avoidance of admitting what one thinks. "So you don't think he's going to leave me? He's going to leave me, isn't he?" What is important here is not what the questioner suggests is important. My view can be right or wrong. Who's to say? The questioner, however, seems to want confirmation, so instead of saying directly "I think he's going to leave me," the responsibility is thrown onto me to either agree or argue, and we may never get any further than that. Yet the questioner really needs to examine what is actually happening between herself and her lover, as well as facing her own fears and projections. My opinion is being solicited so that she can take on the role of the victim, and not as a genuine request for clarity.

Be wary, also, of the word 'but'. But is the way we say one thing and then immediately negate it, leaving some doubt as to what we may in fact mean.

"I like it, but I'll take the other one..." This is a way of making a statement, or seeming to make a statement, only to withdraw it. Or try this one: "I love you, but I don't want to marry you." There's a minefield if ever I saw one. It can be clarified a little if we take it that everything that precedes the 'but' is insincere. After all, if, to us, love means marriage then the person who qualifies the statement with a but is the one who is saying that he or she does not love us in the same way we expect to be loved. At their worst, 'but..' statements leave us uncertain as to which half of the sentence is true and cover the speaker's own confusion.

A version of this is seen in the way some people choose to reverse pronouns. "You'll love it," someone may say, when what is meant is that she loves it. Similarly, "How's it going?" is not the same as asking: "How are you?" because the 'you' has disappeared. How is what going? Since none of us is an 'it' we are entitled to ask why our humanity has been ignored, and why the speaker doesn't want to see us as human.

Perhaps the most famous example of this is the by now standard routine of Good Guy and Bad Guy. Policemen do it; car salesmen do it; everyone does it at some time. "I'd like to give you a break on the price (Because I'm the Nice Guy) but my boss won't let me..." The boss becomes the 'bad' guy who won't agree, even though he or she may never appear. Variously known as 'hiding behind the rules' and 'avoiding responsibility' it is a tactic used by many. The only way to break the deadlock is to take everything that's said and react as if it comes from the 'bad guy'. This is the only way to get behind what's being said to what is really meant. Look at the difference between these two statements: "I'd like to go with you tonight but my boss says that I have to..." Notice the 'but' and the 'have to'. Compare this to: "I'm not going with you tonight. I have work to do." This may seem bleak, but it has the virtue of being honest.

And here is the whole crux of this book, and why I'm choosing to focus on vocabulary here. This book has been designed to give you the chance to be honest with yourself. This is not an easy thing. So much of our social world is based on polite fictions, those little half-truths that allow us all to get along harmoniously. They are to be valued. The trouble is they've become all-pervasive so that even the speakers who use them, which is all of us, have become enmeshed in their uncertainties. If the limits of my language are the limits of my knowledge I will do well to be aware of those limits. Reclaiming our language involves saying what we mean - how can our life passages be meaningful unless we have confidence in our words? How can we know what we mean if we don't know what the words say? How can we be truly present in the moment if our perceptions, linked to language, cannot emerge fully?

And that's the challenge.

The valuing of the present moment might seem perhaps to be a form of self-indulgence. After all, the future is important too. We should most certainly plan for the future and be mindful of our possibilities. I've spent much of this book asking you to look into the past so you can free yourself for the future, and you can do that by being free in the present, and staying free each moment.

The crux here is that many of us routinely give our freedoms away. This country guarantees us certain freedoms. They're named in the Constitution, and even though the framers of that document did not specify women and blacks, those freedoms do exist now. Many other countries have no such freedoms, nor do they have written constitutions. Britain, once the most powerful nation on earth, has no written constitution. Putting it bluntly you'll see that the governments of many countries allow their citizens freedom only when it suits them to do so. In the U.S. freedom is practically guaranteed.

We give away our freedoms whenever we agree to do those things that limit us. I've worked with many people and I'm always surprised at the number of men and women who jump from one constricting relationship or job to the next equally stifling commitment. This fear of being alone, of feeling freedom in all its frightening and exhilarating force, is often too much for many of us.

Another way this manifests itself is in the way some people prefer to live in the past, in reminiscences, in roles that were adopted years before. Or perhaps we choose only to live in the future, in dreams, fantasies, and hopes that all will come right without our efforts. These are both ways of not being present, now.

What I'm asking you to do is to see and assess your life by using the past and the future, but using them as servants of the present. Frederick Buechner called it "listening to your life" - being as fully aware as possible, now, of all the things that have shaped and will shape your life. For if we give away our freedom carelessly it is a freedom that is not worth giving. It is only when we deliberately choose to give up freedom that it has value. So, you can choose to give up some freedoms in order to be with the one you love, and that choice, consciously made, is a validation of the worth of the freedom to choose. If I choose to give up a bachelor life-style in order to nurture my emotional life and invest my love in a relationship with another person then I am choosing what I want over what I do not want as much. That is freedom of choice. If, however, I stumble into an ill-advised relationship for no better reason than that I am lonely and bored, then I am acting without awareness, without even the consciousness of choice. I become a victim of my compulsions and confusions. I'm refusing to be free at all.

And this leads me to another consideration, also to do with the Constitution: 'the pursuit of happiness'. I'd argue that this single phrase has done as much harm as good. For happiness is not a game animal. It cannot be pursued, tracked, killed, and dragged back to the homestead. If anything happiness is something that we have to allow to catch us. If we sit still, remain calm and alert, happiness will come to us. We can earn happiness only in the way I've been suggesting, by freeing our minds so that we can recognize it when it arrives. It's not hard to do. We've all done it, whenever we've smiled in delight at some casual joyous thing - flowers in a yard on a city block, the butterfly that settles by your hand as you repair the car. The challenge is to keep being aware of it, and to live the happiness that arrives in whatever form it takes. Sometimes we even have to train ourselves to recognize it. The mother who is fully occupied with small children may well be fulfilled and happy, if she takes time and lets herself feel it. The mother with children and a job that is unrewarding but pays the rent may be just as happy. She has made a choice to do the job so that she can support the children adequately, and it is by seeing the job as a choice necessary for her happiness that her sense of joy can be maintained in a far-from-perfect world. The fact that our lives may not be exactly as we'd like them to be is less important than we might think. After all, our governmental systems are not perfect, yet we'd be foolish to allow our reactions to them to dictate our emotional state to us.

A comparison springs to mind. When I worked in a maximum-security prison the exit procedure was that one waited by a steel door until the guard behind bullet-proof glass pressed the switch. A buzzer would then let us know when the lock was disengaged so we could push the door open. Several of us were waiting by a particular door one day, in the middle segment of a series of three such doors, expecting the buzzer. After a few minutes we began to get restless. It never usually took this long to go through the trap. Four minutes into our stay a young man squeezed through the crowd and reached up to rattle the door, to get the guard's attention. That was when we realized the door wasn't locked. Seven of us had stood like statues beside an unlocked door. That's what I mean about giving up freedom. We can walk through the door whenever be want, but so often we assume it's locked, that we're not free, that someone else has to open it for us. Until we claim our freedom we're unlikely to be able to experience real happiness.

Chapter Twenty

EPILOGUE

At the time of writing, summer 1999, the United States is once more engaged in military action, this time in the Balkans.

In future centuries I imagine that our descendants will look back on this era and conclude that two of the things we did more successfully than ever before were to wage war and to kill each other. The Imperial War Museum in London, in 1995, estimated that 100 million people had died worldwide as a direct result of war this century. From the Armenian Genocide in 1915, to the Holocaust, Stalin's Pogroms, Pol Pot's killing fields, Rwanda, and the Balkans, there seems no chance of mass killings slowing down.

Beside such tragedy - and it is a tragedy for all of us to have to witness these events, too - this little book is insignificant. Yet I make so bold as to state here that it is not valueless. Any nation that can bring itself to pursue a genocide is a sick nation, a nation possessed by terrible demons that can bring only misery. Genocides are the manifestations of a mental disease that may have taken decades to develop, that may have required generations of personal and imaginative deprivation for an entire populace before this horrifying way of thinking could come into being.

I contend, humbly, that it is the failure of people to be allowed to become themselves, to be fully human that robs them of humanity. And once they no longer have that, crimes against humanity are not far away.

So, use this little book for yourself. Enhance your creativity, enrich your personal awareness, and free yourself of your emotional baggage. And then, please, be aware that your new self is something the world needs more than ever before.

BIBLIOGRAPHY

I have purposely omitted references from the text in order not to distract the reader. I have occasionally included publication dates of texts which are mentioned, but only when this seemed relevant. All authors whose ideas are specifically mentioned in the text will be found listed here, as well as others whose contributions are less direct, whose work the reader may wish to explore.

Bernays, Anne, and Painter, P. *What If?* New York: HarperCollins, 1995

Berne, Eric *Games People Play*. New York: Ballantine, 1985

----------*Transactional Analysis in Psychotherapy*. New York: Ballantine, 1986

Benson, Herb *The Relaxation Response*. New York: Random House, 1992

---------- *Beyond The Relaxation Response*. New York: Berkeley, 1985

Bettelhein, B. & Freedgood, A. *A Good Enough Parent*. New York,: Vintage, 1988

Bolen, Jean Shinoda *Goddesses in Everywoman*. New York, Harper and Row, 1984

---------- *Gods in Everyman*. New York, HarperCollins, 1990

Bradbury, Ray, *Zen In The Art of Writing*. Santa Barbara: Odell, 1994

Brande, Dorothea *Becoming A Writer*. Boston: Houghton Mifflin, 1934

Branden, Nathaniel *The Six Pillars of Self-Esteem*. New York: Bantam, 1994

Brooks, Tim *Signs of Life*. New York: Times Books, 1997

Byock, Ira *Dying Well*. New York: Riverhead, 1997

Cameron, Julia *The Artist's Way*. New York: Putnam, 1992

---------- *The Vein of Gold*. New York: Putnam, 1996

---------- *The Right to Write*. New York: Putnam, 1998

Carlson, Richard *You Can Be Happy No Matter What*. Novato: New World, 1992

Chierichetti, Sandro *St. Francis*. Milan: Industrie Grafiche Nicola Moneta, 1940

Cowens, D. and Monte, T. *A Gift For Healing*. New York: Crown, 1996

Erikson, Erik *Identity*. London: Faber, 1968

---------- *Childhood and Society*. St. Alban's: Paladin, 1977

Dalai Lama, *The Art of Happiness*. Riverhead: New York, 1998

Ferguson, Niall *The Pity of War*. Oxford: OUP. 1998

Freud, Sigmund *The Psychopathology of Everyday Life*. (widely reprinted)

Gardner, Howard *Multiple Intelligences*. New York: Basic Books, 1993

---------- *Frames of Mind*. New York, Basic Books, 1993

Gilligan, Carol *In A Different Voice.* Cambridge: Harvard Univ. Press, 1982

Goldberg, Natalie *Writing Down the Bones.* Boston, Shambhala, 1986

---------- *Wild Mind.* New York, Bantam, 1990

---------- *Long Quiet Highway.* New York, Bantam, 1993

Hodgkinson, Tom "The Seven Deadly Virtues" *Utne* Reader, Sept/Oct 1996

---------- (ed.) *The Idler's Companion.* New York: HarperCollins, 1997

Hughes, Elaine *Writing from the Inner Self.* San Francisco, HarperCollins, 1991

Hunter, Allan *The Sanity Manual: The Therapeutic Uses of Writing.* New York, Kroshka, 1996

Jung, C.G. *Man and His Symbols.* New York: Doubleday, 1964

Kuhbler-Ross, Elisabeth *On Death and Dying.* New York: Macmillan, 1991

Lamott, Anne *Bird by Bird.* New York: Pantheon, 1994

Lasch, Christopher *The Culture of Narcissism.* New York: Norton, 1991

Levine, Stephen *A Year to Live.* New York: Crown, 1997

Lozoff, Bo *We're All Doing Time.* Durham, N.C., Human Kindness Foundation, 1985

Manchester, William *A World lit Only By Fire.* New York, Little, Brown, & Co, 1993

Mendelsohn, Robert S. *Confessions of a Medical Heretic.* Chicago: Contemporary Books, 1979

Metzger, Deena *Writing for Your Life.* San Francisco, HarperCollins, 1992

Miller, Jean Baker *Towards a New Psychology of Women.* Boston: Beacon Press, 1986

Moore, Thomas *Care of the Soul.* New York, HarperCollins, 1992

Myss, Caroline Why People Don't Heal and How They Can. New York: Harmony Books, 1998

Newman, Leslea *Writing from the Heart.* Freedom: Crossing Press, 1993

Pennebaker, James *Opening Up.* Guildford: New York, 1990

Phillips, Adam *On Kissing, Tickling, and Being Bored.* Cambridge: Harvard, 1993

Price, Reynolds *A Whole New Life.* New York: Athenaeum, 1994

---------- *Clear Pictures.* New York: Athenaeum, 1989

Remen, Naomi Rachel *Wounded Healers.* Mill Valley: Wounded Healer, 1994

---------- *Kitchen Table Wisdom: Stories that Heal.* New York: Riverhead, 1996

Richardson, Peter *Four Spiritualities.* Palo Alto: Davis-Black, 1996

Rico, Gabriele *Writing the Natural Way.* Los Angeles: Tarcher, 1983

Rogers, Carl *Client Centered Therapy.* Boston: Hoghton Mifflin, 1951

Starhawk, *Dreaming The Dark.* Boston: Beacon Press, 1982

Sulloway, Frank *Born to Rebel.* Cambridge: Harvard, 1996

Tannen, Deborah *You Just Don't Understand.* New York: Ballantine, 1990

Varon, Lee, *Adapting On Your Own: The Complete Guide to Adoption for Single Parents.* New York: FSG, 2000

Wakefield, Dan *The Story of Your Life.* Boston: Beacon Press, 1990

Webb, Marilyn *The Good Death.* New York: Bantam, 1997

Weenolsen, Patricia *The Art of Dying.* Boston: St. Martin's, 1997

Winnicott, D.W. *The Child, The Family, and the Outside World.* Harmondsworth. Penguin, 1964

INDEX